High Praise for M. Jo

"John Fayhee is the OG of literary outdoor writing in the modern era. His accounts of these several hundred hikes serve as contemplations on his life, trails, trucks, and abiding respect for the land he walks upon. There is a lot of hard-won wisdom in this book. And, oh yeah, it's funny as hell."
— **Tim Cahill, author of *Hold the Enlightenment, Road Fever,* and *Jaguars Ripped My Flesh***

"With the right guide, armchair hiking—like armchair travel—can be almost as good as the real thing. John Fayhee's lifelong passion for hiking is likely to inspire you, at the very least, to remember your own encounters with rock and sun and cactus, that "talisman" emergency kit you always carry but haven't needed yet, and the way your thoughts ramble so pleasantly along with your feet. You might even find yourself getting up from the chair and taking a walk—and that's the best kind of reading experience! (The dog, by the way, as John admits, steals the show.)
— **Sharman Apt Russell, Burroughs Award-winning author of *Diary of a Citizen Scientist* and *Songs of the Fluteplayer***

"Science recently confirmed what every writer knows: walking promotes thinking. In this memoir, veteran outdoors writer John Fayhee ruminates on blown knees, love, hallucinogens, childhood, regret, and inspiration, while he and his dog encounter coyote, wild boar, thorns, and the occasional wandering human, over 367 days on the trails in and around the Gila National Forest. A book as piercing as a New Mexico sunset."
— **Nina Burleigh, author of *The Fatal Gift of Beauty: The Trials of Amanda Knox* and *The Trump Women: Part of the Deal***

"This romp through the woods with Fayhee and his dog is a joy from start to finish. While their adventures and Fayhee's musings always entertain, the book is also a meditation on how companionship and the natural world can provide solace for that perennial ailment: getting old. A brilliant achievement."
— JJ Amaworo Wilson, author of *Damnificados* and *Nazaré*

"Fayhee has always been on my list of inspiring writing walkers (or is it walking writers?) including Husserl, Wordsworth, Thoreau, and Solnit. Yes, walking generates creativity, conjures image and memory, creates new stories. Here, however, John takes us a step further: walking is the way to a new dimension—where vehicles become conscious, God is a dog, an emergency kit (stubby pencil, safety pin, and paraffin fire starter) shifts from tool to talisman exactly when needed. Where 'Little Hope' is a tiny Baptist Church, and the opposite of what I got reading this book. Read it and walk."
— Brooke Williams, author of *Mary Jane Wild: Two Walks and a Rant*

"Reading John Fayhee's book is the closest many of us will get to having a beer with him. But it is great consolation since we'll be able to read and revisit our favorite riffs again and again. You'll gain insight to the madness of the long-distance hiker, and an appreciation for his long-suffering and saintly wife, Gay. And for his trusting, beloved dog, Casey, who eagerly goes the distance. Buy the book and enjoy the belly laughs, and look forward to your next beer with the man himself. It's an excellent barstool companion for any wanderer."
— Greg Poschman, documentary filmmaker and member of the Pitkin County (Colorado) Board of County Commissioners

"John Fayhee is an original—creative and hilarious. He is a treasure."
— Alison Osius, former senior editor at *Rock and Ice* and *Climbing* magazines, now senior editor in travel at *Outside* magazine

"Hike every day for a year? Fayhee is up to his old tricks as he leads us down the trail (with his dog, Casey) while pondering his mortality, his marriage, and his misadventures hiking the mountains, canyons, and deserts of the American West. Companion, guide, and storyteller, Fayhee at his aging best."

— **Vince Welch, author of** *The Doing of the Thing—The Brief, Brilliant Whitewater Career of Buzz Holmstrom* **and** *The Last Voyageur— Amos Burg and the Rivers of the West*

"Fayhee is acerbic, funny, and folksy, without being annoying about it. This is an entertaining read and if you're not careful, you may come away with some deeper insights about the human condition."

— **Jay Cowan, author of** *Hunter S. Thompson: An Insider's View of Deranged, Depraved, Drugged Out Brilliance* **and** *In the Land of Living Dangerously: Bali, Borneo & Beyond*

"An unforgettable, year-long journey by foot through New Mexico and into the mind of one of outdoor literature's great writers, Fayhee's 'A Long Tangent' is an instant classic, a writer at his best with a faithful canine companion by his side."

— **Mike Rogge, editor of the** *Mountain Gazette*

"John Fayhee, a gifted, prolific, and intuitive writer. Imagine John Nichols writing nonfiction instead of fiction. These days he, accurately enough, self-identifies as a 'hiking museum piece,' as he continues to pump out books laden with random and well-chosen thumbnail biographies and detailed and humorous recall of his unlikely adventures."

— **Jon Kovash, Moab-based radio and print journalist**

"On one level, John Fayhee relates his adventures with his four-legged trail companion during a solid year of daily hiking, a bond that any dog lover will relate to. But Fayhee goes deeper too; his hikes are a launchpad for musings on life's fragility, the meaning often found in unexpected places and a deep appreciation for the natural world. Like a good raconteur occupying the next barstool, Fayhee delivers these observations via a hilariously skewed perspective, enlivened by his ongoing curiosity and off-kilter wit."

— **Cindy Hirschfeld, editor-in-chief, *Cross Country Skier* magazine and author of *Canine Colorado: Where to Go and What to Do with Your Dog***

"Drink in this glorious stream of consciousness that is Fayhee's writing at its best. Part hiking story, part love letter to life, 'A Long Tangent' will make you laugh out loud (a lot) and ruminate on why we're all here. It's a sensitive and informed dissection by one of mountain living's classic chroniclers, who's not too proud to admit that he is 'winding down.'"

— **Devon O'Neil, correspondent, *Outside* magazine**

"Not just a book for hikers or dog owners, John Fayhee's book is a lovely tribute to nature and friendship with a dash of life philosophy. If you are a dog owner, you can't help but chuckle, gasp, and be in awe of the retelling of John's adventures, seeing yourself in his 'dog dad' reactions. While you see the world through John's eyes, he fully admits up front that Casey is 'the star of the show.' The reader is lucky to have the opportunity to join in on their amazing adventures together. John's book is a lovely read that will have you hugging your own pup and plotting new experiences together."

— **Wendy Newell, freelance writer for *Dogster* magazine**

"The literature of walking is a rich one, from Bruce Chatwin and Paddy Fermor back to Saint Augustine, with his immortal words of *solvitur ambulando* ('it is solved by walking'). John Fayhee has penned a worthy addition to the canon, a collection of adventures and memories steeped in sweat and trail dust and cactus spines and the happy reek of his carcass-loving dog-friend, Casey. Fayhee was walking deserts and the alpine vastness for decades before he started the hike-a-day project to celebrate his sexagenarian years and defy its limitations. This is a life's chronicle of revelry and ribald tales, with an undercurrent of joy, like looking up from the second beer in a small-town saloon far from home to see an old friend, utterly unexpected, outlined in the doorway by the fierce New Mexico sunlight. These are indeed the good ol' days, as Fayhee tells it, 'because every day is a future good ol' day for someone. Hopefully, me too.' St. Augustine couldn't have put it better, because St. Augustine missed the American West, the greatest wandering country on this planet. Fayhee missed not a single thing."

— **Hal Herring, contributing editor,** *Field & Stream* **magazine**

"John Fayhee, dogs, and hiking suggest a magical trinity of reasons to be outdoors for me. To be invited to join him and the beautiful yellow Lab mix, Casey, for a year on the trail is to plunge down a path of time-stopping, mountain-sky moments, and laugh-out-loud memories. This is a book that makes you remember what it means to be here. Especially with the pup. I'm grateful John took the time to take the notes. And have a beer!"

— **Peter Kray, author of** *The God of Skiing* **and** *American Snow*

A LONG TANGENT

Also By M. John Fayhee

When in Doubt, Go Higher: A Mountain Gazette Anthology

The Colorado Mountain Companion: A Potpourri of Useful Miscellany
from the Highest Parts of the Highest State

Smoke Signals: Wayward Journeys
through the Old Heart of the New West

Bottoms Up: M. John Fayhee's Greatest Hits
from the Mountain Gazette

Up at Altitude: A Celebration of Life in the High Country

Along the Colorado Trail

A Colorado Winter

Mexico's Copper Canyon Country:
A Hiking and Backpacking Guide

Along Colorado's Continental Divide Trail

Colorado Mountain Dogs

Along the Arizona Trail

A LONG TANGENT

Musings by an old man & his young dog
hiking every day for a year

By **M. JOHN FAYHEE**

Photography by Gay Gangel-Fayhee

MIMBRES PRESS
of Western New Mexico University

MIMBRES PRESS
of Western New Mexico University

Mimbres Press of Western New Mexico University
www.mimbrespress.wnmu.edu

Some sections of this book have previously appeared in print:

- An earlier version of Days 56 and 356 appeared in issue #16 (Summer 2021) of *The Gulch* magazine.

- An earlier version of Day 70 appeared in the August/September 2021 issue of *The Canyon Country Zephyr*.

- An earlier version of Day 130 appeared in the November 7, 2021, issue of the *Aspen Daily News*.

- An earlier version of Day 150 appeared in the December 2022 issue of *Desert Exposure*.

- An earlier version of Day 301 appeared in *Mountain Gazette* issue #199 (Spring 2023).

Media and Publisher Inquiries:

Mimbres Press of WNMU
1000 West College Ave.
Silver City, NM 88062

Photography and Cover Inspiration by Gay Gangel-Fayhee
Cover and interior design GKS Creative
Editing by Shelley Chung and Cindy Doty

978-1-958870-07-5 (hardcover)
978-1-958870-08-2 (paperback)
978-1-958870-09-9 (e-book)

FIRST EDITION

First printed in the United States

Library of Congress Case # 1-12792705971

This book is dedicated to Michael Fleming, who has been one of my closest friends since we were both youngsters at Western New Mexico University way back before dirt was invented. Gracias por la amistad, amigo.

"A dog doesn't care if you're rich or poor, big or small, young or old. He doesn't care if you're not smart, not popular, not a good joke-teller, not the best athlete, nor the best-looking person. To your dog, you are the greatest, the smartest, the nicest human being who was ever born. You are his friend and protector."

— Louis Sabin

CONTENTS

FOREWORD

Walk. Verb, to go on foot. Noun, the doing of the thing. Or crawl if that's an option. Run if it's downhill, you're in a hurry, or you've decided this is an appropriate response to being chased. But no faster. Beyond the physical human pace, perspective is out the window.

Driving is ridiculous, trains worse, and airplanes spin your head like a top, landing you on the other side of the planet in half a day. What we were designed to do by a creator, by evolution, is walk.

Wealcan is the Old English word, circa AD 1200, meaning to roll, toss, move around, or to turn in the mind, to scheme. The word was not specific to feet, applied to snakes crossing ground and what one does with a horse after riding. Old High German *walchan* is to knead, known in Dutch to make full, to spread out, as if a lump of dough or a cut of fabric you'd tread across to flatten.

Walking stretches out the world, not like swifter mechanical methods that leave blank swaths behind you, places where you didn't reach down and pick up a feather or a pebble. It is knowing the distances you cross. In an older sense of the word, we walk with our fingers, eyes, whatever we have. When there came carts and buggies, and soon cars, trains, and airplanes, we identified ourselves by this way of locomotion. Our bodies thought to do what nothing else does, typical human hubris, as if a stone doesn't walk across the ground after you toss it, as if snakes don't do it as they slip ahead of you through the grass. The origin of the word says it is intrinsic, applied to those things that cover ground.

The word hike is a finer and more recent description, narrowing a walk to something more arduous, possibly in complex terrain. In eighteenth and nineteenth century English, *yike* and *hyke* meant moving vigorously, leaning toward the negative, as in be gone with you, go take a yike, a hyke, a hike.

It was applied in the 1800s to the action of pulling up your pants, a jerking motion. It is walking with a dig, doing it with deliberation. It is walking made into a tincture and dropped sizzling on the tongue.

I cannot think of a more satisfying action in life. Sleep, sex, eating, and drinking are well enough, but walking, hiking, listening to your own breath and footsteps, letting the world thread through your senses, is the most primal. Without walking, there is no sleep, sex, eating, or drinking. You have to get there first.

The book you have in your hand goes there. In a year of hiking, Fayhee's words come to about three miles per hour, which is how fast a person should read, space enough to pause and look around, easily finding your bearings. True to the origin of the word, his walking is not with feet alone, but with characters and ideas, with a young dog at his side and a mind meant for roaming. He spreads life out like fabric and treads across it to stretch it out. These are not epic quests full of doubt and danger, but the kinds of journeys any of us might want, finding along the way Mexican food, beer, prayer, and an understanding of what it's like to be an oddball, or at least an eccentric, in a ludicrous sea of normalcy.

In the industry, this book would be called a memoir, a lifetime told one step after another. Or you might call it a gospel, the wisdom of a wild-haired wanderer living in an empty quarter of the United States as he inches toward elderhood, embarrassed to walk faster than those older than him. The meanders he takes are not all in the wild. An encounter while trekking through Walmart becomes one of the most touching moments of his year. You never know where you're going to find what you need, which is why you have to get up from your seat and go there. That is Fayhee's genius. Lace up your shoes or boots or do it barefoot if that's your way. Put some water in your pack, a little food, and a coat in case it gets cold. Find a starting place, a trailhead, a nick in the woods showing a way, or any open door. This is what we were meant to do. Now, go.

— **Craig Childs**

PREFACE

My dreams are dominated by hiking.

Last night, for instance, I was waiting on the side of a well-worn path—vaguely the 850-mile Arizona Trail, which I completed in one fell swoop more than twenty years ago—for a partner in wilderness crime from way back in my college days. We used to hike together all over New Mexico's Gila National Forest with the kind of reckless abandon that can only be sustained by youthful legs and a pointed lack of adult responsibilities. We'd pick up and go on a whim for weeks at a time, surviving on instant oatmeal, peanut butter, homemade trail mix, and plastic film cannisters filled with cheap Colombian weed. My friend, who I hadn't seen in many years, arrived in my dream from out of nowhere. We shook hands, exchanged basic "so-how-ya-been?"-type greetings and, as it was being hoisted, his pack morphed into a camera the size and complexity of the Hubble Space Telescope. My friend pointed the lens straight at me as he said, "Let's go."

I arose severely out of focus.

The night before that, I was in a gear store in the Colorado High Country, my home range for a quarter century. The store purveyed but one item. Not one *type* of item, mind you—I mean, the shelves contained only a single, faded green, beat-up, external-frame Kelty Tioga pack, which once represented the pinnacle of both technology and avarice among early-era trail junkies. These days, with the ubiquity of ultralight, minimalist gear, the beefy Tioga is considered more worthy of a museum than the boondocks.

I enthusiastically bought the pack and immediately took it out into the heart of Breckenridge, an affluent ski town where my wife and I once owned a hovel. The Tioga, though empty, was so heavy I could barely lift it. I started walking, but I had to stop and catch my breath numerous times. Pudgy tourists from the flatlands and young couples pushing baby strollers overtook me with ease. I tried to quicken my pace, to lengthen my stride, but I kept falling farther behind.

I overslept.

Last week, I was guiding a gaggle of tourists in New Mexico's remote Bootheel, which I have been exploring of late. Only a few minutes into the hike, a dorky teenager pointed a better trail out, one I had never seen before, despite having passed it many times. The group opted to follow the teenager, leaving me standing at the junction, scratching my head, wondering which way to go, wondering what had happened. My dog, Casey, stood at my feet, torn between a natural canine instinct to keep the pack intact and an equally natural canine desire to remain faithfully at the side of her human companion, no matter the consequences.

When my eyes parted at dawn, I did not know where I was. I barely knew *who* I was.

I rise from these recurring somnambulant peregrinations stiffer, more achy, and more fatigued than I would have had I in reality laced my leather boots, cinched my pack, and ventured forth for an extended trip into the extensive and rugged turf that has surrounded almost every home in which I have dwelled for most of my life.

It does not take a student of Freud to interpret these messages from the Land of Nod: Much as I try to ignore—if not deny—the inevitable, I am winding down. My left knee aches when I hike uphill, and there is an awful lot of vertical topography where I live. I have a bulging L4/L5 disk, which often incapacitates me. Surgery on my right shoulder did more harm than good. I cannot count the times I have had to turn back toward the trailhead because of a vicious attack of gastric reflux. My stamina and agility are far from what they once were. There are many more trail miles behind me than there are ahead. That much is not a dream.

Casey's dreams are likewise dominated by hiking.

At least I think they are. When she sleeps, her legs twitch in rhythm and she yelps and yowls as though she is bounding through our local forests. I watch and try to ascertain if she is stalking some hapless member of the lower rungs of the food chain—a rabbit, squirrel, deer, or quail, all of which are thick hereabouts—or if she is being pursued by one of the many dangerous creatures that inhabit our turf—wolves, bears, mountain lions, bobcats, et al.

Last year, she and I together were chased—a hundred yards from our front door—by an irate javelina boar, its intimidating tusks glimmering in the groggy early-morning light. A few months back, I got between Casey and the biggest coyote I have ever seen. It was six feet from her posterior, teeth bared and gaining fast. She once got ganged up on by a troop of agitated coatimundis. So maybe that's what Casey dreams about.

When she wakes, she is confused, like she's wondering how she came to be lying on the living room floor when, scant seconds prior, she was staring down a herd of mule deer or jumping into a creek.

I have no way of telling if Casey is actually dreaming about hiking. For all I know, those yelps and yowls could be coming from whatever her existence was before she joined me on the trail when she was six months old.

The brain has a real problem differentiating dreams from reality.

This is both a blessing and a curse.

There's good reason why our dreams are dominated by hiking: Our waking lives are dominated by hiking. Since the universe overlapped our paths, Casey and I have covered thousands of miles together.

This has been my life since I was a tyke growing up in the northern Adirondack Mountains of New York State, far closer to Montreal than any sizeable American city. My mom fit every hard-ass stereotype one can associate with Englishwomen who spent their formative years looking up into the smoky sky and seeing Luftwaffe bombers raining fire down upon their childhood.

Much psychological baggage traveled with my mom from the desolation of postwar London to the U.S., not the least of which being that she had mental health issues that often manifested themselves in violence. I became adept at a survival strategy based primarily upon duck and run. Fortunately for me, the thick-wooded Adirondacks provided ample opportunity to escape a domestic environment defined by frequent volcanic eruptions and tectonic-level continental drift.

Equally fortunate for me, there was an upside to my mom's rock-hard personality: As the eldest child of a female Brit with a very stiff upper lip, I was expected to be independent. I was given wide latitude to wander far and wide pretty much from the time I was old enough to find my weary and wary way home at the end of the day. I was a free-range child long before the term was coined.

Casey has also grown up on trails. I know few specifics of her life prior to my wife and I adopting her. She had been apprehended running at large in hardscrabble Artesia, New Mexico, and saved from euthanasia shortly thereafter by a rescue group that specialized in Labradors, Lab mixes and, fortunately for Casey, mutts that had at least a random strand of Lab DNA. It was soon obvious that Casey carried her own psychological baggage into our relationship. There is little doubt that, like me, violence was part of her formative years.

Even as we were working our way through those and other issues, Casey and I came to feel more comfortable in each other's presence while hiking together through deep canyons, across bone-dry mesas in ninety-five-degree heat and toward the cactus-covered mountains that rise above the desert lands of southwest New Mexico.

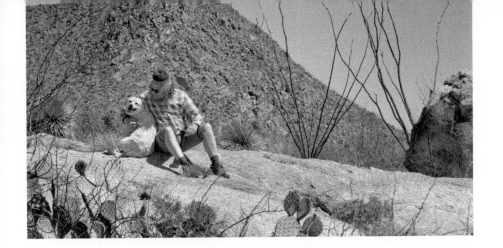

INTRODUCTION

"There's nothing wrong with a good delusion."
— **Quark (Armin Shimerman)**,
from the *Star Trek: Deep Space Nine* episode, "The Passenger"

With imminent sexagenarianism looming on my personal event horizon, I decided to do something of relative note. Part celebration that I am not yet dead and part personal challenge to see if I yet retained the physical ability and mental fortitude to complete an endeavor arduous enough that I could brag about it at my local watering hole.

Circumstances did not allow me to, say, attempt the Pacific Crest Trail, as I had several work projects on the front burner that I did not want to abandon, even temporarily. Plus, there was a good possibility my wife, Gay, would justifiably have divorced me had I yet again slung my pack and headed to the hills, leaving her behind to keep the domestic ship afloat. I needed something close to home, something I could integrate into my increasingly staid domestic status quo without too much disruption. This undertaking had to take the form of a lifestyle tangent rather than a full break.

I decided to try to hike every day for an entire year.

1

The idea began to germinate while sitting on a barstool so familiar it bears a permanent imprint of my posterior. I had just returned from a long day hike with Casey. While quaffing a well-earned pint, I mentally reconnected with a similar, albeit less ambitious, mission. The previous year, I had hiked forty-one straight days in what turned out to be a futile effort to drop a few pounds before my fortieth high school reunion. Up until that point, my longest on-trail streak had been twenty-one consecutive days, during midwinter, sometimes on Nordic skis, sometimes on snowshoes, back when I lived at an elevation of 9,600 feet in the Rocky Mountains. Even during my various multi-month backpacking trips along the Appalachian, Colorado, Continental Divide, and Arizona trails—I never went more than a fortnight without taking what is now known in hiking circles as a "zero day."

"How about hiking a hundred days in a row?" I asked the cocktail napkin upon which I was absentmindedly scribbling various attainable adventuresome alternatives. The cocktail napkin was shockingly legible.

When I wobbled back to my vehicle—a malodorous 1999 Toyota 4Runner nicknamed "Pronto"—I turned to Casey, who was snoozing contentedly on the back seat. "You up to hiking a hundred straight days?" I asked. She answered with a standard semi-enthusiastic, semi-perplexed canine-companion facial expression that I read to mean, "Whatever you do, I do too."

During the seven-minute drive home, my mind, undoubtedly fortified by the beverages I had consumed, began to wander further afield. By the time I walked through my front door, I was feeling my ancient oats. "To hell with a hundred days!" I exclaimed. "We're going for a solid year!"

There it was.

Etched in stone. Porous stone, yes, but stone, nonetheless.

There would be only two rules, which were the same as my previous forty-one-day personal record:

1)   Each hike had to be for a minimum of sixty minutes (though most days I hiked for longer than that) and

2)   Each hike had to take place in the woods. Walking around my neighborhood, hilly though it is, would not count.

I fully understood hiking every day for a year would not earn me any lifetime achievement awards from the Explorers Club. Bear Grylls would likely not come calling, seeking advice.

Be that as it may—I am ancient, and I am beaten up and tired from a life that has not been lived cautiously, sedentarily, or responsibly. I have a litany of orthopedic aches and pains commensurate with a man of my vintage. This tale is largely about getting old, which, let me tell you, is no walk in the park. But, as the tired bromide states, it is indeed better than the alternative. Most days. If you, too, are old, you understand. If you are young, maybe one day you will.

I would try to hike every day for a year and, by so doing, see where I landed. Pretty much the way I have careened through six decades.

What could possibly go wrong?

The following text comes from a combination of journal entries, scribblings upon soggy beer coasters, social media posts and garrulous bullshit sessions at assorted watering holes and subsequently recalled over the course of the intervening years with varying degrees of accuracy. Some sights, sounds, or experiences jogged my memory and, thus, I shamelessly intertwined past events and thoughts into this loose narrative. Basically, things I noticed, experienced, or pondered on a given day all became fair game for inclusion in this meandering tale.

Many days, nothing of note happened while I was on the trail and my mind was blank. "Today I hiked some more; sweated profusely; that's it" would have grown old after use number seventy-one. Thus, there are temporal gaps. Feel free to read between the lines.

Some chapters covered material that was spread over several days or even months. I had to make command decisions regarding where to splice those sections into the text.

A few times, this journey even took me indoors, where a shocking amount of weirdness happens.

As well, there is a considerable amount of material born behind the wheel of Pronto. That's one of the things about hikers: We spend a lot of time driving to and from the trail. Our carbon footprint is often much larger than our actual footprint.

The text has been ornamented with photographs, some of which were taken by me, a man whose photographic skills are defined by hope and occasional luck, with an antiquated iPhone or a $300 Nikon rangefinder camera.

Most of the images, thankfully, were taken by Gay, who accompanied me on many of the hikes herein described, armed with considerably higher-end gear and a significantly higher level of photographic competence. It is easy to tell which images are hers and which are mine: Hers are well composed and sharp.

With me almost every step of the way on this year-long mission was Casey, who was five when this quest commenced and six when it ended, and who, as you will soon see, was the real star of this show.

A note on proper place names

Throughout the process of compiling this manuscript, I was vexed by the subject of proper place names. I have long held the firm belief that outdoor recreationists of all stripes ought to foreswear publicizing the locales they visit. Basically, keep your mouth shut, do not engage in geotagging, provide inaccurate information if the situation merits and, when you post selfies on Instagram or TikTok, lie about your whereabouts. If you are a professional influencer, reconsider your vocational calling. Even well-meaning people often do not seem to comprehend the potential negative impact that comes from outing specific locations via public venues.

I take this seriously enough that I spent several frustrating weeks attempting to set the following tale in a totally fictitious setting. Northern Bethelmesbia, or some such. Failing that, I considered setting it in a faraway locale that was likely not overwhelmed by the ever-increasing hiking hordes. Siberia came to mind.

Alas, neither option worked with the narrative.

I had but three choices: Set this manuscript on fire, rationalize the use of proper place names by invoking a lame "higher good" or "no harm" argument, or fudge the truth. As is my inclination in most things, I chose the latter.

In the end, there was no hiding the fact that I live in southwest New Mexico and hike primarily in the Gila National Forest (known colloquially simply as "the Gila," a term that covers as much spiritual, cultural, and psychological ground as it does geographic). That said, with a few unavoidable exceptions, all other proper place names in these pages are fabricated.

A high percentage of the hikes herein portrayed took place on a single series of trails close to my home that I will refer to only as "Trail System-X" (TS-X)—partly because its proper name is too long to repeat 500 times and partly because, like almost every square inch of the American West, it does not need additional publicity.

Though I doubt any readers will be inclined to follow in my footsteps, even in the most general sense, I have endeavored to make certain my words will dissuade people from venturing to this desiccated country, which is thick with snakes and scorpions. Those who might be inclined to investigate the trails that have snaked their way into these pages will have to engage in some manner of detective work. If you get lost in the process, all the better. That's how compelling stories are born.

Either way, mea culpa, muchachos. Caveat emptor.

DAY 1

Even unexceptional quests are best commenced with some manner of ceremony serious enough that, if the endeavor fails, regret and embarrassment will ensue. The very best such ceremonies, of course, include shots of tequila shared with a gaggle of compadres who may or may not know or care about what it is they are toasting. Given the nature of this particular undertaking, however, I considered it appropriate to postpone the lubricated bonhomie until after I launched the endeavor in suitable fashion: Doing something physically demanding, borderline dangerous, and sufficiently stressful enough that it had the potential of serving as a motivational springboard, or, in the worst-case scenario, as an indication that maybe this full-year quest wasn't such a good idea for a man of my advanced years.

Casey and I drove five miles down a bumpy and rutted dirt road that breaks off state highway blacktop well outside town. Southwest New Mexico is dirt road nirvana, and that trait is one of the main reasons I have chosen to cast my lot with this parched land.

This particular dirt road, like most hereabouts, is not exactly on the tourist circuit. Few soccer moms piloting shiny crossovers come this way. It is used almost exclusively by ranchers driving monster dually pickup trucks looking to tend their haggard cattle and firearms enthusiasts driving monster SUVs looking to assert their Second Amendment rights in the general direction of drained whiskey bottles and crumpled cans of Bud Light.

The road—impassable during monsoon season, barely passable the rest of the year—accesses a picturesque, though altitudinally unimpressive, topographic feature I will call Pimple Peak, which sports a sheer rock face on its southern side, the side most visible from the highway. When I have described this promontory to local residents, visages go blank. They will then pause for a few seconds and ask, "Is it the one with the big cleft in the cliff?" (It is.) Some may even comment about how radiant the escarpment becomes at sunset. No one ever says, "I have climbed that mountain." It is mentioned in no guidebook. There was no available information to aid in the route-finding decision. My favorite kind of hike.

The plan, if you want to call a near-absolute lack of a plan a plan, was to plow directly up the big cleft in the cliff. The footing was lousy, loose rock defining the entire ascent. I would take one step on my tippy toes and slide back down three-quarters of the length of the previous stride. Forward progress, yes—but not much. Analogous of my life. Casey had no problem, though she cheated, as she employs real-time four-wheel drive. She powered ahead, turned, looked down at my flailing efforts and sighed, half worried, half exasperated, half amused. "Keep it up," I told her. "The tables will be turned on the way down."

I had to make numerous tactical route-finding decisions that included skirting a few precipitous drop-offs and pulling myself up using various types of vegetation, which is rarely advisable in these parts, as 1) a high percentage of our local flora sports spines, needles, stickers, or brambles and 2) you never know how solidly a given plant is connected to terra firma until you end up holding an uprooted bush that you were wholeheartedly depending upon for both stability and forward progress. Many have been the times I have tumbled while clenching a branch or stem that was no longer attached to anything save my fingers.

An arduous hour later, we topped out. I was adorned with a few scratches, contusions, and bruises—standard fare for an old man bushwhacking his way through the Gila. With a bit of scrambling that necessitated lifting Casey up and over several rock outcroppings, we reached a pinnacle that, despite its relatively low elevation, was scenic both near and far, inside and out. A couple of tree-dense canyons—otherwise hidden in topographic folds—became visible. I vowed to explore them at a later date. With a squint, I could see into Old Mexico.

But ogling the vista was a secondary reason for this climb. The main purpose was to vow, via a resonant bellow, that come rain, cold, heat, lightning, flash floods, sore body parts, alien invasions (hey—this is New Mexico—such things are therefore a distinct possibility) or debilitating hangovers, I would hike every day for a solid year!

Casey wagged her tail.

To capture the moment, I pulled my iPhone out, fired it up and proceeded to take the first selfie of my life, which was more challenging than I would've liked, for this modest summit was surprisingly precarious. I've seen those Internet stories about people who, while immortalizing their idiotic decision-making, fall off skyscrapers or waterfalls. It would be humiliating in the extreme to expire before officially commencing my year-long quest.

While holding on to a rock knob with one hand, I raised my phone, pointed it in the general direction of my head and, after several ineffectual attempts to locate an on-screen red dot that was barely visible in the bright sunlight, I heard a faux shutter release indicating that my opening ceremony had been pixelated. When I got home, I realized the only thing my dramatic photographic effort captured was the topmost part of my tousled bouffant.

Given a lack of apparent alternatives, we ended slip-sliding down the same cleft up which we had so recently climbed. Steep downhills are challenging for dogs. Humans, of course, handle such inclines lower-body first. Dogs can't do that. They must descend headfirst. So, they are forced by not-so-intelligent design to take leaps of faith. They must either have confidence in their own ability to apply the brakes before flying off a precipice into a grove of cactus, or they have to trust their human companion to intercede on their behalf as they are careening by.

When my confidence in Casey's onboard braking system wavers, I tell her to stay while I go ahead. I then brace against a boulder or a tree and encourage her to follow. She usually takes a deep breath and displays an expression that indicates she wishes she had been adopted by a suburban family with three small children whose most adventuresome undertakings took place in a well-manicured dog park. Eventually, she launches. Then I reach out as she passes, her eyes wide.

Though this process is almost always totally successful, it is marginally successful or completely unsuccessful often enough that Casey approaches each such occasion with justified trepidation. Though it took a while, she now clearly believes that I will try my best to catch her. I'm not sure she has complete faith in my ability to do so. And who can blame her? She has dislodged me a few times, which has often resulted in subsequent bonding experiences that can best be described as rolling ass-over-teakettle together down the side of whatever it was we were trying with all our might to not roll down. There have been scuffs, yowls, curses, and clouds of dust rising in the landing zone, but, when choices are limited, it is the method we use, because it is the only one available, save limiting our jaunts to more benign territory or staying home, neither of which is an option.

Casey had to put her fate in my hands several times as we inched our way down the cleft.

But we made it. We always make it.

On the dentition-rattling drive out, I reflected upon the enormity of the oath I had uttered on Pimple Peak. Adhering to that oath would come to define my life for what turned out—because I finished on the same date I started, and because it was a leap year—to be 367 days.

Then I went to a bar and consumed shots of tequila with a gaggle of compadres who did not know what it was they were toasting. Nor did they care.

I, however, *did* care.

The next chapter of my wayward life had begun.

DAY 2

The iPhone alarm function, which I only recently learned to use, is a decided step up from the poorly wired $7 Walmart clock that has—because its volume switch has been stuck on "maximum" since I first pulled it out of the box—been jolting me awake for many years. Instead of being blasted into disoriented consciousness by what sounds at 5:30 a.m. like a mating ritual between a bull elephant and a sousaphone, I am now gently roused by a tone called "silk"—digitally produced strings lightly plucked, seemingly by elves, maybe even stoned elves, who, although very sorry to have interrupted my various journeys through dreamland, are excited to coax me into the lovely late-May dawn.

This morning, however, day two of my quest, "silk" sounded like a battalion of Orcs pounding their battle drums in frenzied fashion.

Under the best of circumstances, this is not my preferred temporal ecosystem. I am inclined to let the sun creep above the eastern horizon unsullied by my bleary-eyed observation. However, during the hot months— generally mid-May to mid-September—if I am going to hike, it has to be early to beat the desert heat. I dwell in southwest New Mexico *despite* the summers, not because of them. Temperatures in the nineties debilitate me. Casey too. I try to be on the trail by 6:30 and home by 8:30. I would rather hike in late afternoon or early evening, but I can do so only when it cools down come autumn.

That said, I would not describe my state of being this morning as "the best of circumstances."

Now would be a good time to talk about the debilitating hangovers I mentioned in the preceding chapter, like they were not only a joke, but a rarely occurring joke, an anomaly inserted into the text merely to add levity to the series onto which it was added as an afterthought.

But no joke, no levity, no afterthought.

When the "silk" alarm alarmed me this morning, I gave serious thought to abandoning my quest before it ever really got started. I mean, the reprobates with whom I consumed far too many beverages the night before would have no recollection whatsoever of my boastful proclamations. Even if they did, they would not hold it against me if I bailed halfway between the first and second days of what was supposed to have been a twelve-month undertaking. That's one of the more alluring things about New Mexico sociology—merely mentioning, much less overtly proclaiming, your intent to undertake a project is considered an accomplishment. Few people expect you to actually complete whatever it was you talked about commencing.

My main challenge—not only on the trail, but in life—is that I am half Irish and half English. My genetic heritage inclines me toward—as I'm sure you have by now concluded—draining a pint or three several times a week. It is not uncommon for that inherited characteristic to translate to ensuing days that can best be described as "not optimally energetic or productive." Days when the mere thought of reaching from the couch for the remote control is challenging and, thus, I while away painful afternoons watching *Gilligan's Island* reruns. (Ginger or Mary Ann? Mary Ann or Ginger?)

Yes, I suffer from debilitating hangovers. Were it not for this fluke of liver-based internal chemistry, I would likely have been the town drunk in every hamlet I have called home.

The concern, of course, is that my unfortunate hangover habit (some might call it a drinking habit, but what do they know?) could well derail my desire to hike every day for a year. I would clearly have to come to terms with this proclivity if I stood any chance of making it.

Like, here we are in the early hours of day two, attempting to answer the pre-dawn call of the drum-pounding Orcs, and I am already wondering if maybe I ought not consider the previous day's ascent of Pimple Peak to be an opening-ceremony mulligan. I could regroup and begin anew tomorrow.

But I did not. I dragged my haggard carcass out of bed, ate enough ibuprofen to cure cancer, chugged eleven glasses of water, laced my trail shoes (took several tries), drove erratically to the TS-X trailhead, hoisted my day pack and, with Casey bounding gleefully ahead, staggered off, leaving a wake of acrid sweat.

It turned out to be a beautiful day.

DAY 10

I do not know when the signs—which included no words, only a cartoonish rendering of a human form holding a leash attached to a sitting dog—were posted at one of the area's busiest trailheads. Seemed like they were fairly recent. But I am not known for my powers of observation. Or maybe it's a case of being subconsciously selective in what I notice and heed. Either way, we pulled in close to a pickup truck with Colorado license plates and, as I hoisted my pack, the owner—a fit-looking, well-trimmed man probably in his 40s who had on a leash one of those fashionable canine mixes that has "-doodle" tacked on to the end—theatrically cleared his throat and pointed to the sign.

As he did so, several other vehicles pulled up and out of each jumped some manner of mixed-breed mutt that likely had never seen a leash in its entire life.

"Hmmm," I said. "Wonder how long that's been there." Then I hiked on, Casey sans leash at my side.

The Colorado man looked like maybe he had taken a wrong turn somewhere near the 37th parallel north latitude.

There is, of course, much in the way of justified finger-wagging associated with allowing one's canine companion to hike off leash. (Let me stress that I am not talking about city parks and such. I'm talking about the vast tracts of national forest and Bureau of Land Management turf found in the Mountain Time Zone.) Plenty are the places where it is required to keep Fido under physical restraint. This is one of the main reasons I opted to part ways with increasingly gentrified Colorado and return to the scene of my youthful crimes in New Mexico: More and more trailheads in the Centennial State—which, when I moved there in 1982, was still a card-carrying part of the laissez-faire Wild West—started displaying signage indicating in no uncertain terms that leash laws were "strictly enforced."

The pro-leash arguments were many. As Colorado's resident and visitation numbers increased exponentially, simple population-density issues—which included more dogs as well as more people—by numeric default mandated a more severe regulatory overlay. Well-meaning folks pointed out—not entirely incorrectly—that unleashed dogs often harassed wildlife. There were also concerns raised about the safety, or lack thereof, of unleased dogs. They could (as we shall see in subsequent chapters) run off and never be heard from again. They could get killed by coyotes. Again, these are not invalid concerns. I have two friends whose little dog was dispatched by a coyote right before their very eyes.

At the top of the list, however, was the indisputable fact that, when it comes to managing their dogs, most people are clueless. The near-universal anecdote that is repeated most frequently (usually through clenched teeth) is something along the lines of: "Right before the pair of two-hundred-pound, salivating Rottweilers named Cujo and T-Rex mauled my dog, the owner, who was at least fifty yards away, jabbering on a cell phone, yelled, 'Don't worry, they're friendly.'"

I get it. But my operational mantra is and always has been that I will work hard to make sure my dog does not harass wildlife, does not run up to other people on the trail, and does not get killed by a mountain lion.

The first real hike Casey and I took together—two days after we adopted her—followed a benign path that accesses a too-well-known petroglyph. As was then my habit, I had Casey attached to a heavy-duty sixteen-foot retractable leash, which gave her enough leeway to wander and sniff but not enough leeway to scram. She handled it mainly by dislocating my shoulder every twelve seconds. The physics of her immediate situation seemed to be escaping her. This oft-repeated action was accompanied by verbalizations on my part that did not appear to translate perfectly to puppy-speak. After each attempt by Casey to lengthen my humerus, she would look at me and sigh, like, "Why on earth are you continuing to restrain me?"

I kept waiting for the lightbulb to go on. It was a long time coming.

I scoured the canine behavioral literature and found precious little information regarding a structured transition from leash walking to leashless hiking through wild country. There was plenty of material about teaching the "heel" command, but not much regarding how to properly indoctrinate a would-be hiking companion who might one day be allowed to range unchained.

So, I continued to use the retractable leash in hopes that Casey would eventually get that sixteen feet was plus or minus the maximum distance allowable between her and I while we were on the trail. When she approached that boundary, I would say, "Too far." Little by little, she came to understand that was a warning indicating that, if she did not ease off, she would once more find herself reaching the end of both her tether and mine.

Casey did improve, insofar as she ripped my arm from its socket less often. It was, however, incremental. There were times when, exasperated, I considered detaching ourselves while saying something along the lines of, "I release you to your fate, best of luck," and seeing what then ensued. But I knew what the likely outcome would be: An eventual call from someone who read the word "reward" on the customized identification tag on Casey's top-dollar collar would surely also come. And—oh, yes—spousal fury. There would surely be plenty of that.

After we had had her for three months, I decided it was time. Gay was concerned enough that she preprinted a stack of "lost dog" fliers that included both a photo of Casey and, once again, the word REWARD, followed by a long row of $$$$$ signs. We drove to a trail close to town on a sunny spring Saturday, figuring that, if—when—Casey bolted, there would be plenty of other people around to snag her.

After hiking on a leash for about a half mile, with no fanfare, no loquacious statements regarding the significance of the event, I snuck up behind Casey while she was sniffing a bush and unclipped the leash quickly enough that she did not realize she had been set free. She stayed within sixteen feet for a while. Then, tentatively, she moved a bit farther away. She began to run in ever-larger concentric circles, with Gay and I being at the center of her orbit. When I said, "Too far," she throttled back. All the many miles we have hiked together, she has only ever taken off once, a tense situation I will talk about a bit later.

That was the last time Casey ever had to endure a leash, with the exception of very brief on-trail situations or when we are downtown or at the vet's office. It was like she realized that life with me would, from then on, be defined by romping relatively unfettered.

It was then a matter of fine-tuning the protocols, which consisted of and still consist of the following:

- She has to remain within the line of sight.
- She is not allowed to chase critters, except lizards, which she has zero hope of ever catching. (We all need at least one vice.)
- When other trail users approach, she is required to immediately return to me and sit on the side of the trail until they pass.

We have at least an 80 percent compliance rate on each of those, which, by rural New Mexico standards, is downright magna cum laude.

Besides those three edicts, she was, and still is, allowed to be a dog living in the heart of wild country.

Run, sniff, frolic, swim.

Repeat daily.

When we got back to the trailhead, the Colorado man and his whatever-doodle were gone. Likely looking for somewhere with a higher regulation compliance rate.

My mongrel-doodle and I hopped into Pronto and drove home via a very scenic route, windows open, dust pouring in, wind in our hair.

DAY 11

It is a given that the American Southwest is thick with numerous species of spiky and spiny plants, many of which come into my here and now because, no matter how tough Casey's paw pads might be from all the hiking we do, and no matter that she—a lifelong desert dog—is very aware of the piercing power of the local flora, she still manages to occasionally step on a sticker, briar, bramble, or needle.

Particularly notorious—at least partially because they are light enough to be borne by the faintest breeze to locales distant from their easily identifiable host plant—are these little buggers I call prickly pear buds. Though smaller than a dime, they still manage to retain and deploy six or eight needles that are sheathed in a layer of venom that would do a poison dart frog proud and are, on a microscopic level, as barbed as a whale harpoon. To get pierced by one provides evidence that big pain often comes from small packages. Like burning the tip of your finger on a match head or getting bit by a saltwater mosquito.

When Casey steps on a prickly pear bud, fast action on my part is required, because she will invariably attempt to remove it from her paw via the only means available: her mouth. This is yet another example of the hit-and-miss nature of natural selection. Most times, upon observing a sudden limp, I am able to shout "NO!" quickly and vehemently enough that Casey freezes before touching lips to needles. Today I did not react accordingly when she winced, whimpered, parked her posterior in the middle of the trail and began gnawing on the bottom of her right forepaw in hopes of removing the painful spines from her pad.

She succeeded. But it was a Pyrrhic victory, as the bud ended up stuck about halfway back on Casey's tongue. Judging from her body language, I assumed this was a very uncomfortable situation.

Shit.

What to do?

I pulled out my ever-present Swiss Army knife. The plan was to use the tip of the small blade to very gently dislodge the bud from her tongue. This would require some degree of cooperation on Casey's part. Such was not forthcoming.

I tried to make her sit (no easy task, given the circumstances). Instead, she plopped onto her back. I forced her mouth open with one hand, which was also holding the knife with the extended blade, grabbed her tongue with the other hand and pulled that slimy organ as far out of Casey's head as physiologically possible. These combined acts resulted in resistance that was reminiscent of a bronc bucking in a rodeo arena. Then there was the high-pitched squealing.

True to my karmic form, at that exact moment, an elderly woman day hiker, likely reacting to Casey's yowling, walked around the bend and saw me with a dog tongue in one hand and a knife in the other.

I mean, what are the chances?

"What are you doing to that dog!?" the woman shrieked, which did nothing to calm Casey.

21

I'll admit, it must have looked somewhat suspicious.

"My dog nearly swallowed some cactus," I replied somewhat lamely, before, in exasperation, simply reaching into Casey's mouth and grabbing hold of the prickly pear bud with my thumb and forefinger, which meant that those nasty, barbed, poison-covered spines were now embedded in my digits instead of my dog's tongue.

Then I skulked off while cursing and futilely trying to flick away a stubborn prickly pear bud. Casey bounded ahead, tongue intact, seemingly with scarcely a care in the world.

Meanwhile, I'm certain that an elderly woman day hiker was calling police dispatch to report a crazy man trying to amputate a dog's tongue on the side of the trail.

DAY 15

 Every scenic photograph is enhanced by the sudden appearance of a canine rectum.

DAY 17

Given that I would be spending a lot of time over the course of the next twelve months in remote locales, I opted to upgrade the survival-based components of my day pack. I ordered an emergency bivouac shelter, additional first-aid supplies, and some waterproof matches sealed in a screw-top plastic container. I thought about getting one of those emergency beacon devices that can connect to a slew of satellites orbiting way above the Earth, but, with a price tag exceeding $350, I opted for what is considered in survival circles to be the next best thing: a whistle. Matter of fact, I bought two. One for me and one for Gay, who, upon being informed that I had a present for her, was expecting a bottle of wine or piece of jewelry. Sensing her disappointment at being handed a whistle, I suggested she could use it to adorn a necklace. It had a fashionable lanyard and would accessorize most any ensemble. Practical shabby chic.

She wasn't buying it.

I was astounded at the variety of whistles for sale at REI. There was a tri-power whistle, a titanium whistle, a classic safety whistle, a JetScream floating whistle, a hurricane whistle, and a sternum strap with a built-in whistle. There was a four-function whistle that, among three other non-whistle things, included a thermometer. There was a six-function whistle that, among five other non-whistle things, included a magnifying lens.

In addition, a high percentage of pieces of emergency gear that, at least superficially, have nothing to do with whistles, include, yes, whistles. Bombproof flashlights, waterproof blankets and giant, multifuel lighters that can set the world on fire during an Old Testament-like deluge often come with conjoined whistles.

You can never have too many whistles.

The only time I ever remember tooting a whistle was one winter when, desperate for cash while flailing my way through a community college in eastern Virginia, I worked for a parks and recreation department officiating youth basketball games—mainly girls, aged six to nine, a competitive demographic that did not require much in the way of training, experience, competence, or sobriety for referees.

I would empty the entire contents of my lungs into my shiny official referee's whistle every two minutes or so just to make those sugar-addled little shits freeze in their tracks so I could call some manner of fabricated transgression like "contrary vexation" or "refusal to capitulate." Whatever it was, it would likely never be called again, because the chances of me recollecting the individual infractions were nil, given how much pot I smoked in those days.

That was recreational whistleblowing. Were I to find cause to engage my newly procured wilderness survival whistle, it would almost assuredly be because something was amiss enough that I needed to beckon help.

I don't know why I consider the potential of having to be rescued so foreboding. Frightens me far more than the thought of whatever it is that would cause me to have to be rescued in the first place. Broken leg? Snake bite? Heart attack? Bear attack? All would surely suck and, given the amount of time I have spent outdoors, it's a flat-out miracle I have not experienced at least one of them. As long as I could drag my bleeding, poison-infused posterior out to the trailhead, I could accept and deal with the pain. Worst-case scenario, I could live with trying to put my faith in the cellular gods in hopes of phoning a couple of my drinking buddies and asking if they could please put their mugs down long enough to come give me a hand.

But actually involving official search and rescue? Would I rather die? No, but it would be a close call. I'd likely perish from mortification were I to ever find myself in the position of having to attract the attention of organized help. The humiliation quotient would be lessened somewhat if the means by which I did so had a semblance of dignity. Like, say, a flare gun. Or one of those aforementioned devices that can connect to a slew of satellites orbiting way above the Earth. At least that's somewhat cool in a tech-nerd sort of way. I mean, those devices boast a plethora of buttons and, as we all know, guys like pushing buttons. Whether I could ever figure out which buttons to properly engage is another matter entirely. Instead of search and rescue, I'd probably end up getting connected to a telemarketing firm in Bangladesh or getting a pizza delivered. But, again, those devices are simply too pricy for a starving writer.

The analog nature of whistles is not without merit. Like most things that appear simple, the technology is surprisingly complex. A well-designed, well-built whistle has the ability to produce audible oscillations that cut through whatever else noise might be cluttering up the proximate sound-scape and travel for miles.

There is basic whistle communications protocol. One blast means "How are you?" or "Where are you?" Two blasts mean "I am fine," and/or by extension, "I am right here where the annoying sound of my whis-tle is coming from." Three blasts mean "Help!" Whistle sticklers contend that those three blasts should be three seconds in duration with three seconds in between.

I have difficulty envisioning being on the verge of expiring on the flank of some remote mountain and having the ability to muster the necessary number and duration of whistle blasts to be located and rescued. It's my guess, however, that under life-threatening circumstances, there would be sufficient motivation to tweet (pause) tweet (pause) tweet till my last pitiful whistle-wheeze dying breath.

Dear God, if you exist, please take me out before that point. Let me die with a smidgen of dignity!

Shortly after our new whistles arrived in the mail, I gave each of them an enthusiastic test toot. They worked well enough that Casey jumped up, shrieked, put her tail between her legs and ran as fast as her stubby little legs could carry her around the side of the house, where she stood trembling. So, what I learned was, if I ever end up frantically blowing on my whistle, trying to get rescued, my dog will run off in a completely random direction. Great.

DAY 19

So, I'm getting ready to take a well-deserved post-bush-whack sip from a frothy pint of amber ale when, in front of several witnesses who boast marginally more cultured bona fides than I do, a fairly large twig falls from my admittedly unruly locks and plops directly into my cerveza.

"Jesus," one witness proclaimed, "that twig was big enough that, if my dog was here, he'd try to fetch it from your glass."

"When was the last time you brushed your hair?" queried another prox-imate patron.

"I'm wondering when the two leaves dangling from your whiskers are also going to fall into your beverage," said another.

Yes, OK, maybe I should freshen up between the trail and the bar. Justified castigation vis-à-vis my admittedly lax grooming standards notwith-standing, I found that twig added an earthy tone and a nice lichen-like finish to the amber ale.

A Little Help
from
a
Friend

DAY 22

 With a little help from a friend.

DAY 24

People seem (for reasons I can't for the life of me imagine!) to assume that, when I blather on about navigating a "dentition-rattling" dirt road, I am merely being glib. Well, here's evidence: While driving at a rate of speed some might consider inappropriate down an unpaved track, I noticed something amiss on the molar front. My dentition was indeed rattled. A gold crown had bounced clean out of my mouth and out the window toward what might have been the largest copse of prickly pear I had ever seen. I stopped, got down on my hands and knees, and desperately searched for a good ten minutes. Casey stood there looking at me like, "My dad has finally gone off the deep end." I finally gave up all hope of retrieving my errant crown, which would cost a grand to replace.

Damn! Expensive hike.

Upon reentering Pronto, a gleam on the floor caught my eye. Turns out, the crown had not bounced out the window after all, but rather landed in a mix of sand, gravel, and what looked to be dried cow caca between the gas pedal and the brake. Yes, OK, I should vacuum out my vehicle more often.

A quick wash from my water bottle and the crown was good as new, ready to be reattached when I returned home some hours later.

As I said, I love dirt roads.

DAY 28

Conditional verb tenses can break your heart. Today would have been my mom's eightieth birthday. She passed away at fifty-two. She is frozen in my mind as a perpetual middle-aged woman, almost ten years younger than I am now.

My mom and I had a contentious relationship pretty much from my arrival not long after World War II ended. As stated previously, she was a hard-assed Englishwoman who spent her formative years looking up into the smoky sky and seeing Luftwaffe bombers raining fire down upon her native land. PTSD before puberty. With all the ramifications you can imagine, and many you can't.

Shortly after graduating high school by the skin of my teeth, I fled 2,123.6 miles westward and only rarely thereafter returned to the perpetually disintegrating familial fold. I always say I was running from the humidity. But, much as anything, I was putting distance between my mom and me.

My mom only ever visited me one time in the West. Though already well down the road to the inevitable, she wanted—for once and, it turns out, only once—to join me doing that which I love most: hiking. We went up the East Inlet Trail, in Rocky Mountain National Park, outside altitudinous Grand Lake, Colorado, the town I called home when I met the woman who would become my wife.

It took her a long time to huff and puff her sea-level lungs up the steep subalpine path, which accessed a fairly famous waterfall, our destination. She carried with her a urine bag that hung close to where her bladder once was.

The next time I saw her, she had one foot in the grave. Both feet not long thereafter.

She has now been gone for more than half my life.

I don't think of my mom as often as I should, but every June 26—her birthday—I do. It is a day that, no matter where I am, I toast her memory, usually in a watering hole. This year, though, I was sitting on a rock on the side of a mountain visible from my home. Casey was running around sniffing mysteries not perceivable to the human olfactory system. Gay was nearby, taking photos of century plants in the height of reproductive bliss, during which time they raise thick, green stalks toward the sky at a growth rate that seems impossible. When those stalks reach their zenith, they shoot their seeds skyward. Then the century plants wither and die. Slowly. Having completed the task they were born for. Having fulfilled their destiny.

I hoisted a can of lukewarm beer heavenward and hoped my mom had found more peace in death than she ever did in life.

Were she still alive, I would have arrived at the point when I would have thanked her both for bearing me (breeched, as she never hesitated to point out) and for encouraging me to become the wanderer I have always been.

Eventually, I would have.

Surely, I would have.

DAY 32

At the very bottom of my day pack can be found a little red bag—about the size of a deck of cards—with black trim made out of what feels like canvas. It has a drawstring and a toggle lock. Weighs a few ounces.

It is an MSR emergency kit, which originally contained a signal mirror, a pencil, a slip of paper, a P-38 "dog tag" can opener, a safety pin, waterproof matches, some paraffin fire starter, an itty-bitty pocketknife and mini booklet containing survival tips. There might have been some other components that have been lost since that red bag came my way in what now seems like a previous life.

I have never found cause to use a single item in that kit and suspect I never will. I carry it mainly as an homage to its creator. I pull it out occasionally and empty it just to re-remember what the bag contains and why it retains a permanent home in my pack.

Bill Forrest was a man whose name resided at the top of the mountain-climbing hierarchy in the heady days of the 1960s and '70s when what is now called the "self-propelled outdoor recreation industry" started outgrowing Army-Navy surplus stores and Boy Scout manuals. Forrest had been an avid climber since he was a teenager. After serving in the military in Germany—where he met members of Europe's alpine climbing community—he began making his own gear in the basement of his residence in Denver's Park Hill neighborhood. He invented a wide array of climbing gear and achieved many first ascents on notable routes.

Dude was the real thing.

His business grew enough that, in the early 1970s, he opened Forrest Mountaineering in what is now Denver's post-hipster LoDo area. At the time, it was an abandoned warehouse hobo wasteland, the seediest part of the Mile High City, located as it was across a rusting steel bridge spanning the South Platte River from Larimer Square, which was once a sketchy part of town made famous by the likes of Jack Kerouac and Tom Waits. Forrest Mountaineering was among the first handful of businesses willing to venture to the other side of the tracks, along with *Westword*, Denver's long-lived alternative weekly newspaper, and a venerable imbibery called My Brother's Bar.

Forrest Mountaineering, which published a black-and-white catalog that was more magazine and instruction manual than sales device, was one of the main advertisers in the original incarnation of the *Mountain Gazette*. Forrest sold his company in 1985 and eventually began work on a product that would, a decade later, bring he and I together.

I do not remember the means by which Forrest first contacted me. I was then editing a weekly publication in Frisco, Colorado, called *Summit Outdoors*, which was part of the *Summit Daily News* operation.

We met, and he handed me a couple pairs of snowshoes that looked unlike anything I—an experienced snowshoer—had ever seen. Since divesting his company, he had been working on modernizing a means of wintertime transportation that for centuries had a justified reputation for being a bit on the stodgy side. Think the winter scenes in *Jeremiah Johnson*.

By that time, snowshoeing had already moved past its wood-and-sinew history. In the mid-1990s, Bill Perkins, an ultra-endurance athlete living in Leadville, Colorado, had founded a company called Redfeather that not only revolutionized snowshoe design, but that also morphed snowshoeing into a sport rather than merely a means to shuffle along.

Forrest's efforts marked the next step in snowshoe evolution—a plastic, modular unit that could be modified depending on the snow conditions and which incorporated crampons that ran the full length of the frame. By this time, Forrest had been hired as a research and development specialist by outdoor-gear behemoth Cascade Designs/MSR.

He asked if I would be interested in becoming a prototype guinea pig during the R&D process that would lead to the much-ballyhooed release of the MSR Ascent snowshoes. I answered in an enthusiastic affirmative.

The guinea pig experience included not only many structural failures, but a wide variety of failures occurring almost every time I took those 'shoes out into the Rocky Mountains.

Matter of fact, the closest I have ever been to a genuine "I-may-be-truly-screwed" moment in all my backcountry forays occurred when the binding of yet another malfunctioning pair of Forrest's snowshoes broke two or three miles from the trailhead at an altitude of more than 12,000 feet in Colorado in mid-January at about 3:30 p.m. with snow waist-deep and an ambient temperature of minus seven. And dropping fast.

That made for an enthralling story at the bar several near-frostbitten hours later.

Whenever a design or quality-control defect occurred—and I stopped counting at twenty—I would fill out a report and Forrest would respond not with questions regarding my well-being and whether I wanted to continue working as his guinea pig—unpaid, I might add!—but rather with a series of pointed interrogatives relating to the exact circumstances under which the failure occurred, most of which I did not have the opportunity to note, given that my mind was then usually more concerned with making it out in one piece while limping along on a broken snowshoe than I was recording the angle of descent and the nature of the snowpack.

This is not to indicate for a moment that Forrest, a tall, sort of goofy guy—and affable as could be—was not concerned for my well-being. He probably assumed—correctly—that, since I was there talking to him, I had in fact survived despite the issues with his snowshoes and likely had bullshit-worthy adventures as a result. He was correct. He was a steadfast adherent to the adage that the worst day spent tromping through the woods is better than the best day not tromping through the woods. The entire frustrating process was one of the highlights of my outdoor life—mainly because it solidified my friendship with Forrest.

Forrest invited me several times to accompany him on his annual midwinter bivouac-type snowshoeing trip over Trail Ridge Road, through the heart of Rocky Mountain National Park. It never worked out. We did spend a few hours snowshoeing up Mayflower Gulch—between Copper Mountain ski area and Leadville—one frigid afternoon, but that was it.

Forrest's snowshoes were eventually released on a mass scale by MSR. Though the design was lauded, quality-control issues continued to plague the product for several years. Numerous gear shops I frequented, initially attracted to the cutting-edge design and the low cost of the Ascents, stopped carrying them because of the number of returns. Eventually, those issues were addressed, and Forrest went on to design several upgrades to MSR's ever-expanding line of snowshoes, which long dominated the market. (I still own a pair!)

Forrest shifted his attention to other products, including an emergency kit housed in a little red bag. It never made it past the R&D stage. I think that chagrined him somewhat—Bill Forrest, the man who held seventeen patents for climbing gear that revolutionized the sport—to be designing an emergency kit holding a stubby pencil, a safety pin, and some paraffin fire starter. It seemed from the sidelines to be a humiliating fall for a man who had put up a slew of first ascents of mountains even non-climbers have heard of. He related to me the frustration of sitting in a meeting room trying to make argumentative headway with a gaggle of young corporate suits who likely were not qualified to hold his jockstrap. He harkened back to his days hammering out climbing gear in his basement and wondered why he ever opted to let those days pass by.

"Very few of us are smart enough to realize what we have till it's gone," I said to him.

Forrest left MSR shortly thereafter.

He gave me one of those emergency kits with something of a shrug. It was the last time I saw him.

Forrest died while snowshoeing with his beloved wife, Rosa, on Monarch Pass shortly before Christmas 2012 at age seventy-three. Dude went down not only with his boots on but standing atop snowshoes of his own design.

What a way to go.

I keep that MSR emergency kit in my day pack not because I suspect it will ever help me survive, but rather in memory of the man who gifted it to me. It is more talisman than tool, a reminder that, yes, the worst day tromping through the woods is better than the best day not tromping through the woods.

Besides, maybe I will end up in a sketchy situation where hope for a positive outcome rests upon having at my disposal a stubby pencil, a safety pin, and some paraffin fire starter.

I hope so.

DAY 33

After I felt confident enough to let Casey off her leash, it was another year or so before she found her true trail footing, to learn what my expectations were, to reflexively integrate those expectations into her behavior, and to feel confident enough to explore her own interests without constantly looking over her shoulder and wondering what manner of tersely stated command I might be preparing to fling her way. Those interests mostly consisted, and continue to consist, of two things: sniffing pretty much everything she can touch her nose to and frequently urinating, often upon that which she has just sniffed.

Eventually, I came to perceive Casey's true trail superpower: She is an amazing route finder. Not merely competent, but upper percentile. Once she has been on a trail, no matter how faint, she can find it again, even after several years, even if that trail has been adversely impacted by fire, flood, or neglect—all of which are common in these parts.

This morning, Casey and I detoured to a long-abandoned trail we had not visited since the previous winter. Not only had it become badly overgrown in the interim, but, to complicate matters, we traveled in the opposite direction we normally do, which can be more disorienting than one might think. With thick foliage obliterating what little tread remained, I had to stop several times to get my bearings. Basically, I was unable to discern where the faint trail lay. Each instance, I waited for Casey to catch up—she having been distracted by various odors that I walked right by. Once she arrived, she nonchalantly found the trail, as though she had been there yesterday. I was impressed. And proud. I had a sniffing eye dog.

This ability also extends to places we have never been before. If there is the slightest evidence that a human has passed, Casey can detect it. I have assumed it's mainly a matter of residual waft. There appears to be more to it than lingering scent. She seems able to perceive the slightest indentation in the sand, dirt, or leaf matter. She intuits where trails are, or where they once were.

She has even developed navigational acumen when we bushwhack into unfamiliar areas. She knows which way we should go and scowls and sighs when I head off in a direction that does not meet with her approval.

Of course, just because Casey is good at finding the way does not mean she feels obligated to adhere to whatever trail or goat path she comes across. On many occasions, I have been knee-deep in thorny foliage, mired in mud or standing on the edge of a crumbly precipice because, some period of time prior, I have said, "I can't seem to locate the trail that obviously has not seen anything resembling upkeep since the Great Depression! What should I do? I know! I'll follow Casey! She'll point the way!"—only to realize too late that Casey was not at that moment seeking out a route easily passable for the upright humanoid who provides her with food and shelter but was, rather, hot on the trail of a rabbit that recently hopped by. At which point, she will turn and look at me like, "What insanity inspired you to come this way? The trail is back there!"

It is, however, not unusual for me to override Casey. In cases where she thinks we are angling toward Mortality Ridge because that's what we usually do when we reach a particular trail junction, but in fact, this go-round, I'm inclined to veer down Snakeinfestation Gully, she will hold her ground and stare at me until such time as she concludes that I am set in my ways. Then she will groan, roll her eyes, and reluctantly follow in a manner best described as "hesitantly dutiful."

On rare occasions, I actually am correct, upon which case, Casey will wag her tale in heartfelt gratitude that she hooked up with such a reliable dad.

On most occasions, however, I am *not* actually correct, and I end up returning to where Casey thought all along we ought to have been going.

There are several ways I respond to this latter circumstance. I often pretend I was doing nothing more than "seeing what was up this steep, cactus-infested incline." You know: checking things out. Then, Casey will knowingly smirk.

There are other times when I'll entirely ignore Casey and her goddamned smirk while grinding my teeth and muttering expletives under my breath about being dumber than a rescue dog. This inspires Casey to run in front of me displaying what I call her "gloat stride," which is more a prance than a proper gait, and which, in turn, unbeknownst to her, will ensure that her post-hike treat ration will be cut in half, or maybe forgotten altogether.

Between the two of us, I am generally confident that we'll locate the proper route, arrive where we're going, and end up back where we started in mostly one piece. When we don't, that's OK too. We were not put together by whatever cosmic force oversees such things to be perfect in our pairing. We were put together to rejoice in whatever circumstances we find ourselves in, even if we sometimes incur scrapes and bruises and have no idea where in the whole wide world we are.

DAY 34

Almost since the moment we first brought her home, people have commented on Casey's lovely smile, which is her defining physical feature. The back of her mouth curves upward till it's almost touching her ears. She looks less like she is reacting to a good joke and more like she is simply happy.

Some animal behaviorists contend that what we might perceive as a smile on a dog's face is, at best, mimicry on the part of an animal species that has lived in close proximity of humanoids for something like 30,000 years and, at worst, projection/anthropomorphism on the part of human companions inclined to purchase $100 designer sweaters for canine charges who are only too happy to wallow in dead fish guts whenever the opportunity arises.

I believe when Casey "smiles," it is an authentic expression of overt happiness.

On day thirty-four of our quest to hike every day for a solid year, Casey was in need of her annual shots. At that time, our veterinarian told me a story. He had had multi-year dealings with a remote tribe in Alaska. There had, according to my vet, been some "genetic intermingling" between the tribe he was hanging out with and the next tribe over. The resulting offspring, according to the vet, had popped out of the womb with facial characteristics that included a perpetual smile which, in his opinion, looked just like Casey's. So, he took a photo of my dog and sent a bunch of copies to his amigos in the land of musk oxen and permafrost. For grins and giggles, I would presume.

Afterward, I related this tale to my wife. We both wondered how those photos would be received up in the Last Frontier. Were images of Casey hanging on refrigerators and walls throughout Alaska? Were people up there laughing their heads off at how much Cousin Billy looked like Casey? Or was there a slew of furrowed brows taking some degree of offense that their relatives were being compared to a mixed-breed mutt down in New Mexico?

I asked Casey how she felt about the comparison. She smiled at the thought.

DAY 40

Why have a dog?

I mean, there are plenty of otherwise well-adjusted folks who have successfully gone through life without ever having had to (as but one example of many) stick their hand into one of those little plastic poop bags—which sometimes break—prior to picking up a pile of shockingly malodorous caca the consistency of Cream of Wheat.

So, yeah, why dog?

This is a very good question, especially when you are engaged in the monthly process of categorizing credit and debit card receipts that include mounds of bank-account-depleting paper relating to veterinarian bills, the purchase of upper-crust kibble and accoutrements like toys, rawhide chewies, Dentastix, lotions, unguents, vitamin supplements, and dog-specific outdoor gear, as well as non-refundable pet fees added to motel bills.

It is shockingly expensive to bring a dog into your life. Definitely comparable to keeping many of the pitiful excuses for vehicles I have owned on the road.

There is also a high emotional price—of worrying if your dog is tired or too hot or too cold or hurt or sick or simply going through some manner of mental anguish based upon her lack of confidence because of trauma that occurred before she ever became your dog and you became her human. Some scars are not easily erased. High-priced kibble helps, as does hiking together.

Here would be a good time to interject that when we adopted Casey, I swore she would not be spoiled. That lasted about fourteen seconds. Not sure what the exact definition of "spoiled" is, but, no matter your take, Casey would pretty much serve as the poster child. And that's just fine with me. (I—gulp—guess.)

For many hikers, the answer to that "Why dog?" question is simple: protection. Some research indicates even a wuss dog, like, as but one random example, Casey, dissuades negative behavior from both bipeds and quadrupeds. So far, so good. Since Casey has come into our lives, we have never once been accosted by man or beast.

But, of course, there's more to it than that.

First, I love Casey and enjoy her company, in the woods or at home. And I am of the opinion that the vice is versa. It took a while for this bond to develop, but eventually develop it did. And it has grown deep.

Casey doesn't gripe and seems thankful for every bit of pleasure she experiences. She seems to grok that life—including her relationship with me—is a fast-fleeting blur and you should live each minute to its fullest, except at nap time. It's heartening to seriously undertake the responsibility of giving an animal a good ride.

Whether it's chasing a stick, rooting around in the underbrush or rolling in something foul, it is amusing in the extreme to observe a creature having that much fun. It positively enhances the overall experience. I have heard people with children say much the same thing (right up until the kids start asking for the car keys and the reality of college tuition hits home).

There's even more!

My mind wanders when I hike. Matter of fact, that's one of the main reasons I do so. I get badly (or goodly) lost in thought while on the trail.

I often see neither the forest nor the trees. Having Casey along serves as a much-needed and much-appreciated real-time reality check. She has a special spot reserved in the corner of my brain. My attention rarely wanders so far that I lose track of my canine companion. By using strips of duct tape, I have softened the sound of the three metal tags attached to her collar—identification, rabies inoculation certification, and town dog license—enough that their clinking is not disruptive. But it is still audible. That noise keeps one of my feet solidly anchored in the here and now.

Casey connects me to sounds and smells that pass my senses by. I can see the world through her eyes, ears, and nose. Not literally, but enough that her presence adds a significant overlay to my experience. Those rare times when Casey is not with me on the trail, my senses seem partially muffled. I miss even more things than usual. It's like I've eaten a quaalude and my head is underwater and I'm wearing earplugs.

In his book *Finding Chika*, Mitch Albom wrote: "One of the best things a child can do for an adult is to draw them down, closer to the ground, for clearer reception to the voices of the Earth."

I feel that way about hiking with Casey.

I never had the desire, or better stated, the nerve, to procreate. Whatever minimal parental inclinations I might possess have been well served by adopting a series of dogs and cats. The comparison between being a father and being a pet owner, I understand, is tenuous, maybe even specious, but that reality does not entirely negate the assertion. It has been said that being a father makes men better men. I would hold that being a conscientious dog daddy achieves much the same end.

In a nutshell, there is little sense to it. Only heart. All the best things are only heart. Are at least mainly heart.

Why dog?

I love dog.

Dog love me.

A better question might be: Why not dog?

DAY 43

I kept track of my progress by purely analog means: I marked an "X" in pencil in my Gallery Leather weekly planner next to those days in which I hiked. No annotation. Just my mark, like I was an illiterate character signing a document in an old Western movie.

Some days, I forgot to etch that "X." I would then rectify the oversight the next day. While catching up upon returning from my morning jaunt, I realized that twenty-four hours prior, I had broken my record for consecutive trail days. Seems like that would have been on my mental front burner to the degree that the event, modest though it might be, would have been defined by on-trail rumination. You know—what it all means.

Totally slipped my mind.

Was more concerned with putting one foot after another.

There's no doubt, when I realized my oversight, I flexed my quads a bit and thought, "Cool." I was pleased that I had stuck with my plan this far, but I still had more than 300 days ahead. Too many miles ahead to spend time looking back.

DAY 44

On day forty-four of my year-long quest, a world-class endurance athlete named Scott Jurek completed a record run along the Appalachian Trail, covering 2,100-plus miles from Springer Mountain, Georgia, to Mount Katahdin, Maine, in forty-six days and change—almost exactly to the minute one hundred days *less* than I took on my thru-hike of the AT, back when I was young and spry. (Note: Jurek's record has been bested since.)

Mountain country is increasingly filled with hikers, backpackers, peak-baggers, and trail runners seeking similar long-distance records, "fastest known times (FKTs)" and personal bests while doing things like climbing series of peaks, covering sections of footpath through national parks, and finishing an ever-expanding list of "routes" that have been spliced together by adventurers looking to move past the national scenic trails, which become more crowded each year.

Visitors to the mountains and deserts are moving at a faster pace than ever. I do not know why this is, except perhaps that there will always be a segment of the population that is inclined toward speed, competition, and records.

I guess in a way that my own attempt to hike every day for a solid year might be perceived as an extension of that mentality, especially when coupled with the undeniable fact that I am a fast hiker, not necessarily because I am overly competitive, unless you count the never-ending race against time to be a form of competition. I keep track of how long it takes me to complete certain regular trail itineraries. Then I compare those numbers to past times. If I am still moving as fast as I did, say, two or three years ago, I gloat and flex my calves. If I realize I am slowing down, I try to increase my pace, and, if (when) that fails, I blame Casey, whose inclination to sniff every goddamned twig often slows us down. The territory through which I pass often becomes a blur. There are times when I return to the trailhead and realize that I could not relate a single detail of my hike if you held a gun to my head.

I have to remind myself to stop, or even throttle back, to ogle at the view of distant mountains, or to say howdy to a particular tree I have passed a hundred times, or to stand there with my eyes closed, feeling the touch of the forested world upon my skin. Every year or two, I resolve to park my ass for five minutes somewhere along the way. That lasts a week at most before I forget that the resolution was ever made. I mean, it's not as though I consider sitting silently on a tree stump to be a form of torture. I don't stare at my watch counting the seconds down while wondering if this misery will *ever* end. It's just not the main reason I hike. While hiking, I stop to piss, give water to Casey, and to get a pebble out of my boot, but sitting on a fallen log or a trailside boulder and doing nothing more than breathing? I'm not so good at that.

I have a friend who regularly hikes many of the same trails as I do. We are about the same age and level of fitness. She will take four hours to complete a loop that takes me ninety minutes. She talks to the plants. And they talk back. She gets down on her hands and knees to watch bugs. She sees fairies and chats with them. She meditates. I, on the other hand, hike. I am addicted to movement.

Takes all kinds. To each his or her own.

It was fortuitous that Jurek's well-publicized feat ended less than two months into my quest, as I was already getting tired. My motivation was beginning to wane. I was beginning to entertain the thought of perhaps calling it good at one hundred days and patting myself on the back. I was not certain I could pull off a solid year logistically, motivationally, or physically. But reading about Jurek's feat, which of course dwarfed my quest, served as something of an inspiration.

I kept moving.

DAY 45

Today marks the fortieth anniversary of my arrival in the Mountain Time Zone. I had left the bicentennial madness of Colonial Virginia as the tall ships were entering Chesapeake Bay. I egressed the Tidewater country in a bright red 1967 Opel Kadett station wagon that died an undignified death during rush hour on a 105-degree day in downtown Amarillo. I sold it to a junk dealer for just enough money to put all my gear—which included five pounds of homegrown weed stored in a series of Mason jars that were sealed with wax and hidden in a locked trunk—on a Greyhound bus, but not enough money to also put *me* on the Greyhound bus.

I entered New Mexico—which I had never before been to—with my thumb out. After being dropped off in Clovis ("Please don't let the rest of New Mexico look like Clovis," I muttered) by a fundamentalist Christian who spent most of the drive praying with his eyes closed rather than paying attention to the highway, I got a ride all the way to Alamogordo by a half hippie and half redneck who was driving (at an extremely high rate of speed, I might add) a 1963 Chevelle with an engine so large, there was no room for a hood. He made his living by dealing extremely potent magic mushrooms, which he shared with me during what turned out to be a colorful trip across the moonless desert.

When I finally arrived in Silver City the next day, I was dusty, hot, and disoriented, and I learned that my gear, including the above-referenced five pounds of weed, had mistakenly been sent to San Diego, though I was assured by the bus people that the situation would soon be rectified, which it was. New Mexico lesson number one: Things rarely work out. Then they do.

My first meal in my new hometown was dinner at the old El Paisano restaurant up on Brewer Hill, where the only item I recognized on a menu that otherwise might as well have been penned in Sanskrit was, predictably, tacos. The other items were as foreign to me as the mud grubs the natives eat in New Guinea. It is now unimaginable how scrunched up my face must have been while I parsed delicacies that have become staples in my culinary lexicon. Chiles rellenos. Flautas. Chimichangas. Posole. Tamales. Sopaipillas. Dishes I couldn't possibly live without. I took a culinary shot in the dark and ordered something called "enchiladas." The waitress asked whether I wanted red or green. I kept waiting for an attendant noun to clarify those colorful adjectives. When none was forthcoming, I responded, "Red or green what?" When she answered, my tongue, housebroken by a stereotypical English mom whose sole notion of spice consisted of salt, wondered aloud if I could have the enchiladas with neither red nor green. I learned fast.

Later that evening, while walking downtown for the very first time, I expressed puzzlement to a perfect stranger when noticing that the sidewalks were all about two feet above street level. That very night, enlightenment fell from the sky as a monsoonal gully washer flooded Bullard Street thigh-deep.

When we are young, there is a better than even chance our decisions will be bad and/or wrong and/or stupid. (Like, for instance, carrying five pounds of weed cross-country when you looked as ratty as I then did.) My decision to forgo the buggy humidity of the East—known commodity that it was—to move lock, stock and barrel to southwest New Mexico sight unseen was none of those. Almost purely by accident, I found my place in this magical frontier country at the far edge of a tattered antique map, upon which are drawn the indelible images of Geronimo, Billy the Kid, and Aldo Leopold. I took a curvy right turn and never looked back. Never had to.

DAY 47

Few are the feelings that can match going one-two-three and jumping with all your concentrated might from a slippery rock on one side of a creek to a slippery rock on the other side and noticing, while you're nearing the apex, a blacktail rattlesnake coiled in a shadow within easy striking distance of your projected landing spot. Not a giant snake, mind you—maybe two, two and a half feet long. But big enough to ruin an otherwise nice hike. Big enough to inspire you, from then on, to look before you leap.

Time can simultaneously progress at two completely different speeds under certain captivating circumstances. There you are, moving in what seems like slow motion, having sufficient opportunity to think, "Damn, there's a rattler and, judging from what now amounts to an ill-considered trajectory, my right foot is going to come down arm's length from its flicking tongue. How could I not have noticed that before taking flight?" Then, finger-snap-like, you're fast-forwarding to seemingly unavoidable reptilian envenomation. A species-wide nightmare since Lucy was shuffling around the Ethiopian veldt.

I do not know how I managed to alter my flight path, though I'm certain it came down to a combination of frantic arm flapping, a propulsive release of methane, and a degree of contortionism that would make Houdini proud. I landed far enough away that the snake did not strike, though it rattled furiously.

Sadly, I came down awkwardly on my right ankle.

Casey, who had been obliviously frolicking in a nearby pool while this was transpiring, and I were about two miles from the trailhead, with ten more creek crossings ahead of us. It was a slow limp out.

By nightfall, that complexly constructed joint—home to three major bones, four major ligaments and six tendons—had swollen to the size of a cantaloupe.

By midnight, I could barely walk from my bed to the bathroom.

Here I was, forty-seven days into my quest to hike every day for a year, and I had to hobble to take a leak.

At least I was not laid up in a hospital being treated for a snakebite.

Small blessings.

Full recovery from the injury—which I never had formally diagnosed (I assume it was a sprain)—took almost six weeks, during which time I wore an ankle brace while not on the trail. I popped ibuprofen tablets like peanut M&Ms, used so much ice that I came within a whisker of developing frostbite, gritted my teeth, and hiked on—with a decided list to my gait and a constant grimace.

It would have been mighty easy to throw in the towel, to blame the vagaries of the universe for the premature termination of my quest. And that would have been Fayhee 101, to have presented to me upon a silver platter an excuse to bail. "I surely would have made it those last three hundred and ten days were it not for this bit of physiological misfortune."

Not this time, dammit. Not this time. If I have to limp my way through the next ten months, then so be it. I will not be dissuaded by mere pain. I must continue.

DAY 52

Though she generally keeps her nose down at ground level, Casey occasionally raises her head toward the sky and stares. No overflying birds. No clouds. Only empty blue. What is she looking at? Nothing? Nothing wrong with perceiving and pondering nothingness in all its glorious forms. But what if there's something more than nothing at work when my dog turns her muzzle upward?

I have long wondered if the concept of spirituality and its illogical devolutionary nadir—codified religion—is limited to the human species. Supposedly, that's one of the main things that separates man from beast— our ability to perceive (or invent) and subsequently worship almighty, supernatural entities that inexplicably and improbably dwell in the wild blue yonder, under the earth, or on some imperceptible or barely perceptible plane of existence.

Dogs, at least as far as we know, don't have to deal with all that. Their Sunday mornings are wide open. No giving up, say, Milk-Bones for Lent.

Were I forced to categorize her theology, I would speculate that Casey seems part monotheistic, part secular humanistic. She clearly looks at me as the one true god occupying her personal cosmology. But she does not take it to a nonsensical extreme. She does not seem inclined to compose really shitty songs in my name, though she might consider it if she thought by doing so, she would get an extra jerky treat. There are no formalized supplications, no organized ceremonies that ruin the otherwise direct line of communication between dog and man, the worshipper and the worshipped. Sure, Casey is fully capable of a deep-rooted grovel if she pisses me off. And she can sometimes be over the top with that licking thing.

But Casey does not seem to subscribe to any manner of absolutism. While she may consider me godlike insofar as I have unlocked the inexplicable mysteries associated with driving a vehicle and I can defy the basic laws of physics by producing an inexhaustible supply of dog food from the inside of a small kitchen cabinet—very much like Jesus supposedly did when he fed 5,000 hungry people with five loaves of bread and two fish—she does not consider me to be an omnipotent or almighty entity. She has seen me screw up too many times. Tripping, getting lost, losing stuff, the whole imperfection enchilada. And she has seen Gay regularly set me straight in a manner and to a degree unbecoming a supposed superior metaphysical entity. In that regard, in Casey's eyes, I am more like one of the lesser Greek gods, blundering my way through life, but fully able to wreak havoc when provoked. That unpredictability keeps Casey on her toes. Which, I guess, is one of the foundational components of any organized religion. One day, it's all milk and honey, the next, a long line of furious smiting. Cities vaporized. Planet immersed by a deluge. Jerky treats inexplicably withheld.

Here's the thing, or at least a thing: If I'm going to be even a half-assed, halfhearted god with a worshipful flock numbering only one, I at least want to be a *good* half-assed, halfhearted god—benevolent and fair, but fully capable of free-falling from the sky and landing solidly on my keister in a cloud of dust. This perspective inspires me to steal a line from a million bumper stickers, to be the person my dog already thinks I am. Or pretends to think I am. Or wishes I was. Or I wish I was.

Little doubt, however, that I am reading too much into Casey's occasional skyward glances. What possible use could a well-fed, well-loved canine have for any manner of the institutionalized mass psychosis that has infected so many members of my species?

Possible though that dogs perceive matters paranormal far better than humans, the same way they can use their nose in a way we cannot to tell that last night, a bear passed by this very spot. Unseen, but real as a flash flood rising from a distant thunderstorm.

Who knows? Not me.

And hallelujah for that.

DAY 56

While driving down a dirt road, I saw in a ditch a little paperback book that looked to be aimed at children maybe ten years old. It was titled, *Come On, Rain!* by Karen Hesse, who, come to learn, is both a Newbery Medal winner and a MacArthur Fellow. On its cover was a painting by Jon J. Muth of a little girl named Tessie, the book's main character.

Tessie, whose skin was the color of mocha, appeared to have pigtails, but it was hard to tell because there was a bullet hole through her head. Her lower extremities were likewise obliterated because the book had been riddled by weapons discharge. Small caliber, likely a .22. The aim was too precise to be accidental. It appeared the image of little Tessie was specifically targeted by the person who fired upon this heartwarming tale.

My heart sank.

Given its condition, it was hard to read *Come On, Rain!* in its entirety. One of the still-legible lines, uttered by Tessie, who loved to make sweet tea for her doting mother, was: "A creeper of hope circles 'round my bones."

I keep that desecrated book as a reminder that, even though we live in a world in which someone would shoot up a child's book and leave it on the side of a dirt road, there is always hope.

DAY 57

Two firsts on one hike.

First first: I knew it would eventually happen. While standing in the middle of the trail, waiting for Casey to finish her business off in the brush, a woman coming from the opposite direction with her nose planted atop her smartphone walked directly into me. Head-on collision. She looked up for the briefest of moments confused, said absolutely nothing, replanted her nose atop her smartphone and continued on her way. I had to step aside, lest she run into me again.

Second first: Shortly thereafter, I passed a woman who was reading a book while walking. Though she did not acknowledge my existence in any other way, she at least had the presence of mind to avoid a mishap.

DAY 61

Casey and I returned from a hike that ended up being three hours longer than I had originally planned. By the time we staggered back to the trailhead, it was ninety-something degrees.

Oops.

I plopped down on the couch and the only thing between me and a floor fan set on high was a dog panting so hard she was hyperventilating. I popped a cold beverage and reached for the TV remote control and landed on one of those Lonely Planet-type travel shows that are broadcast by PBS on summer afternoons. I was likely one of about three people watching.

The host, an affable though somewhat goofy Gen-X type, was hiking in an Australian national park, the name of which escapes me, with a stout park ranger. She, while carrying a fully laden backpack, danced through a convoluted hodgepodge of slippery, uneven, sharp rocks.

The ranger's nervous-sounding advice to the host, who was stumbling along carrying a day pack scarcely large enough to hold a Clif Bar and who looked, from his unsteady gait, as though he might take a tumble at any moment, was to "stay above your feet."

Got me thinking about other feet or foot-related sayings, all of which speak to our bipedal heritage, but which have left the realm of perambulation in favor of more sedentary interpretation. There are surely many more.

- Keep one's feet on the ground.
- Stand on one's own two feet.
- On one's toes.
- Drag one's feet.
- Dig in one's heels.
- Get one's feet wet.
- Foot in the door.
- Itchy feet.
- Trip over one's own two feet.
- Stand one's ground.
- Have cold feet.
- Step on someone's toes.
- Out of step.
- Have one foot in the grave.

"Stay above your feet"—at least while hiking—translates to maintaining your balance by being aware of and controlling your center of gravity, which, in the most literal sense, defines everything from stride to not falling on your posterior. I have seen many on-trail mishaps that resulted from hikers not adhering to this advice. People's feet "get out from under them" and, splat, down they go while descending a steep, scree-covered mountainside or trying to rock-hop their way across a stream.

"Stay above your feet" does not appear in any lexicographic source I could hunt down. Its applications to non-trail life are therefore open to interpretation. Mine is: Remain calm but attentive, no matter the circumstances, which could theoretically include everything from being dressed down by your boss in front of co-workers to retaining dispassionate remove while driving through a blizzard.

Of the various foot/feet-related sayings, I am most inclined toward staying above my feet—even while I move through life with itchy feet—and likely will, clear up until I have one foot in the grave.

DAY 62

While scratching Casey's ear, a middle-aged woman I met in the middle of TS-X asked if I lived nearby. When I answered in the affirmative, she sighed and told me how lucky I was. Several times. I did not attempt to balance the conversational scales by asking from where she hailed out of legitimate fear of not being able to disguise my heartfelt sympathy if she answered Jersey City or Hattiesburg—both of which I'm certain are awesome municipalities populated by superlative people, but which, like areas called home by the majority of Americans, are sorely lacking on the geophysical grandeur front. She was nice, and I could tell she was sincere. And she was correct. In a way. To a degree.

From the top of the peak I had just ascended, you can see into Sonora. I have observed on this labyrinth of trails bobcats, bears, javelinas, rattlesnakes, and coyotes. In autumn, wildflowers cover the mountainside. From mid-November to mid-February, there's enough snow and cold to lend a veneer of winter, but not so much that the world seems frozen all the way down to its core, like other places I have lived. Public land—some benign and easily accessible, most of it rugged and remote—reaches to the horizon in every direction.

If you are inclined toward a life that revolves around the outdoors, southwest New Mexico is paradise, and I do indeed consider myself fortunate to hang my hat hereabouts.

After we parted, I realized I had left much unsaid. What I might well have added to that superficial trailside chitchat was this: Luck had nothing to do with my mailing address. I made a conscious decision early in life to live where I can access the lovely wild of the American West, where that wild is as much a part of my daily existence as are the gleaming glass towers, malls, traffic jams, and seas of monoculture subdivisions found in other locales.

This is where I have chosen to plant my flag, to make my stand.

As a result of that decision, I have essentially flushed fiscal opportunity down the toilet—to the degree that my retirement plan consists of never retiring, or maybe taking up with a hunter-gatherer tribe down in the Amazon Basin. As a result of that decision, I have spent my entire adult life living so far from the American mainstream that I often have to use Google to help orient me to the most foundational aspects of our society and culture. I once had to ask someone I know in the East who/what a Kardashian is. He thought I was joking. I was not. And I'm still not exactly certain what a Kardashian actually is, or why I should care. (I don't.)

I live in a town where, unless you count romantic bestsellers located near the checkout aisle of the grocery store, it's hard to buy recently released books without going online. Which is problematic, as our Internet comes and goes. Our sidewalks are crumbling. Our municipal coffers often hover on the edge of depletion. Many people hereabouts experience food insecurity. I dwell in a state many Americans do not realize is actually part of the U.S. I have been asked by people in Virginia, where I went to high school, what manner of currency we use. I was once told by a bank teller in Pennsylvania, upon eyeballing my driver's license, that she would need to see some form of domestic identification to cash a check. She asked if perchance I had my passport on hand. All of us in the Land of Enchantment have stories like that. We tell them at parties. A local monthly publication even has a regular section cataloging our perceived orphan status. Our local heroes are Billy the Kid—who grew up in Silver City—and Geronimo—born nearby. Other parts of the country idolize the heavily polished perfection of George Washington, Daniel Boone, and Sacagawea. We have a gunslinger who killed eight men before he was offed at age twenty-one and a man whose name struck primal fear into the residents of two countries and who spent the last twenty-four years of his life incarcerated as a prisoner of war in faraway Oklahoma.

The trade-off, which, thankfully, the vast majority of my countrymen are unwilling to make, is geophysical stupendousness relatively free of the hiking and biking hordes that have descended on Colorado and Arizona— our scenic and more populated neighbors.

The physical comparison I usually make is to the country of my birth: the United Kingdom, which, in its entirety—including England, Wales, Scotland, Northern Ireland, the Channel Islands and Gibraltar—covers about 93,000 square miles. The UK has a population of sixty-seven million soggy souls. Sunny New Mexico has an area of about 121,000 square miles. A few years ago, much to the consternation of many residents, our state broke the two million inhabitant mark. Thankfully, almost half of those people live in metro Albuquerque, four-plus hours away on the other side of a serpentine mountain road that scares the bejesus out of many drivers so badly that they vow never to return. Or never to leave—depending on their inclination and direction of travel. That road tops out at a pass that serves as a cultural moat that keeps us off the map, off the radar, and well off the path of whatever a Kardashian might be.

By the time the woman and I parted ways—she on her way toward the peak I just went up and me on my way down—Casey had grown impatient.

She was already rooting around in the underbrush, looking for lizards. I stood and bemusedly watched as several skinks easily outwitted their would-be predator, supposedly a descendant of the mighty wolf.

We descended to a parking lot where there were only two cars.

I was feeling lucky. Very lucky.

DAY 63

Scene from the lonely New Mexico highway between Socorro and Truth or Consequences, heading south, at the point in yet another long and arduous road trip when I start feeling like I am home, like I can finally exhale. Dirt, dents, and bug splat defining the windshield. Dust covering the dash. Casey crashed in the back, wiped out from hard hiking, snoring. Only a few fellow travelers ahead and nothing gaining on me. (At least nothing visible.) Windblown hair in the rearview. Mislaid my brush a couple days back. Grooming optional hereabouts. Brontosaurus, procured in a gift shop in Dinosaur National Monument, poking its head above the hood and providing magical protection on the front bumper. (It has never failed me, and we have traveled some serious mileage together, much of it rough.) Plastic hippo providing protection for the interior. It was found lying on the ground outside Leadville while I was being interviewed on the phone by a newspaper reporter I knew but did not know well who later took his own life. Jumped headfirst off a very high bridge. That decision had nothing to do with me, but I still think about it sometimes when I look at that hippo. Medicine bag hanging as it has from the mirror of every vehicle I have owned for more than forty years. Given to me by a young couple from Acoma Pueblo who wanted to thank me for being their friend during a dark time in their lives. Stick on the dashboard picked up from a creek bed south of Jarbidge, Nevada, probably the most remote town in the lower forty-eight. I had smoked some weed and consumed a few adult beverages at a bar called the Outdoor Inn. The stick looked like a wizard's wand. I've used it to cast a few spells (mostly good). While I was first waving that stick, Katrina was drowning New Orleans. I didn't find out about the hurricane till three days later while I was on the side of Wheeler Peak looking for the famous thousand-year-old bristlecone pines. A park ranger caught me up on current events. She also told me to stay on the trail. I told her such a thing was highly unlikely. She blushed flirtatiously and waved a citation book under my nose.

DAY 64

On a hot desert day, we gave serious consideration to driving a couple hours down to the closest city, where we could hang out in an air-conditioned mall, where we could then interface with food-court cuisine and the retail component of American consumerism. Maybe buy some stylish socks. Instead, we opted to drive a couple hours in exactly the opposite direction, where, after a multi-mile, sweat-soaked hike through briars and brambles, we interfaced with sun, bugs, sandy cheese sandwiches with mayonnaise bubbling in the heat, and swimming holes. Stylish socks optional. We made the right choice.

DAY 65

Up a side-side-side canyon. Heard a faint trickle as we were bushwhacking by. Gay was willing to crawl through the dense underbrush, definitely slippery when wet, to overlay her photographic skills onto a scene that's only there during rare rainfalls. My job was to watch for snakes. Job well done.

DAY 66

Any time the words "it began as a normal day" are invoked, you know shit is about to hit the fan and splatter all over your face.

Casey and I got up early and, per usual in the dead of summer, drove to TS-X and got in a solid hike before the heat sent us scurrying indoors for the rest of the day. Casey crashed out next to the cooler vent in our hallway. Late morning, I put her outside for a potty break, as is our custom. When she came back in an hour and a half later, her eyes looked a bit odd, which I ascribed to nothing more than a trick of the light. Right up until she walked directly into a kitchen wall. I kneeled down and checked her view pods a bit more closely. My jaw dropped as my heart sank.

In the time she had been outside, the inexplicable had happened: Casey's eyes looked like something out of a horror movie, like she had been possessed by the devil. Both orbs were bright red and, shortly thereafter, appeared covered with horrible cataracts. I'm talking something out of a *National*

Geographic photo of a hundred-year-old woman from rural China in the 1920s. It was apparent she could make out basic shapes but, other than that, her vision was badly compromised. She could barely keep her blood-rimmed eyes open. She was obviously confused and disoriented.

I rushed her to the vet, but the staff was beyond flummoxed. Employees who have known her since she was a pup were coming into the examination room and exclaiming, "OH MY GOD! WHAT HAPPENED TO CASEY?"—which did nothing to mitigate the fact that I was essentially puking with fear. The vet suggested I take her home and wait a few days to see if the condition cleared up. Like, yeah, that's what I was going to do.

I called the Southern Arizona Veterinary Specialty and Emergency Center in Tucson—four hours away—and was informed that the next opening for their staff ophthalmologist was the following week. By this time, I was hyperventilating and wondering how having a blind dog was going to negatively impact the lives of me, Gay and, well, poor Casey. To say nothing of my quest to hike every day for an entire year, which, without warning, was relegated to second-fiddle status. I replied, appointment or not, that I was going to drive down to Tucson the next morning and they were going to see my dog and I didn't give a damn if I had to bust through their front door. The receptionist called me back a few minutes later and said they could squeeze us in after lunch, but we would have to pay inflated emergency fees. Fine.

By the time the sun rose, Casey was completely blind. I dashed out to TS-X for a hike that was not one second longer than sixty minutes and lifted Casey into Pronto, where she curled up.

The whole incinerator-hot drive to Tucson, my mind was reeling. What could *possibly* have occurred in that short period of time? Did Casey get stung by a scorpion or a centipede? Did someone spray something in her eyes?

Casey shook the entire way. She was so scared. She whimpered for every one of those four hours, wanting me to keep a hand on her. Wanting me to tell her everything was going to be OK. I'm certain she perceived that I was unconvinced. Still, she seemed glad to hear the words, to hear my voice.

The ophthalmologist, a very nice lady named Emily Moeller, was remarkably calm and reassuring. She almost immediately diagnosed Casey as having something-Latin-something-something, in which the protective casing around the eyes gets compromised and allows blood fat to flow in. Moeller said most such cases are usually a result of a dog eating an entire vat of turkey fat or a pound of bacon—neither of which Casey had done.

In addition to numerous tests that looked very uncomfortable, Casey had to endure a steroid shot in each eye, which I was not allowed to observe (thank goodness). Moeller said she was 90 percent certain that Casey's vision would start to improve within a couple days and return to normal within two weeks. She added that the healing process might take the form of two steps forward, one step back. Hiking was off the table till things cleared up. Casey was put on a slew of meds and scheduled for a follow-up. All we could do at that point was wait and puke.

DAY 69

Three days after she went blind, as per Emily Moeller's prediction, Casey's eyes were looking slightly less hideous, but she was nowhere near ready to join me on the trail. Didn't want her walking headlong into a tree. Didn't want to hear any jokes about the blind leading the blind. Thing is, we hike upon the very same trails often enough that she could likely find her way solely via habit and sense of smell.

Though TS-X boasts innumerable loops, there are only about five that Casey and I normally traverse. Creatures of habit. We know almost every detail about those loops. How long they take. Which ones boast the best shade in the summer and the best sun in the winter. On each of our regular routes, there is a set spot—about halfway through—where I pull my pack off so I can give Casey a drink of water. She knows the loops, and she knows where we stop. There's the gnarled oak with the remnant nub of a branch where I can easily hang my pack. There's the little box canyon with a boulder upon which I sit while Casey drinks. There's the junction where someone long ago constructed a rock bench.

I was hiking the loop that passed the gnarled oak. When I got there, I reflexively de-packed and started to pull Casey's water bowl out. Something was amiss. I looked for Casey, but she was not there. I thought for a fleeting moment that she had yet to catch up.

Then I remembered: She was at home with Gay. Lying on her bed. Still scared about the fact that, one day, she could see as well as she ever could, while the next, her world went dark. It was clearly getting lighter, but we still did not know if her eyesight would ever return to normal.

I put the water bowl back in the side pocket and hoisted my pack.

Casey rose at the sound of my return and wagged her tail a bit. She knew it was me. She sniffed my shoes for a long time. They smelled of the woods she knows so well.

DAY 70

A couple years ago, a friend was suffering from a hip issue that was causing him severe distress. I watched as he hobbled into our local organic grocery store with a limp grave enough that he could not mitigate, much less hide, his listing stride. He tried mightily though, understanding full well what an outward manifestation of any manner of malady in Gila Country portends.

Sadly, his gallant attempt to walk normally failed. As a result, customers and employees alike, sensing wounded prey unable to run away, streamed down the aisles toward my ailing amigo, obviously regaling in the opportunity to offer unsolicited advice. It was like they had been waiting for such an opportunity all day and, when it arose, they pounced.

With nary a syllable uttered by my friend providing so much as a hint regarding the source of his affliction or any previous medical diagnoses he may have received from stethoscope-bearing professionals who know how to operate equipment like X-ray and MRI machines, he instantly found himself in the midst of a veritable volcano of recommendations erupting from people old and young, tall and short, hippies, outdoor athletes, male, female, and whatever lies between.

Suggestions like applying poultices made from prickly pear cactus pulp extracted by the light of a harvest moon; smearing unguents derived from the anal sacs of female coatimundis; practicing one-legged yoga on a cliff top while wearing a paisley sari and facing east at sunrise; and engaging in guttural chanting while inhaling smoke generated from a fire fueled by a combination of mesquite branches, wild rose blossoms, and the ass hairs of a javelina.

Folks were crawling atop one another to shout about Rolfing, the liberal application of holy water, chakra realignment, acupuncture, static stretching, dynamic stretching, Grandma's surefire homemade ointment, chelation, pot brownies, praying, exorcism, fasting, ceremonial dancing, orthopedic acupuncture, massage, healing touch, tantric sex, sexual abstinence, tequila infusions, meditation, aromatherapy, sound therapy, sensory deprivation, colon cleansing, and on and on.

People were running down the well-stocked pill/supplement/snake oil aisle grabbing fistfuls of products, sometimes randomly, sometimes with apparent purpose, and shoving vials, bottles, jars, and ampoules into my friend's face and instructing him to take three of these foul-tasting pills or to rub globs of this stinky green slime made from kelp on his ailing hip before bed while burning a cinnamon-infused candle.

There was enough in the way of boisterous bedlam that no one noticed when my friend quietly procured and paid for a small bag of free-range potato chips and shuffled his way out the front door.

He ended up getting several rounds of surgery and has, to the best of my knowledge, fully recovered.

Maybe it's this way the whole world round, but Gila Country seems thick with folks who not only have the inclination but consider it a divine imperative and mission to impart unbidden healing-type wisdom upon people they know and perfect strangers alike. It does not seem to matter one whit if the entirety of their expertise in the medicinal arts consists of having once applied a Band-Aid to a paper cut.

I'm certain they mean well.

I had made two interrelated mistakes. The first was posting on social media a solicitation for "good vibes" (or "healing thoughts" or some such) after Casey went blind. In that post, I outlined the basics: I had put her out in the yard and, when she came back in, she could not see.

The second mistake was, despite the fact—or maybe because of it—that I was still somewhat in shock about my dog's sudden ocular circumstance, I ventured forth for restorative libations that evening. The regular crowd was already chatting full bore about Casey's mysterious condition when I arrived. Numerous participants were tickled pink that, given the nature of her affliction, they could pontificate both on potential cause and potential options for treatment.

"It's my guess that she came in close proximity to a mother skunk and got sprayed directly in the face at point-blank range," one cowboy/carpenter drawled. "My granddaddy told me that back in nineteen thirty-six, same thing happened to his ol' coonhound named Bessie. He fed her a passel of collard greens mixed with gunpowder and bound in possum sinew and she was right as rain in two days!"

I mentioned something about how, if indeed Casey had been sprayed by a skunk—which has happened before—she would likely smell like she had been sprayed by a skunk.

"Coulda been a dry spray," the man responded, sagely, to what I would classify as tepid affirmation by those within earshot.

"Probably a spider bite," a young hipster suggested.

That's another thing about Gila Country: Spider bites are the default diagnosis for a host of afflictions covering the gamut from hangnails to brain cancer. If you don't know what it was, it was likely a spider bite. You could walk in with your arm ripped off to a nub or your skin glowing bright orange with oozing pustules and someone in the room would proffer that, to them, it looked as though you had suffered a spider bite.

I mean, there would have to be populations of hyper-venomous arachnids the size of stegosaurs that have somehow managed to evade the long reach of taxonomy to impart the number, variety, and severity of spider bites accounted for in southwest New Mexico.

The young hipster had heard somewhere along the line that a salve made from baking soda, ground-up aspirin, and plaster of paris applied directly to the spider bite would do the trick. Casey's eyesight would be restored!

Except, I told him that upon examination in the expensive canine ophthalmologist's office down in Tucson, which included going over most of Casey's body with a high-powered magnifying glass, no evidence of a spider bite was found.

"Maybe it was a rattler then," he countered, like the vet would not have noticed a snake bite during her detailed examination.

A lady wearing about two hundred pounds of crystal and turquoise speculated that it was likely an allergic reaction to some manner of pollen mixture, most likely juniper and cholla. I started to mention that at the expensive canine ophthalmologist's office, they did a complete set of allergy tests, which came back negative, but could not find an opportunity to insert that snippet into the increasingly agitated discourse because the crystal/turquoise-wearing woman—who had already jotted down a recipe for me to give to Casey that consisted, if memory serves, primarily of eye of newt mixed with fairy dust—got into an argument with an Eastern mystic, who contended that Casey's situation came about not because of anything my dog did, but rather as an extension of some bad, but frustratingly abstruse, karmic thing *I* did—maybe even in a past life—that somehow rubbed off on my otherwise innocent dog and we would need to engage in an unspecified manner of purification ceremony, preferably in the River Ganges.

An eavesdropping shaman lady sitting two tables over offered to blow some sacred smoke up Casey's nose. Or maybe it was up her rectum.

By the time I drank a few pints, the discussion had died down enough that I was able to wedge in that in the three days since I had taken her to the expensive canine ophthalmologist's office, Casey's eyes seemed to be gradually on the mend.

Despite that, the mystic suggested we all hold hands and, as I had solicited in my social media post fourteen hours prior, send healing thoughts in Casey's general metaphysical direction. Appreciating the input and intent, I bought a round for the house. Not long thereafter, the conversation organically shifted from Casey toward the best cures for hangovers. You can imagine where that went.

When I rose at dawn, Casey's sight had improved. There was still a milky-white glaze covering her eyes, but it was dissipating. She followed me to the front door, clearly wanting to go hiking with me. Since she had spent the previous few days cowering in a dark corner, this was cause for cautious celebration. She was under strict doctor's orders to take it easy for a while. So, I did not take her with me when I drove out to the Gila that morning. But it was heartening that she wanted to go.

The power of healing thoughts should never be underestimated.

DAY 72

I know what you're going to think even before you think it (and I do not blame you): I was drunk or stoned or having some manner of psychotic episode or probably all three simultaneously. Nothing could be further from the truth! Sure, I had partaken of one very small hit of weed, and I was halfway through my second cerveza. By my standards, and the standards of most the people I associate with, that amounts to a near-angelic level of sobriety. As for the psychotic episode part, well, possibly. Depends on your definition, I guess.

It was twenty-six days after I twisted my ankle trying to avoid landing directly atop a rattlesnake. Though the injury was very incrementally getting better, it still pained me to hike, and that reality was beginning to wear on me.

It was six days after Casey lost her eyesight and five days after I had spent almost a grand (money well spent, it turned out) at the canine ophthalmologist's in Tucson. Though the doctor had been confident that Casey would get better, she could not guarantee a full recovery. Casey's eyes were still puffy, red, and swollen. It was obvious that her world remained something of a disoriented blur. My stomach was still tied in knots.

Most every summer evening, I sit on my front porch, comfortable in the shade provided by a particular piñon pine. There is a small, circular-shaped gap in the branches. When the sun reaches that gap on its downward arc toward the ridgetop of the Silver City Range, it's like a powerful searchlight beam pointed directly at my face gets flipped on. Sometimes I preemptively scoot my chair a bit to the left. Most times, I'm so lost in thought, I forget. (I would not have been a very conscientious clock-keeper at Stonehenge. I would likely have missed the winter solstice altogether, screwing up the tribe's mating season or some such.) When I forget to move my chair, it's shade-shade-shade-BOOM—the unimpeded sunlight hits my pupils, which suddenly constrict to pinhole size, which causes momentary disorientation.

One of the best parts about sitting in the shade on my front porch in the evening is the hummingbirds. I don't know where southwest New Mexico ranks on the world's hummingbird-o-meter, but we have plenty, and because we have numerous flowering plants potted in our front yard, those cute little buggers flit around with predictable regularity as I'm sitting there sipping a beverage. Raises my spirits.

Here we get to the part of this tale where a skeptical reader might wonder whether I was being honest and comprehensive when listing my intoxicant intake a few sentences back. Some might wonder if I perhaps inadvertently neglected to include, say, three hits of blotter acid. To that I respond: I have not ingested any manner of hallucinogen in more than thirty years, though I have lately been wondering why that is. I have been considering the possibility of taking one last trip. To that end, if you know where I can get some decent LSD, or for that matter mescaline, psilocybin, or peyote, please let me know (surreptitiously, por favor).

This evening, at the exact instant the sun hit that circular-shaped gap in the shade-making piñon pine—I had once again forgotten to preemptively move my chair—a hummingbird flew up and hovered directly in front of my face, no more than two feet away, something that has never happened before. And it stayed there for probably thirty seconds or more—which is a long time for a hummingbird to remain stationary—with the bright New Mexico summer sun at its back, making it glow. As I ogled, transfixed, it transformed into a flying fairylike creature. Almost Tinkerbell-ish. Its wings became bifurcated, and though I could not make out details, I could discern that its face had morphed from that of a beak-dominated hummingbird to something near human.

At first, it did nothing more than stare at me staring at it. Then, it moved closer, almost nose to nose, looked me square in the eye and clearly said, "Everything is going to be all right." With that, it zipped away, a regular hummingbird once more.

I finished my beer. Fetched another. Hoped the hummingbird would return, because, ever the journalist, I had a few follow-up questions. I needed additional clarification. Was the bird talking about Casey specifically? My ankle? Or the world in general? Or did the bird mistakenly think I was someone else?

By then, the sun had started to set and all the hummingbirds had flown away to wherever they go at night. I used to think it was back to their nests. Now I'm thinking it's a quick flutter to a different plane of existence.

By morning, Casey's eyes were pretty much back to normal, though we still had to drive down to Tucson for a follow-up to the canine ophthalmologist.

And my ankle felt the best it had since I almost landed atop the rattlesnake.

"Everything" was not necessarily "all right," but things were moving in the right direction.

DAY 75

Follow-up with the canine ophthalmologist complete: clean bill of health! Casey's vision has returned! Green light to start hiking with me again!

Almost immediately, she was back to doing stupid dog stuff, like leaping off rock faces sans well-conceived landing plans and dashing full bore through brush-choked creek beds—all as if nothing had ever happened.

We never were able to ascertain what Casey might have gotten into. I searched my property high and low to see if there was a pile of half-eaten roadkill or if perchance there was an empty bacon package lying under a bush. Nothing. A mystery that will remain with us forevermore.

It's shocking how one minute, your life is sailing along with worries no larger than deciding whether to have a sandwich or a burrito for lunch, then the next nanosecond, you're freaking out because your young dog looks like an alien and is walking into walls.

Reminded me to take nothing for granted. Ever. Reminded me to hug my dog every day and to be thankful for the pleasure she brings me, thankful for those rare times when all's well that ends well.

Time to get back on track.

DAY 77

Twenty-nine years ago (plus or minus; neither of us can recollect the exact year), Gay and I tied the knot in the back of a lower-level courtroom of the Denver City and County Building. The presiding judge called a recess in the middle of testimony for what appeared to be a very serious criminal trial. I mean, there was a man sweating in the witness box! We self-consciously walked through the middle of a courtroom packed with stressed-out-looking people. The quest for justice could wait while the judge earned an extra $50—which we had to pay up front in cash—to make us man and wife. He asked if we had rings. He seemed pleased when we said we did, like such was not always the case.

We had had a "real" wedding scheduled back on the family farm in eastern Virginia. A justice of the peace had been hired. Best man agreed to stay mostly sober. Caterers scheduled. Airline tickets purchased by distant family members.

And then a call came: My mother was too ill. The stress of the festivities might kill her. Plans cancelled at the very last minute. Airline tickets turned in for a refund. No new date set.

Four months later, Gay walked into the bedroom of our little apartment in the Mile High City and said, "If we're gonna do it, let's do it. Now." I donned my best tennis shirt, and we drove to the City and County Building and interrupted a trial.

Honeymooned in the mountains of northern New Mexico. Mostly in a tent.

When I asked this morning if she wanted to go "out" for an anniversary lunch, she, likely envisioning green chile and cold beer, answered in an enthusiastic affirmative. What she got was yet another soggy PB&J sitting on a rock under a juniper tree several hours from the closest air conditioning with a dog panting behind her. Silly woman. She's been falling for that same line since Reagan's first term. When will she ever learn?

I often worry. I wonder if she regrets having signed on to this life with me. It has not been easy for her. Lots of trail miles. Lots of soggy sandwiches. Often in support of my various protracted undertakings along long trails that crisscross the Mountain Time Zone.

She grew up in Colorado's Arkansas River Valley, and her family—which included four siblings—was active. During winter, they skied almost every weekend at Monarch, Crested Butte, and Breckenridge, back when the outdoor-recreation craze was still in its infancy. During the summer, the clan—waterskiing fanatics all—car-camped alongside various warm-water reservoirs that lined the lower reaches of the Arkansas. So, basically, what I am saying is that outdoor life is intertwined into the fabric of my wife's being.

Still.

I know she appreciates many aspects of our existence here in the heart of America's Empty Quarter—especially because she is an enthusiastic photographer. I am of the opinion, however, that she would have been happier in the long run had she become attached to someone with a regular income who spent his free time perusing museums or art galleries instead of tromping up mountains and down canyons. I occasionally joke about this. She smiles in such a way that I have trouble reading her thoughts.

I promise that someday I will make it up to her. I do not know when. I do not know how.

When the judge next ran for reelection, Gay voted for him for no other reason, she said, than he bound the two of us together. I considered that to be a good sign. I hope all these years later she would still vote for him.

Later that evening, after we returned from what turned out to be a long and exhausting hike, we celebrated properly, in a restaurant with green chile and cold beer. We laughed about interrupting that trial, as we do every year on this date.

DAY 82

In the South of my teenage years, whenever it was raining while the sun was shining—meteorologically known (simultaneously poetically and prosaically) as a "sun-shower"—some grizzled, half-prophetic old-timer with chaw juice dribbling down his chin would drawl as though the great orator in the sky had hardwired itself directly to the man's larynx, "The devil is beating his wife." All the other grizzled old-timers within earshot would then simultaneously sympathetically shake and knowingly nod their noggins.

Even when I was too young to entertain the theological implications of this statement (including, but not limited to, overt cultural insanity), this phrase bothered me on numerous levels. It bothers me still. It is an ugly phrase for such a lovely phenomenon.

First: I did not know the devil had a wife. That was not mentioned during Sunday school at Ware Episcopal Church, which I was forced to attend until I turned sixteen, at which time I followed a different path. Who exactly is

Mrs. Satan and what did she do to deserve such an ignominious connubial circumstance? Did she meet her future better half at a biker bar? Via the personal ads in the back of an alternative newspaper? Had she always been attracted to bad boys? Did she bring Satan home to meet her parents before tying the knot? If so, what was their reaction? ("You'd better have our daughter home by eleven, or there'll be hell to pay!")

More than that, though, was my specific concern for Mrs. Satan. I mean, on her best day, her life is probably pretty rough. Who does she go shopping with? Who are the other members of her book club? Does she occasionally bake goodies for the damned? ("Who wants more devil's food cake?") Does she ever give Satan grief for coming home drunk? And, germane to the original observation, what could she possibly do to deserve getting beaten under any circumstance, much less during one of the most glorious natural occurrences imaginable, one that, when you get right down to it, ought not even be visible down there in the fiery depths?

In most of the rest of the world, a sun-shower is a sign that some creature—a fox, hyena, bear, deer, raven, monkey, whatever—is either getting married (sometimes across species lines) or giving birth. (In the Dominican Republic, it is a witch who is getting married.)

Only in the American South, and perplexingly in Hungary, do people contend that a sun-shower signals spousal abuse in a setting specifically designed to promulgate the most hideous forms of maltreatment upon a significant percentage of the population for all of eternity.

For me, whenever I see a sun-shower, I'll now go with the Tanzanian interpretation: A lioness is right then producing a new litter of cubs. A beautiful vision, both literally and metaphorically—unless, perhaps, you are a member of a species upon which lions are prone to dine.

DAY 83

Save Gay and Casey, I do not often hike with others. My circle of trail companions has diminished over the years via a combination of people moving away, age-related attrition (a category that unfortunately includes several deaths), and interpersonal fallings-out. I occasionally wonder if my inclination to hike solo is not a sign of an unhealthy level of misanthropy. Seems unlikely, given that, post hike, I often head to a bar to share convivial beverages with my amigos, a few of which are also enthusiastic hikers who, like me, prefer to experience the outdoors unaccompanied. Though I envy those of who seek out on-trail camaraderie, I find solo hiking to be easier on the logistics front. The only person I ever have to worry about being tardy is me, and I am rarely tardy. Solo hiking encourages, or at least allows, the daydreaming that defines most of my jaunts. The chances of me ever joining the local hiking club are next to nil—though I keep track of that group's schedule so I know what times and trails to avoid.

One shockingly toasty midsummer morning last week, Casey and I joined a chum who likewise is inclined toward solitary hiking. He wanted to get my opinion on a feature he had found that looked for all the world like a child's footprint set in ancient stone. Like something you would expect to see in Olduvai Gorge. Once we jointly marveled at that impression and speculated about its provenance, it became almost awkward, like we were both wondering whether from that point on we should pretend the other was not there. Maybe right then go our separate directions, with plans to meet up toward happy hour time. I have read that Americans are uncomfortable with long periods of silence when in the company of others. We prefer to jabber about *something*—even if it's contrived and/or trite—rather than enduring quietude.

One of our forced snippets of discourse centered upon a mutual acquaintance, who my companion described as a "good hiker." He meant that the person in question could hike far and fast. When the conversation subsequently fizzled, I began to consider—and not for the first time—what additional characteristics make a hiker "good." While an ability to hike far and fast can certainly be a component of that definition, it is not the only part. Maybe not even the most important part.

Here I would point out that you don't have to be good at an activity to find pleasure in that activity. You don't have to be Jimmy Connors to enjoy tennis, but if you can't get the ball across the net, you're not going to have much fun. Same way, if you can't make it up a short hill without gasping for breath or you get directionally discombobulated every time you step foot on a trail, the subject of how to define a good hiker has some value.

While hiking with Casey this morning, I thought about what traits and abilities make for a "good" hiker and, when I returned home, concocted a list that likely is simultaneously incomplete, too complete and possibly inaccurate. Maybe even foolish.

I limited the list to actual on-trail areas of competence, opting to forgo such nebulous characteristics as public-lands-preservation proselytization, political activism, and volunteerism.

1. There is no doubt that if a person is not fit enough to hike, if he or she does not have the physical wherewithal to make it out and back, it would be hard to consider them a good hiker.

2. A good hiker is prepared on the gear front for basic emergency situations.

3. A good hiker boasts palpable trail skills. He or she knows how to avoid getting lost, how to treat blisters, how to read the weather, how to cross a river safely, etc.

4. Good hikers understand the impacts they have on the land and work hard to mitigate those impacts. They know the proper way to relieve themselves and subscribe at least halfheartedly to the tenets of Leave No Trace.

5. What about natural history awareness and knowledge? Things like knowing the names of plants and maybe even having a broader understanding of ecosystem dynamics.

6. What about practicing trail manners? Like, say, giving other trail users their space—e.g., not stopping for lunch or pitching a tent close to another party when other options present themselves?

7. Then there is actual technique. Must a good hiker give thought to kinesiology and at least attempt to translate that thought to physiological action? Is paying as much attention to counterbalancing arm swing and torso rotation with leg motion and hip rotation as does a tennis player working on the timing of a backhand a trait of a good hiker? Or coordinating breathing with gait?*

8. Must a hiker hike "a lot" to be good? Frequency? Distance? I mean, you can have someone living in Manhattan who has completed the Triple Crown, who only hikes when he or she is on a multi-month trip. Seems to me that person can still be a good hiker. And there are those who hike often, but maybe not all that far.

9. A good hiker must be able to walk though pain and discomfort, often over long and rugged distances.

10. Does a good hiker keep secret the places she/he visits?

By my own criteria, I wondered if I am a good hiker.

Looking back on my list, I ascribed one point for "newbie" or "incompetent," and up to five points for "accomplished." Given that there are ten observations/questions on my list, a top score would be fifty and a bottom score would be ten.

1. Though likely more resolute than I was in my younger years, I am not as fit as I was a half century ago. I guess I could argue that I am in reasonably good shape for a man of my age who swills as much beer as I do. Still, I could work harder on conditioning. Three.

2. I carry plenty of gear. Well, actually, too much gear. I am generally over-prepared. (Famous last words.) Five.

3. Despite my extensive experience, I still have much to learn. I remain fully capable of getting directionally discombobulated and my fire-building skills are mediocre at best. But I know how to cross streams and treat blisters, and I read the weather fairly well. Three.

4. I am old school enough that by current perspectives, my comportment could stand some improvement. I make number two in a cathole instead of carrying my waste out in a wag bag. I still build fires. I bushwhack a lot. That said, by the standards of my generation, I make certain my impact is as minimal as possible. Three.

5. This one I suck at, though I have absorbed some basic information via osmosis. Two.

6. There are those who would consider the fact that I hike with my dog off leash to be bad manners. That I have worked hard to train

my dog mitigates that transgression somewhat. In every other way I can think of, I take trail manners very seriously. Four.

7. I pay studious attention to the mechanics of hiking. Four.

8. I hike a lot and always have. And I have done numerous multi-month backpacking trips. Four.

9. I have hiked very long distances hungry, wet, cold, hot, dehydrated and with severe pain, covering the gamut from debilitating blisters to shin splints to aching joints to excruciating back pain to a badly twisted ankle. Four.

10. I share specific trail details only with people I know and trust. Four.

So, by my own measuring system, my score is an undistinguished thirty-six—on average, a 3.6 rating per question.

I can at least get the ball back across the net. That's good. But, even after all these years and all these miles, there is much to improve upon. That, or much to redefine.

* I once penned an article for *Backpacker* magazine titled "The Radical Repeaters." One of the backpackers I interviewed (via phone) had completed the Appalachian Trail like eight times. I met her in person at a trails conference some years later. She walked like the Penguin of *Batman* fame. She twitched as she strode, as though she were receiving sporadic jolts of electricity. Yet, this woman was a legitimate thirty-mile-per-day backpacker. So, perfect gait is not required to be a "good" hiker.

DAY 84

There was this lady I dated in college. Well, maybe "dated" is not the most accurate way to put it. She had a serious boyfriend in Tucson. One weekend a month, she went to Tucson, and one weekend a month, Tucson came to Silver City. Then there were those other two weekends. I was plan B, which suited me perfectly.

She was a native of southern New Mexico, an Anglo hippie chick who grew up in dry country. Whenever precipitation moved in, she would call me up or come by my hovel unannounced and entice me to walk with her in the rain. Soft drizzle or gully washer, it did not matter. I was lately arrived from soggy-wet eastern Virginia, where there are often long periods that inspire waterlogged residents to wonder aloud if the rain will *ever* stop. I thought her precipitation fixation was somewhat eccentric. She taught me to think otherwise. About both walking in the rain and eccentricity. Her feminine wiles always won the day, and I started walking with her in the rain whenever she beckoned. I don't know that she was necessarily a happy person by nature, but she always laughed when walking in the rain.

She had self-invented names for various types of rain.

There was "skinny-dipping rain," which described a heavy downpour late at night in the middle of monsoon season, when the rain was bathwater warm and so heavy that the instant you stepped outside, you were soaked down to your skivvies. Rain so heavy it was hard to breathe.

There was "hand-holding rain," which described a light shower at dusk, when the moisture made your skin tingle and the last rays of sun illuminated the translucent clouds, seemingly from within.

There were others, long forgotten.

One that stuck with me the most was "perfume rain," which was enough wetness to make the world smell wonderful, but not enough to make mud. Subtle, not overdone.

That's the kind of rain we had last night. This morning, when Casey and I hiked, the air was perfumed and there was no mud and it reminded me of that hippie chick.

I don't know whatever happened to her. Lost track long ago. It's my guess she ended up moving to Tucson, where rain is far less frequent, but when it does come, it pours hard enough to scour the earth clear down to bedrock.

DAY 88

PART I

During my quest to hike every day for a solid year, I took a half dozen modest backpacking trips, totaling a mere eleven nights. By personal standards established over the course of my entire adult life, that's an almost inconceivably low number. But, given the shaky state of my lower back, I now tread lightly when it comes to carrying heavy loads over long, rugged distances. I fear the days of being out for more than a night or two are likely behind me.

The first of those was a boot-printed palimpsest.

I first arrived in Gila Country in the summer of 1976 to attend Western New Mexico University, then one of the few institutions of higher education in the entire country that would let me within a mile of their campus, unless it was to sweep the floors or clean out the sewer lines. Given that I had managed to attain a grade point average (and I am not making this up) of .6 (yes … point six, as in: about halfway between an F and a D. Though, I am proud to stress that it was slightly closer to a D than an F) at a small community college in the Old Dominion, I was granted a "conditional acceptance," a status that, according to a friend who worked in the registrar's office, they made up specifically for yours truly, given that WNMU had open enrollment. Basically, at that time (things have been tightened up significantly on the academic front in the interim) anyone with a heartbeat who didn't drool too much could attend, with few, if any, questions asked. Till they saw my transcripts. Then they, looking to increase their enrollment numbers by any means necessary, scrambled to concoct an entirely new classification bearing my name. I would have been much better off had I written on my application that I was an escapee from a mental institution and was trying to get my life back on track via a wild stab at higher education.

Even before I memorized a class schedule I would soon come to ignore, I decided to connect with that which first drew my attention to this remote part of the world: the Gila.

My maiden multiday trek into my new backyard would follow an old Jeep track that ascended toward the western flank of a prominent ridge connecting a double summit called the Dos Chichis, located pretty much directly atop the Continental Divide. By a combination of geographic default and geographic ignorance, my takeout point was to be a crumbling Army fort that was established in the late 1800s to help eradicate the local indigenous population. All told, maybe ten or twelve miles. Or maybe thirty. I had no idea.

I hoisted a bright-orange Sears Roebuck external-frame backpack given to me several years prior as a Christmas gift by my mom, who, a mere twelve years later, would be dead. The pack was too small, but my young self, then unfamiliar with the concept of retail returns and exchanges, said nothing for fear of offending a woman who did not know the first thing about outdoor gear but whose intentions were good.

I intended to follow that Jeep track only long enough to pass the national forest boundary sign, at which point I would begin a cross-country bushwhack that had a specific goal: a spring I pretty much chose because a cannabis seed popped out of my pipe and landed on my map Right There. A sign from on high, if ever there was such a thing.

From a retrospective position defined by the passage of more than forty years, I should point out how foolhardy that plan was. At the time, though, it was pretty comprehensive coming from someone who looked at stale bong water as a perfectly acceptable breakfast beverage.

The official map covering the Gila's 3.3 million acres has a scale of which is 1:126720 — meaning that one inch covers about two miles. Two two-dimensional miles, that is, as the map does not include topographic contours. Three-dimensional reality is not portrayed. Ergo: One inch might very well amount to three or four miles when slogging through serious vertical reality. That map is the cartographic equivalent of a novel classified as "magical realism." A precision orientation device it assuredly was not.

My optimism/ignorance coefficient was evidenced by the fact that I carried with me but a single quart canteen to cover a distance I could not accurately gauge across rough, cactus-covered country in hopes of locating a teeny spring icon that, for all I knew, might well have been dry for years. And it was August. Hot.

Off I went—me, my stupidity, and the bliss of my cognitive dissonance all walking arm in arm.

Several ripped-skin hours later, I experienced a *Hallelujah Chorus*-level miracle: I walked directly by that spring, which was flowing wonderfully. It was as though I knew where I was going and what I was doing. I wasn't even shocked or relieved. I just drank it all in and accepted my good fortune without batting a sweat-encrusted eye.

I decided to camp near the gurgling fount. Level ground, however, was hard to come by, so I laid my pack in the very bottom of an arroyo I now know to be the headwaters of Dos Chichis Creek, which, most often, is a bit lacking on the "creek" part. I had never heard the words "flash flood" or "monsoon season." This was the time of year when a storm could have come through and washed my moronic posterior down toward Texas with no evidence of me ever having passed and no one knowing where I was, as I didn't yet know anyone with whom I could share an itinerary that was ill-conceived at best. Sometime later in the semester, an employee at the university might say to a coworker, "I wonder whatever happened to that kid from Virginia."

And the fellow worker would respond, "You mean that moron who was—hee-hee—conditionally accepted into an open-enrollment college?"

"Yeah … he doesn't seem to have attended any of his classes."

"Well, that's how you get a point six grade point average at a community college. Maybe he decided that academia was not for him."

And they would then close my file.

I had a $3 plastic tube tent I used as a ground cloth and could make into a very basic shelter if the weather turned bad. I also had a Class Five Nickel Cigar down sleeping bag, one of my first pieces of backpacking gear that wasn't Boy Scouts or Army-Navy surplus. I laid the bag on top of the tube tent/ground cloth.

Toward dusk, I made a fire ring about fifteen feet from my bedding. I gathered tinder, kindling, sticks, and logs, just like I learned in the Scouts. I then poured an injudicious quantity of white gas from a metal cannister used to fill my one other piece of real backpacking gear—a Svea 123 stove—upon the mound of wood and dropped a match into its center. The flames instantaneously whooshed head high.

Later in the evening, when those flames began to dwindle, I kneeled and leaned forward to blow on what was left of the fire. As I exhaled, an explosion knocked me flat on my keister. And I'm not talking about a pine twig popping in the heat. I mean BOOM!!! Sitting in the dirt, nonplussed, with a ringing in my right ear that would not dissipate for several days, I shook my head and wondered what in the world had just happened. I rose unsteadily to my feet and came to the only plausible conclusion, the same conclusion, I reckoned, that any right-minded person in similar circumstances would reach: Someone unseen had, for unfathomable reasons, tossed an explosive device into the fire! An M-80 at the very least. Maybe even a stick of dynamite. There could be no other explanation!

In response to the unseen threat, I staggered behind a nearby ponderosa pine and crouched, convinced that moving to New Mexico had not been such a good idea. I tentatively emerged some unmeasured amount of time later (I did not own a watch until I was almost middle-aged), my head still ringing. I scoured the area with a weak flashlight beam and saw nothing save a thick wall of innocent trees. I suspected that the mad bomber who had tried to blow my head off had surreptitiously moved on in search of other dipshit newcomers to the Gila.

I then noticed that one of the rocks I had used to build my fire ring—one placed directly next to where my head had been when I blew on the flames—was fractured. Half the rock was gone. Vaporized. For reasons I did not learn until I related this tale to more experienced local campers, if there is one thing you definitely do not do in this part of the world, it's use river rocks to build a campfire ring.

"Pockets of air are often trapped in those rocks and, when heated, the trapped air expands," I was told. "Most times, that expansion only causes the rock to crack, but, sometimes, an explosion occurs."

Some months later, sitting around a campfire down in the Bootheel with a cadre of newfound amigos, I told the story of my near-decapitation, and everyone went real quiet real fast. I am a Sagittarius, a zodiac sign defined by the insertion of one's hiking boot directly into one's big mouth. I knew the instant the words had passed my lips that I had for the millionth time in my life inadvertently said the Wrong Thing. Turns out that the brother of one of the men listening as I related my tale had been killed a few years prior by an exploding river rock. I had relocated to a state where murderous rocks seemed to be fairly common.

When I finally moved toward my sleeping bag there in the bottom of the arroyo, I saw that when the rock exploded, it had sent a fusillade of red-hot shards cascading into the night sky and they had landed in a perfect row upon my plastic tube tent/ground cloth, mere inches from my Class Five Nickel Cigar, and burned through to the ground. That not one of those shards had touched my bag was a miracle. That a fragment had not entered my right temple as I blew upon the fire was an even bigger miracle. It was as though I was being issued a warning that said: "Young man, this is not the East. You are now in Gila Country. You had better get your shit together."

That Class Five Nickel Cigar sleeping bag stayed with me for many years. It was with me when I hiked the Appalachian Trail end-to-end. It was with me the first time I traveled deep into Latin America. It covered me and the woman who is now my wife the very first night we ever spent together in the woods. When it finally died of old age, no longer able to keep its loft, I built a big fire and sent its mortal remains toward the star-filled New Mexico sky.

PART II

Inspired by my quest to hike every day for a year, I decided to recreate that hike at almost exactly the same time of year, forty years after the exploding rock almost blew my head off. (I promise, I have learned a few things in the interim.)

I left Casey at home because it had been a disappointing monsoon season and I suspected the spring, even if I could somehow locate it, would be bone dry. I did not want to have to carry water for one human and one quadruped.

When I decided to move from the Colorado High Country, where I lived mostly happily for a quarter century, back to New Mexico, the reaction from my snow-covered compadres was predictable. I was accused of trying to outrun the gray tide by returning to the scene of my unfettered juvenescence, a time defined by boundless (though directionless) energy and (equally directionless) hypermobility. A time when I rarely lived in one domicile for more than a couple months. A time when my life was defined by forays into the boonies at the expense of what few responsibilities I then had, including but not limited to attending classes and remembering to let whatever lady I was dating know I would be out of touch for an unforeseeable amount of time.

I protested, perhaps a bit too much. "I am not trying to reconnect with my lost youth!" I exclaimed. "I am moving back because I miss the area! Besides, I'm getting tired of freezing my ass off seven months a year!"

Indeed, in the time I had been back in Silver City, I had rarely sought out the venues that served as settings for my transition from unfocused youngster to unfocused old fart. I never passed the young M. John on the trail or sat next to him at a bar. I never visited any of my numerous college-era dwellings. Perhaps I have been purposefully avoiding my previous incarnation to prove my suspicious Colorado cohorts wrong.

This short trip would mark the first time I purposefully went looking for size 11 boot prints long since blown away.

I climbed to the base of the Dos Chichis, where I plopped into the dirt and dined upon a partially melted, peanut butter-flavored PowerBar and a rock-hard red delicious apple, likely genetically modified. On that inaugural hike shortly after I moved to southwest New Mexico in 1976, I scampered up both of those 8,000-foot peaks. The summits are connected by a bright-white rock bridge, upon which, all those years ago, I sat and gleefully snarfed handful after handful of trail mix, purchased from Silver City's first health food store.

The trail mix contained raisins, peanuts, sunflower seeds, chunks of dried fruit, carob chips, and coconut flakes. Hardly exotic ingredients, but to a young man who went to high school in a backwater county where snacks consumed among the trees still consisted primarily of canned Vienna sausages smeared on saltine crackers, this shit might as well have been prepared by Wolfgang Puck. I could not get my fill. I consumed trail mix by the bucketful, out in the Gila and in the sparsely furnished college dormitory room I called home until a better domestic alternative landed in my lap. Yet, despite caloric intake measured in gigawatts, that young man remained refugee-camp scrawny.

These days, I can't eat a raisin without gaining five pounds.

I looked up at that rock bridge, trying to reconcile all that passed time with the unfortunate metabolic reality that verily defines the aging process. I now rely heavily on muscle memory to maintain headway that is increasingly being co-opted by Newton's damned First Law of Motion.

I wondered what that young man sitting on the rock bridge connecting the Dos Chichis would say if he looked down and saw a decrepit version of himself hobbling down below. Would he be pleased that he was still out there, pack upon his back—that he had survived to a ripe old age? Or would he be appalled by what he saw? Would he stare at the infirmed sexagenarian and weigh the supposed benefits of an extended lifespan? Simultaneously, I wondered what I might yell up that steep slope to the previous me. Something only he and I would understand, like maybe: "You were very lucky that you did not get arrested for felony drug possession with intent to distribute when you were pulled over by that state trooper in Kentucky on your journey out here from Virginia with five pounds of weed in the back of your Opel Kadett station wagon. You would still be in prison!"

His eyes might then widen in disbelief.

That fictional conversation could wait till I was comfortably ensconced in camp, lukewarm 90 Shilling in hand (I packed in four cans, in case of emergencies), rumination glands secreting full bore.

Bushwhacking would not be necessary—or even possible—this go-round, given that the entire area surrounding the Dos Chichis is now thick with well-marked trails.

On the backside of the Dos Chichis, I slowed my pace, looking for signs of the spring I located without even trying forty years prior. I examined every side drainage for several miles and found nary a molecule of water. I dropped my pack and walked back and forth a few times, finally giving up and picking a campsite on a rise above the bone-dry bed of Dos Chichis

Creek, in the basic vicinity of where I almost got my head blown off by that exploding river rock.

I uncharacteristically opted to not build a fire. It was far too dry, and my paltry water supply would stand little chance of dousing any runaway flames.

I ate an egg salad sandwich, which, given that it had been in my pack all day, was beginning to smell somewhat sulfuric. I was pleased that my various parts were feeling better than expected. A few bones creaked as I parked in my camp chair, but nothing of consequence hurt any more than usual. As a precaution, I ingested a fistful of over-the-counter anti-inflammatories.

Predictably, my mind wandered back to that river rock explosion, which I count as one of only two instances of surefire near-death I had ever experienced, the other being when the driver of a vehicle in which I was a hitchhiking passenger fell asleep and came within a whisker of rear-ending a parked semi at eighty miles per hour in western Iowa on a bone-chilling winter day.

As the sun moved behind the Dos Chichis, I lit a bowl and settled in for a long-overdue, verb-tense-challenged confab with the wild child I used to be.

Old Me: I thought I might find you here. Do you know who I am?

Young Me: You look familiar.

Old Me: I am you, aged sixty.

(Young Me recoils a bit, staring intently at Old Me's face, framed with scraggly gray facial hair, searching for recognition. He glances down at Old Me's paunch.)

Young Me: I can see a resemblance, but it is not possible that you are me. I mean, look at you. I will never be anything save slender.

Old Me: You haven't yet developed a taste for beer.

Young Me: Beer? I don't even drink. I especially hate beer. If you were me, or, if I were you, or whatever, you would know that. Our mom—my mom—is an alcoholic and the last thing I want is to turn out like her.

Old Me: I know all that, and more. You will one day in the future learn that our dad, too, was an alcoholic. He will die with a bottle in his hand just as we were getting to know each other. But there will be this one very hot summer day when you'll be working in your backyard garden in Denver and a neighbor will be standing there sipping an ice-cold Michelob and you will see the condensation droplets running tantalizingly down the side of the bottle and you will ask him for a sip. That single act will have more bearing on the rest of your life than any other, except perhaps your decision to take the reporter gig in Granby, Colorado, rather than the editor gig in Driggs, Idaho.

Young Me: OK, let's say I believe you—which I don't. But, wait, Denver? What am I doing in Denver? I hate cities.

Old Me: You got laid off your job writing for the *El Paso Times* and became an economic refugee to Colorado. You had no choice.

Young Me: So, it sounds like I will actually make it as a writer.

Old Me: To a certain extent. It has been—will be for you—hit and miss. You will end up spending a lot more time covering small-town school board meetings than penning cool magazine articles and books, though there will be plenty of that as well.

Young Me: That's heartening. Why was taking the reporter gig in Granby so important?

Old Me: Because that's where you will meet the woman who will become your wife. Who is still your wife. She dropped me off at the trailhead earlier today.

Young Me: Wait, what, wife? I'm never going to get married! My domestic history does not speak well to the concept of wedlock. Plus, I like being single. Presents more opportunities.

Old Me: I understand completely. But, when you meet her, your perspective will morph. There was more to the fortuitous and, quite frankly, accidental Granby decision. It's also where you will meet people who will become close friends and important business contacts. This is a good example of following your gut rather than your brain.

111

Young Me: So, what you're saying is …

Old Me: Stop. These types of conversations are invariably one-sided. They generally take the form of the older version speaking to the younger version and dispensing words of wisdom gleaned from a lifetime doing a lot of stupid shit and a small amount of smart shit. Lots of college commencement addresses take that form. I am far more curious to hear from you because I now realize I have long forgotten who I once was. Tell me: What are your aspirations?

Young Me: To stay mobile. To travel as much as possible. To eventually make a living as a writer. Though, as you know, my inability to concentrate and plan ahead presents a challenge. I like to party too much to establish any life goals or specific vocational objectives. Why do you ask?

Old Me: Because, somewhere along the line, I lost track of all that. My life got heavy, and I really didn't notice it was happening until it was too late to reverse course. I own three vehicles, I have a mortgage, and, with each passing year, the concept of hypermobility gets more challenging. We talk about buying a camper trailer and hitting the road for a couple years, but we never seem to get that done. The house needs constant work, and my wife looks after her father, who is suffering from Alzheimer's. I spend almost every evening sitting in front of a TV. It would be easy to say that's all part of the process of maturation. Becoming more grounded is what we are *supposed* to do. But it is weighing on me. I miss being able to store all of my possessions in a backpack and a trunk. I'm wondering where I strayed off that path.

Young Me: Let me get this straight. You're looking to a twenty-year-old version of yourself, one that still drinks bong water and has no car, has about $11 to his name, and was just conditionally accepted into an open-enrollment college for advice?

Old Me: That about covers it.

Young Me: If you want to be more like you were forty years ago, get off your fat ass. It's easy to pack up and let go. Couple weeks ago, I loaded up a car and left my life in Virginia behind.

Old Me: Thing is, I like a lot of things about my life. I like my stuff, even though I don't necessarily like *having* stuff.

Young Me: You can't have it both ways. At least not without cheating. Seems to me that you have long been living a lie. That makes me sad.

Old Me: And, yet, here I am, backpacking the same trail as you.

Young Me: Sounds like life is a complicated journey. Is there any advice you could lay on me to help me navigate that journey?

Old Me: Try to be kinder. Talk less—a lot less—and listen more. Don't be so quick to abandon people, pets, and places. Use condoms. Read more. Tell Mom that you love her. The way she was, it wasn't all her fault, though she certainly deserved some blame.

Young Me: Is Mom gone?

Old Me: Yes, she died after a seven-year battle with cancer.

Young Me: Where was I during that time?

Old Me: You were living in Colorado. You only ever went back to Virginia a couple times during her illness. You could not stand to see her wither away, and she did not want her eldest child to see her like that.

Young Me: Should I warn her to change her ways?

Old Me: Fat chance of her taking heed.

Young Me: Sigh.

Old Me: Sigh.

Young Me: Should I try to turn out like you?

Old Me: I am far less than you imagined you would be, but I am far more than you should have been, slacker that you are. I have made more bad choices than good and, as it turns out, my main operational emotion is regret. I regret that.

Young Me: This is disconcerting. Seems like I should alter what little direction I have before it's too late. Maybe join the Marines, or the Hare Krishnas. Maybe I should end this conversation now.

Old Me: If you do, you will regret it.

Young Me: You are overweight, you drink too much, and, as you said, you spend almost every evening glued to a TV set. Man, I don't own a TV and did not think I ever would. I don't drink and I'm so skinny, I could slide through a straw without touching the sides. You have grown slothful while my energy knows no bounds. I am worried about becoming you.

Old Me: As I said before, a lot of that has to do with simply getting older. Your metabolism slows dramatically. You get tired from a life of activity. Dude, I have accomplished a lot. Earned a black belt in tae kwon do. Played competitive tennis for twenty years. Hiked tens of thousands of miles. Traveled all over the world. Owned two businesses. Did you honestly think for even a minute you would do those things?

Young Me: Never gave it much thought. Till now. Damn. I'll have to think about all this.

Old Me: Good idea. And, if it makes you feel any better about your future, we now have more than 200 channels! TV has never been better!

PART III

I slept well, a rare blessing for a lifelong insomniac. I was calmed by the nocturnal sounds — the breeze through the trees, random bird noises, crickets, and various unidentifiable movements through the surrounding understory. Mice, maybe, or a skunk. Other possible culprits: bear, bobcat, javelina, raccoon, mountain lion, coatimundi, jaguarundi, ringtail cat, coyote, or Mexican gray wolf. I was not concerned. I had hung my food bag well away from camp and did not feel even slightly threatened by the creatures that dwell hereabouts.

I arose early and easily, drank several cups of instant coffee, ate some instant oatmeal, broke camp in a leisurely fashion and gingerly lifted my pack.

It was a beautiful day to move through land I had come to know and love.

Young Me arose forty years ago bleary-eyed. He ached all over. He consumed the last of his trail mix. He packed sloppily. Before he left, he looked once again at the fractured rock that had exploded next to his head and wondered, "What next?"

The temperature rose fast. He was wearing fatigue-type pants purchased at the local Salvation Army store and a long-sleeved flannel shirt. Soon, he was sweating profusely. Yet he did not stop to change into lighter clothes. He wanted more than anything to arrive at the crumbling Army fort, from where he would thumb eight miles back to Silver City as quickly as possible.

He followed an ancient wagon trail that was hand-hewn by the famous Buffalo Soldiers, though he cared about this historic footnote not one whit more than he cared about the tall ships sailing into the Chesapeake Bay to celebrate the American Bicentennial at the exact moment he was packing his car and driving west to New Mexico. His gaze did not deviate from the tread upon which he was sprinting. He did not break stride. It was as though he was chasing something while being chased. He did not detour along the side trail to what is purported to be one of the largest trees of its kind in the world. He bypassed nearby Mogollon-era rock art boasting a unique petro-glyph. He flew through expansive fields of blooming flowers. He passed the fort with scarcely a sideways glance and crossed a busy U.S. highway into a village that has since changed its name, where he bought two Snickers bars at a long-gone gas station, sat in the oily shade, and devoured the candy.

After stopping by the college cafeteria, Young Me hobbled to his dorm room, where he remained cloistered for the rest of the day, dozing, and flipping through a magazine he had never before seen that someone had slid under his door. A magazine called the *Mountain Gazette*. A magazine that would inspire him on both the recreational and vocational levels, a magazine that would at a point in the distant future change his life, that would, in a roundabout way, give him some semblance of direction, clear up to the point that as an old man, he would embark upon a quest to hike every day for a solid year.

The next weekend, Young Me backpacked for three days in an area called Frogtail Ridge. Weekend after that, he got invited by a comely vixen to join her on a trip up into the heart of the Gila. His horizons slowly but surely began to expand.

Young Me eventually hiked all over the Gila, sometimes with companions, often alone. Even when he was forced by economic circumstances to move to Colorado, he still came down to the Gila a couple times a year to feel the high desert air upon his skin and to hike with the ever-increasing number of ghosts that populated his ever-expanding past.

Old Me dillydallied on the way to the ancient Army fort, which is now surrounded by an extensive complex of footpaths I often hike upon. I pulled out my cellphone and called Gay to come pick me up at a pre-arranged trailhead. She brought Casey. We spent the afternoon strolling up an arroyo that boasted a seasonal trickle of water, taking photos and lollygagging in the late-summer sun.

Gay asked how the hike went.

I suspected she was outwardly referring to my many maladies but inwardly referring to something else.

"OK," I responded. "I think I will live to hike another day."

DAY 92

The mail arrived as Casey and I were getting ready to pull out for our daily jaunt in the Gila. In the pile of bills, solicitations for donations, and advertisements for special deals at the local fast-food outlets was a letter with an ominous return address: the Social Security Administration. What on earth could that faceless federal bureaucracy want with the faraway likes of me? Turned out they wanted to remind me that sooner rather than later, I would be eligible to start receiving benefits. There were Serious Matters in need of my attention and consideration.

This communique did not exactly raise my spirits, which were already compromised somewhat by the fact that, after my recent backpacking trip, my back and both knees were hurting. I was definitely feeling my age.

I mean, the thought of getting some additional monthly funds was appealing, but I would have much preferred a non-age-related source. Like winning the lottery or inheriting some cash from a long-lost relative.

But there it was.

Guess I earned it.

And, in typical fashion, as I hiked with only Casey for company, many miles away from the closest signs of human habitation, I thought less about how much more traveling I would be able to afford as soon as my Social Security checks started arriving in a couple years and more about the subject of mortality.

Which inspired me some hours later to research longevity statistics for the average American male. That number is 76.2 years for a man of my ethnicity and zip code—a number that did not factor in bad habits and ill-considered undertakings.

Despite my ever-increasing, age-related ache-and-pain quotient, I have definitely long existed in a state of oblivious denial regarding my life expectancy. A buddy once called me a "young sixty-something," which is conceptually akin to being the least-corroded person in the leper colony. Not long ago, I inadvertently referred to myself as "middle-aged." Another buddy sitting on the next barstool guffawed into his merlot and corrected me. "You, my friend, are a senior citizen." I lived for many years in the county with the longest life expectancy in the country. I no longer live there. Maybe I should move back.

Even understanding that sixty is supposedly the new forty, this is cause for some seriously sober reflection.

I know two people who have passed away while tromping by themselves in the Gila.

One was a local writer named Richard Mahler, whose acquaintance I made because I penned a newspaper story about a book he authored, titled, *"The Jaguar's Shadow: Searching for a Mythic Cat."* Mahler never did rub elbows with the world's third-largest feline during his exploratory journeys through the jungles of Central and South America, but he nonetheless came away with a mighty good yarn. Mahler, who was sixty-six when he perished, and I did a few day hikes together. He showed me a trail I did not know, and I reciprocated by showing him a trail he did not know. A very good trade with someone who understood when and with whom to share information and when not to.

Mahler died of a heart attack while installing a series of wildlife cameras—one of his many outdoor-oriented passions—near a remote stretch of river. His fiancé, who I also know, was a member of the local search and rescue team. When Mahler did not return home on schedule, she mustered the troops. It took three days to find his body. Though she was of course heartbroken—they had recently purchased a home together—his fiancé wrote this to me: "On a scale of horrid to perfect, dying in the wilderness is up there at the top. At least if it's a quick death, which Richard's was."

The other person I knew who passed away in the Gila was fairly famous: Micah True, a.k.a. El Caballo Blanco, the man who organized the footrace about which Christopher McDougall's bestselling book, *Born to Run: A Hidden Tribe, Superathletes, and the Greatest Race the World Has Never Seen*, was based.

I first met True at Margarita's Casa de Huespedes in Creel, Chihuahua, the standard jumping-off town for excursions into Mexico's Barrancas del Cobre—Copper Canyon—home to the now world-famous, long-distance-running Tarahumara Indians, who were the stars of *Born to Run*. The first edition of a book I penned about Copper Canyon had come out the previous year, and I was down there guiding backpacking trips into the heart of the barrancas. True at that time was a Copper Canyon neophyte who claimed that my book had inspired him to check out the area that would come to define his life. He was interested in hearing whatever skinny I could lay on him. He said he was a runner, and he said he drove an old truck. We conversed well into the night.

The second time True and I crossed paths was in Boulder, Colorado. *When in Doubt, Go Higher: A Mountain Gazette Anthology*, which I edited and contributed to, had recently been published and I was dashing to some coffee shop on Pearl Street for a live promotional radio interview. I parked behind a battered pickup truck with, of all curious things in the well-coiffed epicenter of cultured Colorado, a faded bumper sticker for Batopilas, one of the most boondock towns in the Copper Canyon area.

As I was blathering into a microphone, I noticed a gangly hombre sitting nearby, observing the proceedings. Though he looked familiar, I could not place him. After the interview, the man came over and said words to the effect of, "You probably don't remember me, but you had a significant effect on my life." Now, when you've been John Fayhee as long as I have been John Fayhee, your natural reaction to words like that is to assume that somewhere in the middle of those syllables lie a pregnant sister or a stint in an alcohol rehab facility. But, no, in this rare case, it was a positive effect.

He was well on his way to becoming not Micah True but, rather, El Caballo Blanco—the White Horse. He was living in Batopilas six months of the year in a house he renovated and was in the process of organizing the race that was immortalized in *Born to Run*. We chatted for maybe thirty minutes before I had to dash off for another interview.

We met again in Batopilas several years later. I had just returned from an extremely arduous ten-day cross-canyon backpacking trip—the type of on-foot journey where you arrive at your destination with your clothes in tatters and campfire smoke forevermore absorbed into your eyelashes. I was beat, and my three compadres and I still had to arrange for transport back to Creel—six or eight hours away—the next morning, so Micah and I did not have much time to catch up. He related a bone-chilling story.

There was only one road connecting Batopilas to the outside world, and that road—dirt, rutted, eroded, and without shoulders—remains an engineering marvel that scares the living shit out of travelers. From the lip of Batopilas Canyon to the Rio Batopilas, it drops 6,000 feet and includes more than forty hairpin switchbacks and more than 200 curves.

Littered in the various arroyos the road crosses are the remains of many vehicles that over the years did not make it. Their brakes might have overheated. A tie rod might have broken. The driver might have been drunk. Whatever the cause, when you're descending into Batopilas Canyon, you see a lot of wreckage that lends a high degree of motivation to your driving efforts, for those off-road vehicular corpses are always trashed, burned, and in a such a state of destruction that you know beyond the shadow of a reasonable doubt the people who were in those cars, pickups, and semis did not survive.

Turns out that Micah's old truck—the one he told me about when we first met and the one that I parked behind in Boulder—was among the wreckage. Yes, he had lost control and down he went. Miraculously, he managed to evade certain doom. He walked away unscathed.

Fast forward. My wife and I were in northern Cameroon, and I had an opportunity to check emails in a sweltering Internet café populated by a shocking number of colorfully attired local tribespeople. There was a message from a runner friend in Colorado, who did not know I was in Africa. "When are you going to write something about Micah True?" he asked.

"Uh, why? What's up?" I responded. It was only then that I learned True had perished, not in the depths of Copper Canyon, but a few miles from my home back in New Mexico.

True had died of a congenital heart malfunction after having left on a solo run along a trail I have followed several times. He was found in a reclining position with his feet in the creek. Rescue personnel later said he looked relaxed.

It is hard to avoid using the words, "Well, at least Richard Mahler and Micah True died doing what they loved in a beautiful place."

I can't help wondering what their last thoughts were, or if they even had the chance to reflect upon their immediate circumstance. Did they have a final few seconds of cogency? Did they lay back listening to the sound of silence, thinking how fulfilling their lives had been? Or did they think words to the effect of, "This sucks." Did their impressive lives flash before them? Did they scream or cry?

The thought of dying alone in the wilderness bothers me not in the least. Matter of fact, it's how I would like to go. I mean, I hope I don't go anytime soon, and I further hope I don't die doing something inordinately bone-headed. I'd prefer it not hurt too badly. It would be nice if my corpse is not too mangled. But, if I end up lying by a stream, like Micah True or Richard Mahler, as my heart starts giving out, I can live with that manner of death.

With any luck, I'll have the opportunity to cash a couple Social Security checks beforehand.

DAY 97

I could put it off no longer: I needed to stock up on doggie supplies. Since Casey is about as spoiled as a canine can be, this chore can't always be fully achieved at the local pet food store, wonderful though it is. A quarterly jaunt to the Big City—which, thankfully, boasts some decent hiking trails nearby—is required.

As she was ringing up what turned out to be a stunningly expensive array of food items for my corpulent canine, the cashier stated enthusiastically while holding a large package of glucosamine-infused, organic, holier-than-thou, free-range chicken jerky treats I intended to purchase, "I think these taste a lot better than the other kind." Her wording caught my attention. Surely, she meant, "My dogs seem to like them better than the competitor's brand." I rationally asked for clarification. "I always try products before I feed them to my babies," she said matter-of-factly while wearing an awkward facial expression that, if I may be judgmental, did not indicate even baseline levels of fundamental social acuity.

My mind quickly raced to the various disgusting store-bought items my dog has devoured. Dried sheep tracheas, pig ears, and cow hooves spring to mind. Surely this woman did not consume stuff like that!

"Oh yes!" she effused. "If something's not good enough for me, then it's certainly not good enough for Woozie and Wiggles." (Two creatures, I am certain, who get up every morning gleefully wondering what weird stuff they can coax their obviously nuts human companion to consume in their name.)

The cashier seemed to notice that my eyes were splayed wide, and my jaw was hyperdistended, an autonomic response to the fact that I was experiencing a disorienting combination of dumbfoundedness and disgust.

"Yeah, I'm the crazy lady who walks around with a pocketful of Milk-Bones just in case ... " she said, her voice trailing off as a small dab of drool seeped from the corner of her mouth while she lustily eyeballed my bag of glucosamine-infused, organic, holier-than-thou, free-range chicken jerky treats. Verily, I had to tug-of-war them from her grip. On my way out, I wondered if I ought to call the psych ward or animal control.

DAY 98

 Sometimes the best course of action is no course of action.

DAY 99

 Sometimes the best course of action is to change course.

DAY 100

When I decided to try to hike every day for a full year, I baked into the conceptual cake a bugout date: one hundred days. I figured that if I made it to the century mark, I would then reevaluate the entire process. Do a head-to-toe reconnoiter to ascertain how many body parts were still functioning within normal operational parameters. Scrutinize my motivation levels. Attempt to determine if Gay was buying into the notion of continuing to revolve a significant chunk of her life around yet another of my harebrained schemes that involves a pack, mud, bugs, snakes, and many meals consisting of energy bars that ought to have been thrown away last year.

Had I decided to bail, I figured I could still hold my head somewhat high, which would have been easy enough, given that, up until that point, with the exception of my opening-ceremony bacchanal—which none of the other participants remembered—I had kept my quest relatively secret. Few related social media posts and little additional mention of my endeavor during happy hour libations. Most of my chums already knew that I hiked a lot, so, upon relating details about recent forays into the Gila, no one thought—or cared—to ask why I had been venturing into the Gila so frequently of late.

Today was the day I set to decide if I was inclined to follow this quest through to an end that, at this juncture, appeared shockingly distant.

I could have split the difference by opting to pursue a more open-ended goal. Something like "see how many consecutive days I could make it," without having in mind a target number. I knew myself too well. Had I opted for that alternative, I would have fizzled at maybe Day 127 and felt like crap about my lack of perseverance.

If I took so much as one step upon a trail today, I was by default committing to the rest of the year.

Gay, Casey, and I drove to a trailhead that accesses a legally designated wilderness area named after one of the world's foremost conservation pioneers. The wildflowers were in full bloom. The creek was tinkling. Aspen leaves were beginning to show the first tentative signs of autumn. Temperature in the low seventies. Nice picnic lunch, shared with a certain canine who knows no shame when it comes to letting me know that, yes, now that I mentioned it, she would be only too happy to relieve me of the last half of my turkey sandwich.

All told: wonderful. The kind of day that makes you reluctant to return home for fear that next time out, similar sublimity could not possibly be replicated.

I can't say I was feeling perfect, but none of my various maladies was any worse than usual, and there were no new aches or pains to report. My ankle was totally healed. Casey's vision was restored. Gay was onboard. And I felt enthusiastic.

OK, then.

Time to start adding an additional layer of motivation by making references to my quest on social media and at my regular haunts. Paint myself into a corner, so to speak.

Full steam ahead.

Or at least some level of steam ahead.

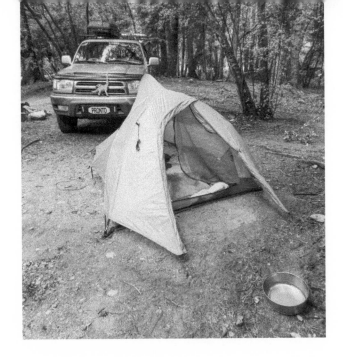

DAY 101

OK, kids: If you skip more classes than you actually attend because you can't for the life of you sit still; drop out of college several times to do things like hang out on beaches in Mexico; accept a series of crappy, low-paying jobs—which you invariably quit because you want to spend the summer backpacking—solely because they are located in beautiful mountain settings; burn bridges with reckless abandon; turn the process of making bad choices into a copyright-able art form; and routinely thumb your nose at anything even remotely resembling an orderly progression into your golden years, then you, too, can become a famous writer and travel in high style and the lap of luxury to the various locations that require your august presence.

DAY 102

It is my most sincere retrospective hope that the couple—probably in their eighties—had not been standing there observing the spasmodic trailside debacle from start to finish. I would like to think they only arrived on the scene during the final discouraging moments, well after the barrage of foul-tempered foul language emanating from my contorted mouth that had recently resonated through the otherwise tranquil forest had dissipated. The couple—turns out they were from Arizona—were gracious.

"Everything OK?" the husband inquired, tentatively, as his wife inched her way behind him.

"Sure, why do you ask?" I responded.

They hiked on and left me standing there trying to act nonchalant holding a trail shoe in one hand while a foot adorned only in a sock stood firmly planted in the dirt.

The couple had witnessed my spasmodic attempts to get a pebble out of my shoe—an increasingly challenging endeavor these days.

Even though I wear ankle gaiters, I still manage, with astonishing frequency, to get all manner of irritating detritus—mostly pebbles—in my hiking footwear. Drives me crazy. My preferred method of dealing with this is to find a boulder, stump, or blowdown upon which I can either sit or station the foot bearing the shoe that needs to be removed, shaken out, and put back on. Alas, often there is nothing that fits the bill readily available. Therefore, I either need to endure the irritation of hiking with a pebble in my shoe, or I need to resolve the situation by kneeling down to remove the shoe or by standing unsteadily on one foot, like an intoxicated flamingo. Neither is an easy task with a bad back and balance that is increasingly falling victim to age.

The goal, of course, is to prevent the now shoeless foot from contacting the ground, for fear of having a sticker, thorn, seed, barb, needle, or spine attaching itself to the naked sock—a near certainty in these parts—which would, when the hopefully now pebble-free shoe is returned to its rightful foot, be worse than having a pebble in my shoe in the first place.

Here's the plan: Raise the foot bearing the footwear with the offending pebble—which usually turns out to be about one-eighth the size of a piece of Grape-Nuts cereal, though it feels as though a full-sized dump truck has unloaded ten yards of gravel directly into my shoe— slowly and smoothly enough that what little remains of my equilibrium is not knocked off kilter. Then, remove the ankle gaiter, untie the shoe, remove the shoe, shake it out, replace the shoe, retie the shoe, reattach the gaiter—all while continuing to stand on one foot—and start happily hiking in pebble-free bliss.

Here's how it usually goes: Raise the foot bearing the shoe with the offending pebble slowly enough that what little remains of my balance is not knocked off kilter. Almost immediately, lose my balance enough that I have to touch the ground with the foot still bearing the shoe with the pebble in it long enough to regain my equilibrium. After several tries, I manage to quickly remove the ankle gaiter, but, while so doing, I once again fail to retain my balance and once again have to do a quick toe-tap. In desperation, I reach for the steadying influence of a nearby tree branch, which causes my hand to be covered in the kind of sap that takes a blowtorch to remove. Absentmindedly, I scratch my nose, thereby getting sap on half my face. I eventually manage to untie, remove, and shake the shoe out. This simple act causes me to once again have to touch the ground with my now shoeless foot, upon which time the exposed sock becomes a repository for every sticker, thorn, seed, barb, needle and spine within ten miles and upon which time I throw my hands up— which causes me to lose my balance even more and let out with a barrage of foul-tempered foul language—which, this go-round, is when I noticed the couple from Arizona standing there—replace the shoe, retie the shoe, reattach the gaiter, and start hiking. Within two steps, I notice that there is now a shockingly wide array of stickers, thorns, seeds, barbs, needles, and spines attached to the sock that had been in direct contact with the ground several times.

I then commence the entire process anew.

There are times when the unforeseeable vicissitudes of the aging process are, shall we say, trying.

Throughout my life, I have been middle of the pack when it comes to speed, strength, and endurance. The only general areas of physical acumen in which I have long excelled are reflexes, coordination, agility, and, at least in theory, *balance*. To see those diminish is truly disheartening and makes me understand that the Road Ends sign is looming ever closer; it's just that I now need progressive trifocals to read it.

This is a tough pill to swallow.

There is a device called a Bosu ball, which is touted as a "balance trainer." I once was able to stand atop a Bosu ball on one foot while executing a slow-motion tae kwon do kick. That seems like yesterday, and like a million years ago.

I have ordered a new Bosu ball, which might be a mistake. I'll probably fall off and break my head. But I will not let those damned little pebbles that make their way into my hiking shoes despite the fact that I wear ankle gaiters impact me without a fight. I swear, I will once again be able to stand on one foot next to a trail in full view of whoever might pass by, and proudly shake my shoe out without aid and without chagrin! I refuse to totally lose the one physical trait I ever possessed that was a teensy bit above average. I will prevail! Soon thereafter, I will likely expire.

DAY 104

A friend almost stepped on a rattlesnake—the first she had ever seen—while hiking on TS-X. Casey and I had passed her on the trail, a couple miles distant from and an hour prior to her encounter, which she described that evening at the bar as "exciting." Based upon her description of both the locale and the snake, it might have been the same one Casey and I came across several years before. It took out after us. That was a sphincter-puckering experience, let me tell you. Big sucker. Ten rattles. Substantial enough to constrict and digest a small dog.

My friend took a photo and posted it on social media. The responses covered a predictable gamut, from "Eek" to "You're lucky you didn't step on it!" At the far end, of course, were observations that she should have killed it, at least partially because it had the audacity to dwell close to a well-trod trail and at least partially because, well, it's a snake! There are plenty of people in these parts who indiscriminately kill pretty much anything that walks, flies, slithers, jumps, crawls, swims, or innocently sits there pretty much for the hell of it.

I have had many rattlesnake encounters. Most times, the snakes were far calmer than I was. They remained curled up in whatever recess they could find—an indentation in a stump, under a rock overhang, within the tangled branches of a bush or in a shadow as an unwary hiker is jumping across a creek. There have been instances where the snake was riled enough to rear up on its hind legs. I have never had a snake strike at me. Damned sure have never been bit.

Many years ago, much to my eternal chagrin, I killed a rattlesnake. I had invited a nubile coed to join me on a backpacking trip into the Gila. She, being a wilderness neophyte, expressed concern about potential dangers, including, but not limited to, rattlesnakes. I assured her that the chances of encountering any member of the Crotalinae subfamily were slim. Yet, less than an hour in, we came toe-to-toe with a juvenile black-tail about eighteen inches long. We saw it in plenty of time, but still, my companion was freaked out enough that she wanted to turn around and go home. To calm her down in hopes that we would, as planned, share a tent that evening, I picked up a rock and lobbed it at the snake, which was sprinting away as fast as it could laterally undulate—clearly demonstrating that it had no intention whatsoever to bite either my companion or me. The rock hit the poor snake directly and killed it instantly, initiating, I will be convinced till my dying breath, a two-year run of extremely bad luck that included two negative interactions with courts of law and ended only after I came within a whisker of getting killed—as I related earlier—when the driver of a vehicle in which I was a back seat passenger fell asleep at the wheel and nearly rear-ended at eighty miles per hour a semi that had pulled off on the shoulder of Interstate 80 in—of all bleak places to perish—western Iowa.

The thought of killing another snake has never crossed my mind, not only because I fear the karmic ramifications, and not only because I understand the undeniable role snakes play in the environment, but because, as I have aged, I have come to loathe the notion of killing anything without just cause. When moths, spiders, scorpions, or centipedes enter my domestic space, I practice catch and release.

But there are circumstances in which the infliction of death, or the attempted infliction of death, is justified.

My philosophy in this regard is simple: Any creature that is biting me or attempting to bite me, I have every right to kill, or attempt to kill. This covers creatures from *Giardia lamblia* parasites taking up residence in my digestive tract to mosquitos, flies, fleas, or ticks inserting, or trying to insert, their nasty proboscises into my flesh, to grizzly bears and white sharks trying to eat me, though, admittedly, those last two are harder to swat.

The ethics of animal killing turn gray when faced with creatures that are giving serious thought to biting me but are not yet biting me. Like a grizzly bear on a predation approach. Were that to happen, on the very off chance that I possessed a high-caliber rifle, I would likely decide to discharge the weapon. Warning shot first. Were I sans weaponry—the most likely scenario—that poor bear would then experience an onslaught of bad language morphing into frantic screams, the likes of which it had never seen or heard before. That would surely teach it a lesson it would never forget!

I draw the line with creatures that are able to bite me, but the chances of them doing so remain slim. I once read that the Greenland shark could very well eat a human—but few humans, especially me, are likely to be swimming among the icebergs. So, Greenland sharks are off the hook. I shall not go out of my way to kill a single one of them.

This same hierarchy of death applies to creatures that are stinging me, trying to sting me, or giving serious thought to stinging me.

There are always exceptions. I once grabbed a desert tortoise that was crawling across a busy highway at a very tortoise-like pace and almost assuredly would have been run over had I not intervened. It thanked me by chowing down on my left index finger. Didn't break the skin, but still, it was uncalled for. I did not kill that tortoise. I relocated it well off the asphalt in the direction it had been traveling and wagged my recently bitten digit at it while it moved away.

I also once rescued a baby raccoon that was in a life-threatening situation. It was a tricky undertaking, made more complicated by the fact that the entire time, the raccoon, oblivious to the fact that I was there to save it, was trying to gnaw on me with razor-sharp teeth. As I was holding it at arm's length, it was trying to rip my nose off. I could hear its incisors snapping together. I raised a baby raccoon while in high school and, therefore, know full well the power of their bite. Understanding that the poor thing had no idea I was a Good Samaritan, I, likewise, did not kill the baby raccoon, though I did give it a stern lecture regarding proper displays of appreciation.

Casey bit me one time. She had only been in my life for a few months. Therefore, she did not yet know who I was or what I was capable of. I was tending to a wound on her paw and evidently tended a bit too forcefully. She yelped and chomped my hand. The resultant look on her face bespoke a fear that I very might kill her. I did not kill her. I hugged her close and apologized for not being dainty enough in my medical ministrations. I told her she had nothing to worry about, that she would always be safe with me. Were she a feline, I believe she would have purred. The moment was interrupted when a swarm of mosquitoes descended upon us. In an instant, I was on my feet, cursing and flailing, trying to kill as many of those vexatious buggers as possible.

Casey did not know what to think. She did, however, seem mighty happy to be alive, despite all the mosquitoes biting her snout.

DAY 107

There comes a point as you're standing there—yet again!—clavicles-deep in near-impenetrable briars and brambles, when you might be inclined to ask—and not for the first time!—if there has ever been another person stupid enough to be standing where you are right now standing?

Then, out of the blue, an answer to your exasperated interrogative magically appears down past your bleeding, abraded shins. Lying on the trail-free ground is a miniature Snickers wrapper!

"Sure, it might have blown in from some less uncomfortable venue. A five-year-old's birthday party in a well-kept backyard, perhaps."

Screw that. It is much better to think there has indeed been another person stupid enough to have stumbled upon this spot. It is somehow reassuring to know you are not the lone resident of the intellectual basement.

DAY 110

It is truly wonderful to experience a trailside chitchat with a pair of pretty young ladies, during which time you have the opportunity to engage your wise man-of-the-mountains persona full throttle, only to get back to your vehicle a half hour later and realize you've got a two-inch snot streamer dangling like a mucous pendulum from your right nostril. I had wondered why those ladies were grimacing as we talked and giggling when they hiked off in the direction from which I had just come.

To make matters worse, they were in my regular bar later than evening. I considered offering to buy them a drink but thought better of it.

DAY 112

It took a few minutes for the unlikely reality to sink in: The cook looked to have expired while preparing my lunch.

It had been a frantic day, crossing featureless expanse at a high rate of speed in hopes of getting to a trail before dark. I had pulled into a low-key-looking dining establishment advertising "the best Mexican food in town." I ordered a combination plate—enchiladas, tamales, rellenos, frijoles. The dining room was mostly full—a good sign. One by one, the other patrons, all seated before I arrived, got their plates, with each order being preceded by a wheezing, barely audible "Order up" coming from the kitchen.

Finally, it looked to be my turn. I heard the first phlegmatic syllables announcing that my meal was about to be served. Thing is, those syllables pretty much ended with the word "Order." At that point, the pronouncement petered out, with only the first wisp of the "u" at the beginning of "up" forthcoming. It was like: "Order uh ... " Then, nothing.

Then, panic.

The next words emanating from the kitchen took frantic exclamatory form: "BERT!!! BERT!!! OH MY GOD!!! SOMEONE CALL NINE ONE ONE!!!"

Much bedlam ensued.

Like the other patrons, I stood and glanced into the kitchen, where, through a cluster of waitress legs, I could clearly see a set of running-shoe-adorned feet, toes pointed upward, sticking out from behind a counter. Presumably, those feet, which were not moving, belonged to poor Bert.

On top of the counter, clearly visible, under a heat lamp, was my order. I could see the steam rising from my enchiladas, tamales, rellenos, and frijoles. I considered tiptoeing in through the unfolding pandemonium and fetching my food, but I thought that would be a bit unseemly, maybe even disrespectful. I stood there, wondering why Bert could not have held on for a little bit longer, long enough for me to consume a repast that very well might have been his last.

I slinked out a side door before officialdom arrived on the scene. My luck, I would be held as a material witness or some such. I went to a greasy spoon down the street. From my booth, I saw a slew of emergency vehicles pulling into the restaurant I had recently left.

Whatever Bert's ultimate fate may have been, I do not know, though I suspected the worst.

I made it to the trail an hour before total darkness and was able to continue my quest to hike every day for a solid year.

While on the trail, I decided it was high time I started eating healthier.

DAY 117

The first day of autumn had arrived. The monsoon season was a dud and hot temperatures persisted till the middle of September. Usually, it cools down when the rains come in July, though they come later and later every year, if at all. Finally, we got one serious storm. More than an inch fell in an hour in the middle of the night. The kind of theatrical meteorological event that freaks Casey out. She sits next to my side of the bed and stares, wondering why her supposedly omnipotent human companion will not rise up and stop the ferocious gale and the lightning flashing one strike following another and the boom of the thunder that rattles the house. She shakes, pants, whimpers, and fidgets. I hug her and stress to her that, like the previous hundred-some-odd such storms she has experienced in her life, we will likely survive. And, if we do not, it has been a good life.

The thermometer dropped a solid twenty degrees overnight, and the day dawned chilly enough that, for the first time since April, I donned a long-sleeved shirt when Casey and I went out. I had to hunt the shirt down, having forgotten where it was stored. I finally located it in a bag reserved for cleaning rags. Gay had thought, given the shirt's tattered state, that I had discarded it. I was aghast, informing the love of my life that she was sorely mistaken, that the shirt had at least another season's worth of life. I did not ask what specific use she had put my shirt to, but it smelled a bit like the chemicals one uses to sanitize a bathroom. Some things are better left unknown.

Since I had only been wearing only T-shirts for the previous six months, it took several tries to slide my arms into long sleeves that were simply not cooperating. One was inside out. The other was twisted. Getting the buttons—half of which were missing—properly aligned was likewise surprisingly problematic.

We arrived at the trail early. The rising sun was hidden by the last wafts of the summer's wildfire smoke, which, on the respiratory front, had made the previous few months feel like one long bong-hit marathon. Though there was nary a cloud, we hiked for more than an hour before we could see what, for many days, had been a bloody sun.

There are times when I wonder how much longer the American Southwest will remain habitable. Though there are some years when we receive above-average precipitation, overall, the region is desiccating before our very eyes and under our very feet. The fires get worse every year. Soon, there will be little left to burn.

Tomorrow, we begin our fall hiking schedule, in which we go out in the late afternoon instead of early morning and venture farther afield than TS-X. I can turn the alarm clock off till spring.

The stoned elves can rest.

DAY 118

PART I:
Fighting over big mounds of cow shit

While tromping down a little-used trail, I came upon what appeared to be a very spirited turf battle between two highly motivated dung beetles. These members of the vowel-heavy superfamily Scarabaeoidea were fighting over what appeared to be a modest-sized, mostly dry pile of cow shit. Nearby were located numerous larger, moister mounds of bovine caca that appeared void of any dung beetle territorial claims. Seemed to me like there was plenty of shit for everyone.

Yet, here these two beetles—inch long and dark black—were slugging it out like six-legged, mixed martial arts cage fighters with antennae and exoskeletons, despite living in an apparent land of plenty (all things being relative in the world of dung, one supposes).

Eventually, one of the dung beetles seemed to tire, and he slinked off, tail between its legs.

The victorious beetle, temporarily distracted by my presence, lost track of his vanquished foe. Once it ascertained that I was likely not a threat, or that I was a threat so off-the-scale-of-comprehension significant that he could do nothing about it had I manifested any sort of anti-dung beetle malice, he started searching intensely for the other beetle, who was hiding a few feet away under a leaf. The triumphant beetle was obviously looking to inflict even more degradation on the defeated dung beetle, to rub his face in the shit.

While the one dung beetle was trying to locate the second dung beetle, yet another dung beetle climbed atop the disputed pile of mostly dry cow shit and seemed to contentedly stake his claim. I believe I might have even heard a snicker.

For a few moments, I started thinking in terms of metaphors and analogies and such. Stuff about greed and wealth distribution and resource management and vocational overspecialization. By the time I walked on, however, I was mainly thinking about how I hope in my next life I don't come back as a dung beetle.

PART II:
Dung beetles push horse turds

A few days later, Gay, Casey, and I were walking down a completely different trail and noticed a completely different kind of dung beetle rolling rounded horse turds down the center of the tread to destinations unknown. What the end use of these turds was to be, who knew?

Anyhow, these beetles were bright green and smaller than the ones I saw fighting over the big piles of mostly dry cow shit. (I mean, how dung-specific are dung beetles?) One of them had rolled a horse nugget into a small depression. It was stuck. No matter how hard it tried, it could not muster the fortitude to get that shit out. It would push the turd about halfway up

145

the side of the depression, lose momentum, then the shit would roll back down, almost crushing the increasingly frustrated dung beetle. And the dung beetle would try again. And again. It had resolve. I wondered if the Sisyphus fable was born down in the dirt, when some random person—an aspiring freelance scribe, perhaps—from ancient Athens was walking along one day and noticed a dung beetle trying and failing to roll a nugget of horse shit out of a depression and thought, "This seems like good myth-making material!"

A few feet from the depression was a mother lode of horse shit. The beetle could have easily abandoned the shit in the depression and gone back for a different turd, one which, hopefully, it could roll around the depression. I finally leaned over and flicked the horse turd out. The dung beetle climbed out of the depression and began rolling the turd to wherever or whatever its goal might be. No expression of gratitude. No offer to share the shit. I was tempted to roll the shit back down into the depression.

Either way, once again, the thought of reincarnation entered my head. I don't know if there's a way a man can preemptively affect what he comes back as. If there is, I will be following the path of righteousness from here on out in hopes that doing things like helping a dung beetle get a horse turd out of a depression will balance the scales in my favor.

DAY 120

The delightfully windy byway had been delightfully winding its way through a dense forest—in the peak of fall colors—for long enough that I was beginning to worry that perhaps I had missed the turnoff to the trailhead that was my goal.

Coming upon a clearing, I saw a man driving an ancient tractor across the road. I pulled behind him into a gravel parking area to ask for directions. I got out of my car, and he stopped, turned his tractor off, and dismounted. After shaking hands, I asked, "Is this the road to the trailhead?"

"I will tell you," the man responded, "but, first, would you pray with me?"

My initial response was to think that, if a man needs to try to establish a cosmic connection with the great GPS satellite in the sky to give a stranger directions to a nearby trailhead, then maybe this is not the right man to be asking for basic orientation.

Then I noticed that we were standing close to a big red building with a cross mounted on top and, in front, a sign that read: Little Hope Baptist Church. Now, if I were to open a church—and I understand that's a conceptual stretch of the first magnitude—I would likely name it something a tad more positive than "Little Hope"—"Moderate Hope" perhaps, or "Some Hope"—but maybe the name is somehow in keeping with the foundational beliefs of this particular congregation. Maybe they are nihilist worshippers. This is not exactly my area of expertise.

The man's facial expression as he eyeballed me indicated that his hope gauge was not exactly redlining at that juncture. But I really wanted to locate this particular trailhead, so I said, "OK."

The man, who was about seventy, looked surprised and bowed his head so intensely that I wondered if his cervical spine had not suddenly liquefied. I mean, his chin was resting comfortably on his xiphoid process. I tilted my head over at about a one-degree angle, hoping that a bolt of lightning would not suddenly flash forth from the sky and fry my sinful corpus into a steaming puddle of sacrilegious goo right there in the Little Hope parking area.

I waited for what seemed like long enough that a prayer ought to have been forthcoming. Maybe my new friend had lost his train of thought, or maybe he had fallen asleep on his feet. Maybe the congregation of Little Hope Baptist Church preferred silent prayers. Finally, the man cleared his throat and said, "Anytime you're ready." Yikes! He was waiting on me to do the actual praying! Sadly, yours truly being the very definition of a theological illiterate, I knew no proper supplications. I could not even mentally muster a vapid Buddhism-ism about one hand clapping or the journey being the destination.

So, I dug deep into my heart and prayed earnestly, for maybe the first time ever. Having spent my first twelve years in the northern Adirondacks, I have been for more than a half century a dedicated fan of the hapless New York Jets, the very definition of little hope, unless you want to take it one step further down, to the depths of "zero hope." So, standing there in front of

Little Hope Baptist Church, I said, while squinting upward into the heavens: "Look, I know you're a football fan, because I see all these players crossing themselves and pointing toward the sky after scoring a touchdown. So, if you could see fit to help us reach the playoffs, Jets fans everywhere would be in your debt. If you just could bestow upon us a little hope, that would be much appreciated too, right up until the point that hope is once again dashed upon the rocks of ineptitude. Amen."

When the man's head once more reconnected with the vertical plain, I think there was the slightest hint of a grin on his face.

"Now, about the trailhead," I said.

"Son," he drawled, staring deep into my eyes, "you're on the right road."

Postscript: The Jets finished the following season at 5-11 and missed the playoffs yet again. So much for the power of prayer. So much for there always being hope.

DAY 122

Speaking of hope, or the lack thereof, a certain someone, while leaning over to take a photo of an amazing fissure in the earth, through which flowed a chilly-willy stream four feet deep, lost her sunglasses, kerplunk-like. Another certain someone disrobed and entered the frigid water in the near-hopeless hope of retrieving them. While standing in the water and experiencing a severe case of genital shrinkage, the second certain someone felt something foreign moving across his toes. Not a fish or a crawdad or a snake. Rather (of all fortuitous things!), it was a pair of sunglasses, heading slowly toward the distant Sea of Cortez!

Even after all these years, it's nice to occasionally be my wife's hero.

DAY 125

I do not wander aimlessly; I wander without aim.

DAY 126

A friend who dwells happily in the heart of the Rocky Mountains, upon hearing me blather on about my attachment to the Gila, speculated that the area "speaks to me." I nodded my head, as though I fully grasped her meaning, which I did not, though I have given the matter some scattered thought in the interim. I suspect she meant that I have both found my proper place in the world and pulled off a way to reside in that proper place. (Hint: Be willing to survive off frijoles.)

This is a more complex subject than it might seem at first blush.

It has been my very good fortune to call home the frosty boreal forests of the northern Adirondacks, the salt marshes lining the Chesapeake Bay and the thin-aired verticality of the Colorado High Country. I appreciated each in their own way. Yet it is the high desert of southwest New Mexico that, well, speaks to me more than any other, or the loudest, or the most convincingly, or the most poetically.

Taking that line of thought one step further, I have come to wonder what the Gila would say were it inclined and able to actually bend my ear, to *literally* speak to me. I refer not to communicative subcomponents—the birds tweeting or the creek babbling. If "it" could speak in a unified voice comprehensible to someone generally incapable of discerning any nature-based message more subtle than a lightning strike, what would it say, and what would its tone be?

I would like to envision that the Gila might take the form of a matronly earth goddess sitting in a mountain meadow with blossoms in her hair who would initiate our discourse by pulling me close to her ample bosom, stroking my hair, commenting on the beauty of the day, and asking after my health.

Or, failing that, the Gila would speak to me in the voice of my dead buddy Fingerless Fred, who, while as cynical as a man could be, still managed to intertwine humor into his gravellly-voiced observations.

Upon further reflection, however, given the havoc my species has wreaked on the natural world in general and the Gila specifically, I suspect, were the Gila to speak to me, the sentiment might be darker. In the past few years, there have been numerous enormous, human-caused wildfires. There is a large herd of feral cattle that is wreaking havoc in one of the Gila's most fragile riparian areas. There are ever-increasing complaints being lodged with the Forest Service about illegal poaching of both fire-wood and wildlife. It would be perfectly understandable if the Gila took on the angry voice of J.R.R. Tolkien's Treebeard character in *The Lord of the Rings* movie as he ranted, "They come with fire! They come with axes! Gnawing, biting, breaking, hacking, burning! Destroyers and usurpers, curse them!"

Me: Good afternoon, Gila!

Gila: Who are you? Get out of here! And take as many of your fellow humans with you as possible. And your little dog too! Don't come back!

Me: Uh …

Gila: Assuming you are going to stay, please get your head out of your ass. Do not operate under the assumption that because you come here almost every day that your presence is somehow beneficial to the forests and deserts through which you pass. It's not! Your presence amounts to a net loss for the places you claim to revere.

Me: OK, but … I've got this Forest Service map that says, "Welcome to the Gila." I have long thought they were speaking for you.

Gila: You're an idiot! Let's for a moment overlook that you likely drove to the trailhead in a car powered by a gas-guzzling internal-combustion engine just so you could stretch your legs for a couple hours. Let's talk only about the time you are actually hiking. The trail you are utilizing was constructed, maybe in the distant past, to expedite commerce or recently to accommodate the blasted outdoor recreation craze. One day, the trail was not there. The next day, it was there, and from the get-go onward, its existence has affected the surrounding environment in a way that has rippled through all the woods you can see as you stand there with a stupid expression on your face. Species have altered their migration routes and changed their nesting habits. Microclimates emerged. The human smell came to permeate everything from the dirt to the treetops. You humans scare the resident wildlife and scar the landscape.

Me: Well, if you would …

Gila: You and your ilk have managed to either ignore this reality or to justify it, increasingly in economic terms. You build new trails and upgrade old trails to attract more visitors and new residents. Few of you are willing to admit that such undertakings result in negative impacts. You assuage whatever minimal amount of guilt you might possess by invoking the words "sustainable," "stewardship," and "mitigation" as though such reflexive invocations absolve you from scrutinizing the fine print that defines the places many of you consider holy.

Me: Thing is …

Gila: You argue that, while, sure, some areas get sold down the river, the fact that they are being "utilized" by the teeming masses means individual members of those teeming masses will end up donating money to environmental groups, volunteering for trail-improvement projects, supporting candidates who will vote to upgrade national monuments to national parks, supporting the establishment of additional wilderness acreage, and to designate rivers as wild and scenic. And maybe you are right. Who knows? I'm just a bunch of trees, squirrels, earthworms, yellowjackets, hawks, lichens, wolves, trout, rocks, water, weeds, and wildflowers speaking to you in a voice that will likely be lost before it ever reaches your ears, much less your consideration.

Me: Yeah, but ...

Gila: I understand that you are addicted to me. You have no more choice to come here than a junkie does to shoot up. So I do not know what to tell you, except maybe to make your fellow hikers look in the mirror, to examine their habits. What have you to say?

Me: I love you.

Gila: Well, just because you love me does not mean I am obligated to love you back.

I hoped that the Gila would tack on to the end of that statement something along the lines of, "But I dislike you less than I dislike some others." All I heard was the ruffling of a sudden breeze.

OK, maybe this "speaks to me" fantasy was not such a good idea.

Good chance I am being too harsh. Maybe the Gila was having a bad day. Some butthead dumped a big bag of trash at a trailhead. Or some other butthead spray-painted graffiti on a rock face or carved his initials in an aspen. Maybe the Gila is disinclined to, or incapable of, differentiating the actions of an individual from the actions of that individual's species. Perhaps, later in the day, the Gila might wish it had toned its message back a bit, that it had spoken more softly, more encouragingly, that it had wished me a pleasant hike.

Casey and I took a late-afternoon walk on a newly rerouted section of a trail a few miles from our house. According to my count, more than three dozen piñon pines, junipers, and Gambel oaks had been cut down to accommodate the tread. Their stumps were still oozing sap. The trees had been dragged away and used to obliterate evidence of the old trail. Their leaves and needles were still green. They did not seem to understand they were now dead. Acceptable losses in the name of outdoor recreation, I guess.

I could not find the proper words to articulate how much this recent carnage bothered me. I apologized to the Gila. For me. For us.

Once you cut down the first tree to build a trail, you enter the realm of rationalization. Once you cut the second tree down, you enter the realm of bullshit.

Off in the distance, a stellar jay was squawking its fool head off. The closer I got, the louder it squawked.

DAY 127

Prior to a three-day car-camping trip, I ventured into a chain grocery store for supplies (read: junk food). Pushing a cart down the salty snacks' aisle, I came up on the starboard quarter of a well-attired gent probably in his midseventies who was eyeballing his iPhone. I assumed it was a shopping list or a message from the missus reminding him to not forget the Metamucil like he did last time.

As I began to pass, he—seemingly thinking I was someone else, a friend, perhaps, who had veered off without his knowledge to the candy section—held the phone up in front of me and enthused, "Look at this one!" So I did, expecting to see a photo of his grandkids or the family dog. I was a bit taken aback to observe on that screen a video of an impressively flexible young couple doing the humpty-dance. Yes, this septuagenarian was surfing porn right there next to the potato chips!

And it was not even surreptitious porn surfing. He was holding his phone chin high and well away from his body. I came close to plowing into a row of Doritos.

Now, in the highly unlikely chance that I was watching porn while walking past stacks of Lay's and Ruffles in a fairly busy grocery store at 4:45 p.m. on a Thursday and I turned and said, "Look at this one," while referring to a limber heterosexual twosome in flagrante delicto to someone who ended up being a perfect stranger, I would expire right there on the floor in front of the bean dip rack.

But this guy just glanced at me and, when he realized I was not who he thought I was (an imaginary friend?), turned around and went looking for whoever the right person might be, his iPhone still held high, like an overhead movie screen on an airplane.

My main thought as I hurriedly put a pillow-sized bag of pretzels into my cart was: I need to work on my flexibility.

DAY 130

I had been invited to drive to Tucson—where it was about 200 degrees—to hike a thirteen-mile section of the Arizona Trail with a Republican member of the U.S. House of Representatives who not long thereafter became a U.S. senator, even though, weirdly enough, she had lost the election (yay democracy!). It was a choreographed event, and I was but one member of what turned out to be a sizeable contingent consisting primarily of the types of socially well-connected individuals you would expect to be invited to accompany a professional politician perceived by many to be on an upward career trajectory.

For me, it was something of a well-timed interaction with memory lane, as exactly twenty years prior, I had become one of the first people to thru-hike the 850-mile AZT. Coincidentally, I had been on the same section the congresswoman and her retinue planned to hike on the exact same date back in 1997.

When I pulled up in Pronto—mud-covered, malodorous, dented, and scratched—eyes squinted and brows furrowed. I would not have been the least bit surprised had one of the supposedly surreptitious security people—camouflaged as trail trash, except they were too well-groomed, wore hyper-pricy footwear, and had wires coming out of their ears—had intercepted me and asked what my business was. (The son of one of the other hikers had been murdered during the 2011 assassination attempt on then-Congresswoman Gabby Giffords, so I could understand the nervousness factor at seeing someone like me drive up in a brontosaurus-adorned SUV that reeked of pot smoke.)

Every other vehicle at the trailhead was fresh off the lot. Rides with blemish-free exteriors, the price tags of which my low-rent brain could scarcely begin to calculate.

New-car smell dominated the rarefied atmosphere.

When we returned late that afternoon, one of the other hikers said of Pronto, "Yep, that sure looks like a New Mexico car." All those within earshot smirked and nodded their heads. I didn't know whether he was being intentionally condescending or backhandedly flattering. I took it as the latter. I thanked him for the compliment, patted my four-wheeled companion on its pockmarked hood, and drove away thinking about vehicles as they relate to self-propelled outdoor recreationists. A worthy topic for high-speed highway contemplation, given that our chummy relationship with the internal combustion engine etches an undeniable hypocrisy-based scarlet letter on the foreheads of those of us who are inclined to shake our fists at the oil and gas industries while simultaneously feeling perfectly comfortable—as but one example—driving a total of eight hours from New Mexico to Tucson to hike for seven hours.

It used to be a point of pride among backpackers that the less you spent on your vehicle, and the less reliable it was, and the uglier it was, the more cachet you brought with you to the trailhead. For a while there, a lot of my hygiene-challenged, pack-toting amigos used as a personality-scrutiny gauge whether you had more money tied up in your hiking gear than you did in your wheels. And the more things your vehicle *didn't* have, the cooler you were considered. Extra image points were awarded for a lack of bumpers, hoods, fenders, and windshield wipers. I once traded a bicycle, a twelve-string guitar and a pound of weed for a long-discarded UPS van that had zero doors. Every time I pulled into a remote parking lot, that pitiful excuse for motorized transportation drew envious oohs and aahs. Anyone who showed up with a car, truck, van, or motorcycle that was made in the same decade in which we were living was considered pretentious and much too arrogant for our lofty anti-loftiness standards.

I don't know exactly when this started to change. Probably when fuel injection began to overtake carburation, giving engines altitude versatility that meant you didn't have to pull out a screwdriver every time you went up or down a few thousand vertical feet. Definitely by the time four-wheel drive and all-wheel drive vehicles started making their way into the consumer mainstream. Or when old-school hikers began to settle down and get real jobs with real incomes and real spouses and real kids. Somewhere along the line, many previously sane people became comfortable with the concept of indenturing themselves to the system by incurring significant debt. Lots of hikers and climbers started traveling to the ends of roads in vehicles that had all their headlights and did not boast a single door and/or fender that was a different color than the rest of the vehicle. Minivans soon followed. Shame should have followed that, but it didn't seem to.

It was simultaneously perplexing and depressing, as things often are when a perfect storm of devolution is afoot.

Right before Gay and I relocated from Colorado to New Mexico, flush (very relatively speaking)—for one of the few times in my life—with a few extra dollars procured from the sale of a house, we purchased Pronto, then only eight years old, with 72,000 miles on the odometer. Pronto had been babied its entire life. It verily glowed when the sun lighted upon its shiny exterior. The man I bought it from was a nonsmoker who owned no pets. It was

161

borderline pristine! Everything worked! No dangling fenders or mismatched colors! I could scarcely believe my good fortune!

It was by far the most top-shelf vehicle I had ever owned—to the point that I was a bit embarrassed to be seen driving it. At the time, I also owned a 1986 Toyota Land Cruiser FJ60—purchased under dubious legal circumstances with money that technically belonged to a now defunct corporation with which I was peripherally involved—that was more rust than metal. So, for several years, I used my shiny 4Runner only for business-type road trips, upon which I would generally leave under cover of darkness, lest one of my compadres see me behind the wheel of such a low-mileage vehicle. Other than that, it stayed hidden away in the garage. Eventually, my Land Cruiser began to decompose to the degree that I had to retire it. I mean, the back seat was pretty much dragging on the pavement. It was heartbreaking to see such a once-noble beast stagger to the finish line. I eventually sold it for parts.

Pronto by that time was ten years old, which gave it enough temporal standing that I could park at any trailhead without hiding my face in shame if confronted by one of the few of my unwashed brethren who was not yet dead, incarcerated, missing in action or—worse—repented of their colorful backgrounds. By then, almost every vehicle I encountered past where the pavement ends cost almost as much as my first hovel. Often, these were colossal pickup trucks carrying mountain bikes with price tags that exceed my annual income, which, of course, isn't saying much, but it's saying something.

I get it. Newer cars are more fuel efficient, more comfortable and more reliable than the oxidized wrecks that have long borne me to the hinterlands. Advancements in safety features are not inconsequential considerations. They orient you! And new vehicles can talk to the stars! They alert responsible people if you have so much as a minor mishap. They come with extended warranties supposedly honored by qualified mechanics. Plus, I guess it's beneficial for our economy if people with high credit scores take loans out on new vehicles on a regular basis. Truth be told, were I not a resident in good stead of the poor house—like if I won one of those giant lotteries you read about—I would maybe consider upgrading my vehicular situation to this century. But I am, so I don't.

My first car was a 1967 Volvo 122S, for which I paid $600. It was named "the Rock," because its gray color and rounded shape resembled a boulder. It even had its own song: "Standing on the Rock," by the Ozark Mountain Daredevils. My second car, a 1967 Ford Econoline van, cost $200. It was named "Atom Heart Mother," after the Pink Floyd album, which was one of the two eight-track tapes that were thrown in as part of the deal. Then there was the 1973 Plymouth Duster I owned when I met Gay, which cost $250. (She was not all that impressed.) That was named "Slick," after the condition of its tires. Of course, all this was many years ago, and inflation has hit even raggedy rides.

While living in Denver in the 1980s, I dropped four grand—which seemed like all the money in the world—on a gnarly 1981 4WD Toyota pickup, named "Truck," that I drove all over the Rocky Mountains, the Southwest deserts, Mexico, and Central America. I ended up—very stupidly—selling Truck a year or so after returning from a multi-month foray to Honduras. It was in need of major repairs I could not financially justify. I could not bear to look at Truck as it was being towed away.

A few years later, Gay and I were day hiking along the road to Kite Lake outside Alma, Colorado—the highest incorporated municipality in the country—and passed a cabin that had next to it a dilapidated shed, in which—of all unlikely occurrences!—was parked Truck. I recognized it immediately because of some modifications I had made to its hull. It had obviously been left to rot. Its eyes lit up when it saw us, then fell downward. It looked so forlorn and embarrassed at its condition. I wanted to say something, but I could not find the proper words. We walked on. I have regretted ever since that I did not try to buy Truck back, even if it could no longer run, even if it just sat in my driveway as a decoration, a reminder of journeys long past. We could have shot the breeze on a daily basis about that trip to Central America, and every other crazy thing we did together.

I still choke up whenever I think of Truck abandoned in that shed, where it might still be. Alone.

What am I saying? That, yet again, I miss the good ol' days? Maybe. I mean, who doesn't? That's OK, because every day is a future good ol' day for someone. Hopefully, me too.

I fully understand that vehicles are nothing more than manufactured aggregations of metal, plastic, and rubber. It is nuts to anthropomorphize them, to look at them as anything save pieces of gear, to give them names, to tell them everything will be all right when they go into the shop for major surgery, to tearfully say goodbye as you're cleaning out your belongings when their time with you is up.

But all those vehicles that have taken me along the potholed dirt roads that have defined my marginal existence have been more than pieces of gear. They are buddies, along for the ride. Chariots of desire that take their mission in life—to get Gay, Casey, and me not only in, but out again—very seriously.

Pronto now has 235,000 miles and counting. It's looking a bit rough around the edges and it's bleeding little oil droplets. I plan to keep it at least until Casey's time on earth is done. She loves Pronto. She has a bed carved out in the back that has been her comfort zone her whole life. Some people have crates for their dogs. I have a 1999 4Runner named Pronto that regularly takes us to destinations most people would not believe. Whenever we walk toward Pronto, Casey's tail wags. While sometimes, sure, we end up at the vet's office, most times we end up hiking through some astounding wild country.

One day, probably sooner rather than later, Pronto will become too tired to travel further. I will then leave it parked in my yard—like I should have done with Truck—where we'll be able to reminisce about past journeys. We can talk about the friends who once rode with us. We can wonder aloud who will outlive who.

By then, perhaps I will have won one of those giant lotteries—upon which case I will truly be able to afford to drive a series of dilapidated wrecks, all with dangling headlights and mismatched fenders. No need to worry about breakdowns or extended warranties if you're rich. I'll be like one of those wonderful rescue establishments that take in only geriatric animals and pamper them right up to the point that the rainbow bridge beckons. I will give them all names and we will drive along the rutted roads that criss-cross the American West until it's time to turn the engine off for the very last time. And we will remember that all that is old once started out new.

DAY 131

To reiterate: In 1997, I became one of the first people to thru-hike the Arizona Trail. I started at the Utah/Arizona border and, over the course of the next two months, made my way toward the trail's southern terminus on the Mexican border. It was one of the toughest of my long-distance hikes, because back then, only about half the Arizona Trail actually existed. The other half consisted of mixing and matching various disconnected paths and dirt roads, and often cross-country bushwhacking with map, compass, and fingers crossed.

When I finally limped, bruised and battered, out of the Miller Peak Wilderness down to Montezuma Pass—literally within sight of Mexico—I was told by Park Service employees that the last mile was closed for at least a week because they were blasting new trail in. I could hear explosions in the distance.

So, after more than 800 miles, I was stopped less than an hour from the end of the hike. This was a frustrating turn of events on several levels, not the least of which being that I was unable to wait for the trail to reopen because the leave of absence I had taken from a gig I could not afford to lose was soon set to expire. I vowed to one day return and finish that last mile, though, as I learned, it was actually 1.7 miles each way.

Midway through my quest to hike every day for a year, and taking advantage of being in the vicinity because of my hike with the Arizona congresswoman, I drove to Montezuma Pass to knock off that last section. I arrived late enough in the day that I hesitated. After dark, this becomes the operational theater of the Dread Minions of the Night: Border Patrol, which had a bank of floodlights set up right at the trailhead. Despite that, I dashed as quickly as I could toward the border, made it in thirty-five minutes, ogled at the beauty of Sonora, took a few quick photos of my ugly mug in front of the monument that marks the southern terminus of the AZT and the saggy barbed wire fence that then separated our two nations, lamented for the millionth time the perplexing nature of border-based politics, and dashed back to my vehicle, arriving just as the Dread Minions of the Night were emerging from their burrows.

Then I pulled into the closest watering hole, which was skanky in the extreme and populated by construction workers who all seemed inclined to beat me up, to celebrate the fact that, after nineteen years, I had finally completed the Arizona Trail. No one in the bar had ever heard of the Arizona Trail. Put things in proper perspective.

Postscript: The southern terminus of the AZT is now located in the shadow of the damned border wall—which was *not* paid for by Mexico—that blocks what was once an unimpeded view into our southern neighbor. But, as we all have been told, it is a beautiful wall.

DAY 133

In the early-morning-shade side of a mountain in the middle of TS-X, I was moving nose-to-the-grindstone-like up a tippy-toe incline when I was startled to see ahead another hiker upon whom I was gaining fast. He also appeared surprised to see someone else on that trail at that hour. He was clearly flustered at having been caught from behind. He turned and quickened his pace. I was stuck behind him on a section of tread that did not sport a passing lane. I had to moderate my velocity to match his. It was interesting to adjust to someone else's cadence and stride. By the time we neared the top-out point, from which there is an unimpeded view of the most majestic mountains in the Gila, I realized that I had not once stopped to catch my breath, which I usually have to do twice on that stretch. Something to be learned, but I never learn.

The man, whose name I never did catch, finally threw in the towel.

"This is the first time anyone has ever caught me from behind," he said dejectedly, breathing hard.

"Well, I've been doing this for a long time," I said. Lame attempt at consolation. (For a man known as a blabber, I often do not know what to say.)

"Me too," he said softly.

He asked my age.

I then asked his. He would be turning seventy-six in three weeks. I told him he was a kick-ass hiker for that age. Even more lame attempt at consolation.

He sighed as he resignedly stepped aside on the narrow path, and I moved ahead. I felt bad about so doing.

"At least we're still out here," I said, by way of an awkward valediction.

I totally understand where that man was coming from. Being dropped like that is one of my biggest worries and is surely one of the main reasons I maintain such a rapid pace while on the trail. I have, of course, been caught and passed plenty of times, most often by Casey, but also by mountain bikers, trail runners, and, a few times, by other hikers. Not often, though. But I understand the inevitable is nipping at my heels. I will be caught and I will be passed. And I will likely be crestfallen, no matter how hard I try to minimize what will surely be a deep bruise to my pride by invoking my age, of bringing my various aches and pains into argumentative play, of saying something along the lines of, "Well, I still hike pretty damned good for an old man who has consumed as many beers as I have."

It sometimes hurts to be so stupid. I mean, you can actually feel the pain deep down to your toes.

I had seen that man on the trails of TS-X several times before, but we had been going in opposite directions. I determined that, when we next passed, I would slow down, exchange names, and ask if he would like to hike together. He likely will say no, that he, like me, prefers to hike solo. But he will surely understand, as I understand: Time always catches us from behind and passes us by.

Postscript: Several weeks later, I saw that same man approaching. Though I had stopped, expecting a trailside chat, all he did was grunt before moving along at a high rate of speed. He was clearly a man on a mission.

DAY 135

Then there's that moment when you're chomping down in famished fashion on a Clif Bar midway through a long hike when you come to realize that the texture could best be described as "overtly decomposition-ish" and, now that you mention it, the flavor resembles what you would expect spider webs to taste like, especially if those webs were mixed with a healthy portion of dirty socks, and you start to wonder just how long that snack item might have been lost in the bottom of your day pack. Years? Many years?

Then you finish it and look to see if there's maybe another one down there somewhere 'cause you're still mighty hungry and you still have a long way to go.

DAY 136

It had finally cooled off enough to start reconnecting with shade-free trails not visited since late spring. One of those accesses a set of Native American petroglyphs. By local standards, it is a small gallery, but the centerpiece is distinct enough that its artistic merit outweighs its diminutive stature. It is a well-advertised and popular hiking destination. That it has never been tagged or otherwise vandalized is a flat-out miracle.

We go there because directly beneath the petroglyphs lie several pools of water large enough for Casey to dog paddle in. While she swims, I admire the delicacy of the carvings. I want to run my hands across the worn indentations, but resist the temptation because it is justifiably considered bad form to touch the art.

Every time I venture forth into the Gila, I fully understand that I do so on occupied land that was not only conquered, but brutally so. By my people. (I guess.) And, in the grand chronological scheme of things, fairly recently. I once interviewed a woman who related living-memory stories from her grandparents about bloody gun battles between settlers/interlopers and Native Americans in the Gila.

It is not only the trails upon which I hike that lie on conquered land, of course. Every inch of southwest New Mexico was forcibly wrested from its longtime occupants. Though of course I should, I don't think about it as much when I go to Walmart or downtown to have a beer. The Native heritage is too deeply buried under the concrete heart of what we call civilization. It's when I'm out among the trees that I consider that my culture is no different than the Romans when they invaded Britannia or the Moors when they occupied the Iberian Peninsula.

I certainly do not mean to limit this observation to southwest New Mexico. It is a grim reality from sea to shining sea. The entire U.S. was built on a one-two punch of slavery and genocide. But this is where I live and this is where I know the most, or misunderstand the least, about the Native culture that once laid claim to the land I call home.

The petroglyphs were likely carved by Mimbreños, a relatively small subtribe of the larger Mogollon culture, who vacated southwest New Mexico somewhere around the year 1450. Anthropologists usually point to long-lasting drought as the main reason for the disembarkation. Some posit that they were absorbed into the Puebloan tribes to the north. Others argue that they migrated to join with the Casas Grandes culture in what is now Chihuahua. Might have been both. Might have been neither. The only evidence of the Mimbreños ever having dwelled here takes the form of petroglyphs, pictographs, abandoned cliff dwellings and pieces of what many consider the finest pottery ever produced in pre-Columbian North America. If there are people hereabouts of verifiable Mimbreño extraction, I have not heard of them. There is no remnant constituency. No one is left to lay claim to the Mimbreño legacy except academicians, museum curators, artists, New Age spiritualists, and black-market artifact dealers.

The most recent Native American residents were the Chiricahua and Warm Springs Apaches, the people of Cochise, Victorio, Mangas Coloradas, Nana, the mystical warrior priestess known as Lozen, and, of course, Geronimo, the man after whom the raid to kill Osama bin Laden was code-named.

Those Chiricahua and Warm Springs Apaches who had not been previously forcibly relocated to the Fort Apache and San Carlos reservations in Arizona were, after Geronimo's final surrender in 1886, rounded up, herded onto trains, and moved, first to Texas, then to Florida, then to Alabama, then, finally, to Fort Sill, Oklahoma—an itinerary from hell if ever there was one. Though some were eventually repatriated to the Mescalero Reservation in south-central New Mexico, most lived out their lives as prisoners of war in the Sooner State. Many of their children had been sent to a boarding school in Pennsylvania, where more than a third perished from tuberculosis.

What a twisted legacy we claim in the name of Manifest Destiny.

When Geronimo and his kin were removed, they took with them the only legal tribal patrimony now recognized by the Bureau of Indian Affairs, the federal agency that oversees most Native matters in the U.S. Thus, the deeply rooted Apache legacy associated with the Gila is now headquartered outside a U.S. Army base in Oklahoma, where Geronimo died in 1909. In order to be a legal member of what is now called the Chiricahua and Warm Springs Apache Tribe (nee Fort Sill Apaches), one must be a direct descendent of those 500 or so souls who were brought to that part of the country in 1894.

I have spent time at Geronimo's grave, located in a cemetery in which dozens of his tribespeople are likewise interred, and have spent time with the then-chief of the Chiricahua and Warm Springs Apache Tribe, who looked like he could be a mandolin player in an Irish band. Though they take their ancestry very seriously, the members of the Chiricahua and Warm Springs Apache Tribe have been gone from southwest New Mexico so long, they are now strangers to their native land.

At the same time, an estimated 250 people living in these parts claim Apache ancestry. I have spent time with them as well, in their homes and at gatherings out in the Gila. They contend that a fair number of Chiricahua and Warm Springs Apaches were not, in fact, rounded up and forcibly relocated by the U.S. Cavalry in the late 1800s. They say their ancestors blended in with the local Hispanic population and waited for the threat to dissipate, which was a long time coming. But, because they were not part of the forced exodus to Oklahoma, in the eyes of the U.S. government, they have no legal standing as Native Americans in general or Apaches specifically.

They live in a sort of cultural limbo. I don't think these people sit around all day lamenting their circumstance, but it's obvious they are bummed that they do not have a legal claim to their heritage or their land.

And here I stand, next to these petroglyphs, wondering about my place in this perpetually chaotic world. I feel like a voyeur peeking through someone's living room window, not only eyeballing their family photos, but claiming them as my own. Yet, I come back to this spot again and again.

If you are alert—or perhaps delusional—you can feel the remnant Native energy percolating up through the soil in Gila Country and, occasionally, you can catch a peripheral glimpse of a fleeting spirit sitting atop a cliff or standing behind a ponderosa pine. It's always like, "What was *that*?" By the time you ask the question, it is too late; the apparition has vanished. The Apaches were masters of camouflage.

Though the Apaches I have met here and in Oklahoma have all been affable, the indigenous vibe in the Gila is not overtly welcoming. Good reason for that. The ghosts understandably look upon us as interlopers whose ancestors killed their ancestors. In the name of greed, and in the name of God.

Which is more than a little disorienting when you're moving through territory that once was teeming with Apache warriors, the least of which could have dispatched me before I even knew he or she was there.

I promise this will be the last time I engage the over- and inappropriately used phrase, "badass." Here it fits. The Chiricahua Apaches were considered badasses among badasses. Tales of the intensity of their coming-of-age rites of passage rituals are eye-popping. Pain, blood, stoic response to pain and blood, that sort of thing. I have read that Apaches could run a hundred miles without stopping, without water, and, upon arrival at their destination, kick the living snot out of whoever it was they were looking to kick the living snot out of. Being taken prisoner by the Apaches was not a desirable outcome of any interaction. Cavalry soldiers operating in what sensitive historians call the Apacheria were purportedly told, if capture seemed imminent, to save their last bullet for themselves.

The thing is, the overwhelming majority of what I have heard or read about the Native legacy hereabouts has been presented by outsiders and filtered through the ears and eyes of an outsider, a man whose relationship with the Gila has not yet reached a half century. I do not know what to believe. I hike far and wide through these lands and hope for the best.

I wonder if there is a chance of some manner of Reconquista.

While they may have standing with the U.S. government, the Chiricahua and Warm Springs Apaches are land poor. They recently purchased a bleak, thirty-acre parcel on the scoured side of Interstate 10. Apache Stronghold is the nation's newest Indian reservation. Population: zero. It was established primarily as the potential site of a casino that has yet to receive approval from the state of New Mexico. It is currently home to a truck stop, restaurant, gift shop and cultural center. According to the chief I interviewed in Oklahoma, the tribe owns numerous other parcels scattered throughout the Southwest. He would not disclose their location. Nor would he let on what their ultimate purpose might be.

The dispossessed Apaches I have spent time with are fighting for some sort of federal recognition. In the meantime, they are reaching out to their Chiricahua and Warm Springs brethren in Oklahoma, offering to reintroduce them to their ancestral homeland in hopes that, together, they can rebirth the Old Ways. I wish them fair winds and following seas.

It took the ancestors of the people we now call Spaniards and Portuguese more than 700 years to expel the Moors from the Iberian Peninsula. "We" have occupied the Apacheria for less than four centuries. There is still ample time for past wrongs to be righted, or at least balanced.

I wonder if the only ethical course of action is to voluntarily vacate premises I love, to hand the keys to my house to one of those dispossessed Apaches and to follow my own manifest destiny back to its origin story in the United Kingdom, which has been invaded, conquered, and liberated so many times it's hard to differentiate between Angles, Saxons, Celts, Normans, Romans, and whatever else might be part of the genetic stew. I do not know on what side of those countless incursions my heritage lies. In my native land, am I the conquered or, once again, the conqueror? Which is neither here nor there, as I wouldn't know a thing about the Old Ways. The songs, dances, and language would all be foreign to me. I'd have to learn how to speak English.

At least the Apaches to this day know who they are and where they truly belong.

Casey is done swimming laps. It is time to walk back to Pronto across a shade-free mesa from which the view is unobstructed for miles in every direction. Then drive home.

DAY 137

Advice to young people: Do not avoid situations that cause you discomfort and pain. Rather, seek them out, for an ability to tolerate discomfort and pain will serve you well once you get old. You don't want to have to learn that skill on the fly when your body breaks down and everything you got starts to ache and hurt.

DAY 138

It was finally time to send my sixteen-year-old Rand McNally Road Atlas to the old atlas home. Its pages were frayed, its staples long unstapled, its print faded, looking like something brittle in a museum from the old-timey days of exploration. A Dead Sea Scrolls of the internal-combustion era.

In these days of Internet-based manifestations of digital cartography, the world is your oyster with the push of a button and few quick bearings-based questions to the perpetually congenial lady who dwells inside your smartphone.

For a few of us, though, no excursion is complete without the feel of real paper in our hands.

While our numbers seem to be rapidly diminishing, there yet remains a die-hard handful of map junkies, those for whom tattered, seared, and stained atlases are far more than the sum of their informational parts; they are, rather, two-dimensional stories of our travels to distant trailheads located in national forests and parks. The only delete button being inevitable decomposition that leaves us trying to reconcile and separate the memories of those countless miles crisscrossing the Rand McNally world.

As I carried the mortal remains of my road atlas toward the recycling bin, I wondered for the first time in years what the inspiration was to circle all those little towns with funny names in green Magic Marker ink.

And whose phone number is that jotted sloppily in the margin next to the inset of Owensboro, Kentucky? I've never been to Owensboro, Kentucky. Don't know anyone who has. Good enough reason to plan a standard deviation when next I am in the vicinity of the lower Ohio River Valley. Maybe dial that number to see who answers. He or she might be able to tell me something about my past.

And what happened to the second page of Maryland—where ought to be found Baltimore, the Chesapeake Bay, and the Eastern Shore? Though the recollection is hazy, seems to me I was camping in Oregon and the perpetual dampness was making it difficult to start a fire. I needed paper reinforcements to assist the process of rapid oxidation. Pickings were slim, but there was my atlas. I thumbed through, trying to decide where I was the least likely to ever drive to. Maryland got sacrificed in the name of warmth and light. A few years later, I was searching for a specific state park in western Massachusetts. There was no page for western Massachusetts in my atlas. Where had it gone? It had gone up in flames with Maryland.

Always a flip side to every coin. Life is nothing if not a constant trade-off.

Atlases are the directional equivalent of analog clocks. They allow you to visualize the whole enchilada, not just a specific moment or a specific place.

Disoriented nostalgia aside, it was time for a new road atlas, preferably Rand McNally, the gold standard of American highways and byways.

The bookstore had atlases of the solar system but not the U.S., Canada, and Mexico. None to be found at the pharmacy or any of the gas stations or convenience stores in town. In desperation, I tried Walmart, though I did not know exactly where to look among aisles so seemingly endless and convoluted, they could use an atlas of their own.

I finally asked a young, blue-frocked "associate," assuming of course in this pixelated era that I would need to draw a map to explain what a map actually was. She knew right away where to look. As we walked the retail equivalent of the Continental Divide Trail, the associate gleefully recounted to me her love of road atlases.

She said her father was a long-haul truck driver who would, upon returning from his extended forays over the blacktop, draw with his finger upon a ratty Rand McNally where his last travels had taken him. He would, she said, relate stories about rivers that flowed green, and gardens populated by elves and coastlines where the sand glowed pink in the dark.

"I knew he was making most of it up," she said. "But I loved hearing his stories. And he loved telling them."

Her father had long since passed away. The young lady kept the old road atlas upon which he used to line out fantasies with his finger. She said it was her most treasured possession, that she would never ever let it go.

"It keeps me grounded," she said. "If I ever have kids, I want to tell them those same stories."

I had entered that Walmart disoriented by canyon walls lined floor to ceiling with cheap plastic shit manufactured in Third World sweatshops. I left with a brand-new Rand McNally Road Atlas, which I likely would not have found without the assistance of a very well-oriented young lady. That trek through retail hell turned out to be among my favorites of the entire year.

DAY 142

Today I crossed paths with three of my favorite two-word combinations:

Pavement ends.

No service.

Gila Wilderness.

Somewhere in there is the heart of a lost haiku.

DAY 145

I learned in a suitably indirect manner that a man I have known and respected since I first arrived in New Mexico claimed to have observed—of all perplexing geophysical phenomena—a brand-new mountain, which, he said, had spontaneously sprouted about fifteen miles north of town. As though some massive tectonic subduction had taken place in a land normally free of such calamitous topographic fireworks. Except that the event was not presaged by so much as a tepid tremor. The mountain, according to my friend, suddenly appeared one otherwise uneventful day. Next day, it was gone. Few days later, it came back. Then disappeared again. There was no evident pattern. It wasn't like it would predictably appear, say, at 8:07 a.m. every other Tuesday.

Given my long tenure dwelling in the land of verticality, I can state unequivocally that this is unusual behavior for mountains. My interest was understandably piqued.

Before venturing further down this booby-trapped rabbit hole, I feel compelled to point out that this particular man, who had just turned eighty, while assuredly hearing the beat of a different drummer, is a fairly normal person. He worked for many years as a professor of English at my alma mater and has also long been a teacher of various martial arts. I mean, he harbors some perspectives that in other parts of the world might be considered a bit out of the ordinary, but, by New Mexico's forgiving sociological standards, nothing too outlandish.

As a casual aside: This is also the man who, in the late 1970s, pierced my left ear lobe with a needle the size of a javelin—a protracted process that was fueled by copious quantities of tequila, the unbridled consumption of which resulted in repeated poor aim on the part of my compadre, which in turn resulted in much arterial bloodshed on my part. By the time the shockingly protracted procedure was complete, I had a hole in my lobe substantial enough to accommodate a strand of barbed wire.

My earlobe-skewering amigo first noticed the spontaneously sprouted mountain while standing in front of the local recreation center, which stands atop a ridge that affords unimpeded views of the Gila's southern reaches. The peak, visible via an indentation formed by two lower and closer mountains, was, according to Ear Piercer, very steep, mostly bare of vegetation, weathered and snowcapped. It had a sandstone color and "looked very tall." Given that the proximate mountains top out at 9,000 feet, my friend estimated that the mountain he saw approached an elevation of 20,000 feet. In other words: Andes high. According to Ear Piercer, at least four other people have witnessed what I have come to call the Misty Mountain.

Ear Piercer, who, for the record, does not ingest hallucinogens, is only a light drinker, and, to the best of my knowledge, harbors mental-health issues no more serious than eccentricity, told me he was not alarmed by the sight because he had had previous experiences with "other realities," including two close encounters with UFOs.

For him, "it was just another confirmation that the reality we believe to be solid and fixed is neither. We are taught that reality already exists whether we are perceiving it or not. It's just *there* and we have to recognize it. Its stability is reassuring to us. Nonetheless, parts of it have a disconcerting habit of just vanishing and sometimes coming back—or not."

This statement did not exactly clear things up.

Ear Piercer had wanted to see firsthand the area where the Misty Mountain had materialized, but, at his advanced age, was concerned it might be too rugged. He had a USGS 7.5-minute quad map with the approximate location of the mountain marked. I convinced him to join me on a hike in the general vicinity where it had appeared. I knew the area well and was therefore able to pick a route that would not be too challenging for an eighty-year-old man.

Before we set out, I decided to interview two others who claimed to have seen the Misty Mountain.

Witness #1 had lived in Colorado Springs—at the base of Pikes Peak—for forty-four years. She knows what high mountains look like.

Witness #1—who once owned a series of businesses that sold material handling and storage equipment to the likes of Honeywell and Hewlett Packard—had been doing tai chi at the recreation center with Ear Piercer, who, before class, asked almost casually if she noticed anything unusual on the northern horizon. She did. She has seen the Misty Mountain numerous times since, sometimes with Ear Piercer and sometimes alone. There have been instances when she saw it and he did not. And vice versa. All told, Witness #1 claims to have seen that mountain—which she describes as structurally similar to the Colorado Rockies, but much taller—close to a dozen times. Mostly, she told me, it is not there.

Witness #2 is a downtown business owner who lives about twenty miles south of Silver City. During her regular morning commute through country anyone would describe as "lonely," she, upon cresting a modest pass, observed, much to her astonishment, an entire mountain range that had seemingly sprung up overnight. Not just a single peak, but an entire cordillera some forty or fifty miles long. Given that the summer had been defined by wildfires, she assumed at first that low-hanging smoke was playing tricks on her perception.

But the smoke did not move. For three straight days, the vision remained static.

She stressed, having made that same drive for twenty-five-plus years, that she knows what the nearby mountains—which she has observed in all climatic conditions—look like.

She said, "I could not believe my eyes. They went up into the sky like you wouldn't believe. They went all the way from the Gila down to the low desert."

She described them as being similar to the regular, run-of-the-mill mountains found in the Gila, but "millions of years older, like they were the original mountains that were here and what we have now is what is left over after erosion. I felt like they were from another timeline. They looked ancient. They had snow on their sides. They went high into the clouds, so high that I couldn't see the tops."

When she drove to work on the fourth day, they were not there.

And they have not returned.

On a sunny November day, Ear Piercer and I drove to a ridgetop where an unmaintained track I have hiked on many times came close to the point marked on his USGS map.

We walked maybe three miles along the headwall of a valley 1,000 vertical feet deep, during which time I asked Ear Piercer on numerous occasions if he "felt anything"—whatever that might mean. He said he was seeing some weird patterns that were causing him balance problems, but he was quick to ascribe those to recurrent eye issues rather than, say, a localized tear in the fabric of the space/time continuum. Which I admired, since almost everyone in New Mexico I know who considers him- or herself plugged into various manifestations of alternative consciousness would, rather than admitting there was "nothing here," have been lying on their back twitching, their eyes rolled back in their head, speaking in tongues about now being one with the Mother Earth goddess and having their chakra auras taken over by the benevolent spirits of the ancient ones.

I could tell Ear Piercer was a bit disappointed that there was not the slightest evidence of the Misty Mountain. Not so much as a molehill. While sipping some beers back at the trailhead, the best that I was able to come away with was that it is likely from another dimension and whatever inter-dimensional rift might be located hereabouts was not right then permeable enough for the Misty Mountain to show its face.

I have returned numerous times to where the Misty Mountain is located on Ear Piercer's map. Casey and I were up there this afternoon. I have, in every kind of weather, at dawn, midday, and dusk, squinted, tilted my head sideways, closed my eyes then opened them again, jumped up and down on one foot, then the other, tried to open my heart and my mind to the possibility of other realities and, well, nothing. Not a damned thing. All the effort produced was orbs filled with grit.

I don't know what Ear Piercer, Witness #1, and Witness #2 saw. I don't believe they conspired to concoct and promulgate a fiction. Given the varied circumstances of their viewings, it's highly unlikely that it was clouds, wild-fire smoke or a weird angle of sunlight. Could it be based upon some sort of groupthink? After all, the three of the people I talked to about Misty Mountain know each other and subscribe to many of the same untradi-tional beliefs. If they had never met each other, would they have still seen those mountains?

Got me.

I may be the only person in New Mexico history who has never had a vision, much less a revelation. No time travel or out-of-body experiences that I can recollect. Never seen a UFO, ghost, or apparition more notewor-thy than having a hippie hummingbird telling me that everything is going to be all right, which is scarcely worth mentioning in these parts.

I sometimes envy those for whom "otherworldly" experiences are part of the normal fabric of life. Inconvenient though they might be on several levels—like getting anally probed or people thinking you're either a liar or nuts—it would be kind of cool to see an alien spacecraft, a spirit, or a significant geological anomaly.

But, as Witness #2 said to me, "You can only see what you believe."

I do not believe anything more than I believe I'll keep going up where Ear Piercer and I hiked together. I'll keep my eyes peeled for seismic abnormalities. Of course, my luck, I'll suddenly be underneath 15,000 feet of solid granite. Or getting sucked into an alternative universe. Look at the bright side: Maybe I'll get to claim a first ascent of an interdimensional mountain. The stories I will then tell!

I can also imagine standing alongside Ear Piercer one day and having him suddenly exclaim while pointing northward, "There it is! Right there! Can't you see it?"

Me being me, I'll see nothing more than what I've seen for all these long years since I first moved here as a young man. That has always been good enough.

DAY 146

During our trek to hunt down the Misty Mountain, Ear Piercer observed, "Something powerful draws people here." (He neglected to mention that "something powerful" also often scares people away.)

Transplant origin stories are a common topic of discussion in southwest New Mexico and part of that usually ends up including conversational digressions into what makes the Gila so "special." What inspires some people to decide that this—among the countless splendid alternatives—is their "place." A recent immigrant I talked with on the trail today said, in response to me asking what has lured him to these remote parts, that the Gila is "magical," which, while a bit vague, is likely as good a description as any.

The Rainbow Family hippies I used to hang out with during my college years contended that the Gila is home to some manner of energy vortex. I can find no evidence of this, though, admittedly, researching that subject does not often lead to peer-reviewable conclusions.

If you follow "ley lines"—which appear to be the most commonly accepted form of mapping energy vortices among a demographic inclined to practice yoga on mountaintops—then the only areas in the U.S. you will be led to are Mount Shasta, California (home to the root chakra of the earth, whatever that might be), and Sedona, Arizona, which is so vortex-dense that it has its own vortex map for tourists seeking enlightenment.

Other sources list Crater Lake, Oregon; Garden of the Gods, Colorado; the Four Corners; the Sandia Mountains east of Albuquerque; Taos; and the Santa Fe Plaza as locales transected by ley lines. All fine spots, I can attest. But, when you learn that some of these same sources also include Birmingham, Alabama, and Roswell, then you realize this is a subject that ought to be examined with a grain of salt.

I have never been able to find mention of vortex-ness anywhere near southwest New Mexico. Matter of fact, it seems like energy vortexes have gone out of their way to avoid the Gila.

Note to self: Never use Rainbow Family hippies as primary research sources.

There is this: Underneath the very ground Casey and I walk on every day lie the remnants of two ancient volcanic calderas, which are responsible for our plethora of hot springs. Over the span of some fifteen million years, the Gila was home to one of the largest and most explosive areas of continuous volcanic activity in the world. There's magma swirling under our feet. I once talked to an American expat living in Santiago Atitlan, Guatemala, which is surrounded by towering volcanoes. She contended that the juju that spews forth from proximate vulcanism attracts some people and repels others. She says, either way, it evokes passion.

Whatever it is, this is an area that grabs ahold of a select cadre of folks who are clearly disinclined to inhabit anything approximating the mainstream and is reluctant to let them go. The Gila either infects you or it does not. Not everyone likes it here. Which is a very good thing. I hope those people find a distant somewhere else that draws them. Birmingham, perhaps.

DAY 148

Casey and I were midway up a hill when, out of an auditory nowhere that seconds before had been defined by the usual birds tweeting and yours truly wheezing, the words, "And then they beheaded them all," suddenly sprang forth. Clear as a bell. And close. I turned on my heels—assuming that there were other hikers—likely ax-wielding serial killers—approaching. There were none.

This was a bit spooky.

Shortly after resuming the ascent, I distinctly heard, "Their swords could pierce human flesh like warm butter."

I turned, and again, nothing. I was hearing voices—not a good realization on the sanity front, though it might translate to a profitable Instagram account/YouTube channel—something along the lines of "#the schizo-phrenic hiker."

Then further, clearly articulated descriptions of various varieties of bloodshed were forthcoming from someone speaking in what, given the nature of the material being related, seemed like an inappropriately dispassionate monotone.

Yet, the only other creature anywhere near me was Casey, and she rarely verbally relates tales of maiming.

The hair on the nape of my neck was by then fully unfurled.

No matter which direction I pivoted, the voice was relating tales of barbaric acts of violence right behind my head.

That would be the part of my pack in which I store my iPhone.

Ding-ding-ding.

I pulled my pack off and retrieved that accursed device, which I assumed had been possessed by malevolent supernatural beings, or worse, Mark Zuckerberg. I was freaked out enough by the continued monologue regarding proper seppuku etiquette that the phone slipped my grip and fell to the dirt, where I ought to have left it. When I mustered the courage to pick it up, I noticed that one of the 2,000 apps that have taken up residence on my phone—most of which I had no idea what their purpose might be or how they got there (Tips? Reminders? Notes? Shortcuts? What *is* that stuff?)—was open. That particular app was titled "Books," which I had never heard of, much less intentionally used, me being attracted to books that have actual paper pages and don't talk to me while I'm hiking. Somehow, I had not only managed to activate the Books app but, while doing so, it had mysteriously dialed up a shockingly graphic nonfiction audio book about ancient samurai warriors. There are many things beyond my comprehension. The world of apps is one of them.

I deleted the Books app and, using a nearby rock, forcefully shut the phone OFF. Bludgeoned it to smithereens, much like a samurai warrior might have done. No, I didn't, but the thought occurred. Then I continued up the hill, with visions of beheadings and seppuku dancing in my head. I mean, why could the Books app not have defaulted to something by Thoreau or Dr. Seuss?

There are people out there whose hikes are not spiced up by the strangeness that seems to follow me wherever I go. I envy them. I feel sorry for them. I should call them. Arrange a play date.

DAY 150

It was the kind of late-model, heavily modified Mercedes Sprinter van that simultaneously elicits eye-rolling and envy from the destitute dirtbag demographic. Lifted, four-wheel drive, total off-road, off-grid package. Probably a hundred grand. Though I hesitate to admit this, I would love to add it to my already bloated vehicular quiver, but sadly I could not even afford the tires adorning that van. I reacted to its presence with a low-volume growl that bespoke jealousy more than irritation. It did not help matters any that the unblemished Sprinter sported license plates from a certain state that most often indicates that some manner of navigational ineptitude is likely to occur before you have time to strategize, much less execute, a workable defensive plan. I pulled Casey close in preparation for some serious evasive maneuvers.

The driver pulled a fast one, though, by approaching slowly and cautiously, rolling down his window and affably saying, "Good morning."

Caught me totally off guard. Made me feel like a douchebag for having, three seconds prior, applied negative stereotypes to his entire existence.

The driver, a man in his seventies, asked directions to a nearby trail. I resisted my normal childish inclination to provide him with a memorable adventure by sending him forty-seven miles down some wretched Jeep track in completely the wrong direction. (There were numerous available options.) But he seemed like a kindred spirit. He also seemed genuinely appreciative of my detailed input. Before pulling away, he said, "That's a really nice hiking stick."

I stood in stunned silence. I don't know what manner of compliment that Sprinter-driving man could have paid me that could top a flattering remark regarding the piece of wood grasped by my left hand. Maybe praising my wife, my dog, or my old 4Runner. That's about it.

That he referred to it as a "stick" instead of a "staff" earned the man extra style points. "Staff" has always grated my plebian sensibilities, making it sound as though the bearer fancies him- or herself a wizard, perhaps even a direct descendent of Gandalf.

One of my favorite things about hiking in the Gila is that it remains a bastion of hiking sticks, which differ from walking sticks, in that hiking sticks are, like, clavicles high and have woodsy applications—which I'll get to here in a minute—whereas walking sticks are more waist high, have decorative metal top pieces and are used solely by tweed-clad English gentlemen sauntering to and from pubs named something like Eagle and Child.

Most hiking sticks are unadorned, but a growing craft industry—probably inspired by *The Lord of the Rings*—now produces ornate sticks that are often decorated with semiprecious stones, representations of runes, and, at the top end, faces of elves or the heads of owls carved into the wood, which is usually exotic in nature. Artisanal hickory or some such. These kinds of sticks can be found for sale at music festivals and art fairs in mountain towns, in between the tie-dyed T-shirt and organic honey stands. Also, many companies purvey high-end hiking sticks online. They are generally far too pretty to consider actually being taken on a trail, lest they be dented or dinged. Kind of like Mercedes Sprinter vans.

My first hiking stick had humble roots. It came to me while camping in a state park in Wisconsin. I was set to embark on a thru-hike of the Appalachian Trail two months hence and had been on the lookout for a stick to compliment a period ensemble that consisted of a flannel shirt, blue jeans, heavy leather Raichle Montagna hiking boots, wool Ragg socks, a green Eddie Bauer felt crusher hat, a green 60/40 parka, and a green poncho. A stick pretty much was a de rigueur component of that very weighty outfit.

The right-of-way of a nearby road had recently been cleared, leaving a treasure trove of felled saplings on the shoulder. I spent an entire morning picking through the arboreal corpses and finally arrived upon one that felt right in my hand. Proper width, height, and heft. I took it back to camp, skinned it, trimmed it, and gave it a name. Given that I had been told by someone who may or may not have known what he was talking about that it was green ash, and given that I was heading toward the Appalachian Trail, I christened my new stick "GrATash," which I considered being an impressively witty portmanteau. Though many of my fellow backpackers on the AT in those days carried a stick, far as I knew, none had had a proper name bestowed upon them.

GrATash, which stayed with me for my entire AT hike, was directly involved in the most serious injury I have ever suffered while hiking. Two buddies—who I'll call Red and Modern Man—had joined me for a couple weeks in North Carolina. The second day out of Hot Springs, we ascended the switchback-free side of Snowbird Mountain. While crossing a small stream, my left foot slipped out from under me, and my left eye came directly down on GrATash's pointed top end. My entire field of view exploded with a crimson hue.

I bellowed, "HELP!!!" down the hill, which was tough, given that I was hyperventilating. When Red arrived—having dropped his pack and sprinted to my location when he heard my high-decibel call for assistance—he was so winded he could scarcely stand. When he saw my bloodied face, his jaw dropped, which did nothing to calm my nerves, which were right then already pretty frayed.

Modern Man, who sauntered up at what I considered to be an overly leisurely pace, by contrast, was shockingly calm, given the immediate eye-gushing-blood situation. He spoke reassuringly, directed me to tilt my head back and said something like, "Well, you don't see that every day." Turns out, my eyelid had nearly been torn off. You could pull it down and see the top of my orb, which might make for an amusing trick at a Halloween party, but, out in the middle of nowhere, it amounted to a stressful turn of events. Modern Man, grimy fingernails and all, plus or minus reattached my eyelid with a couple improvised butterfly bandages and pronounced me patched up enough to resume our hike with the words, "Not sure I lined your eyelid up perfectly, so it might end up looking a bit weird, but it's the best I could do under the circumstances."

For the next few days, whenever we passed other hikers, they would invariably let loose with some variation on the shocked, repulsed exclamation theme. Like: "EWWW!!! GROSS!!!" Their faces would often malform into a grimace I found disconcerting. Since none of us had in our possession a mirror, I had been unable to eyeball my eyeball.

There was some concern that, given the near-tropical climate of western North Carolina in the summer, my entire ocular system could get infected and completely rot away. My onboard medicinal options consisted solely, and predictably, of pot, hash, speed, and a wide array of hallucinogens. And aspirin, in case of dire emergencies.

So, we—three extremely funky longhairs—decided the best course of action would be to hike down a country lane the trail crossed till we located a residence, upon which time we would knock on its front door and ask if the inhabitants happened to have any unexpired antibiotics they could spare. I thought—and I use that word very loosely—my by-then-oozing eye would add a veneer of undeniable authenticity to our pharmaceutical-procurement mission.

Here would be a good time to make some blatantly judgmental socioeconomic observations about that part of the country at that time. If you have seen the movie *Deliverance*, well, this was that—the dark heart of dirt poor, inbred Appalachia. The cluster of houses we eventually found was defined by a bleak tarpaper aesthetic augmented by snarling, tick-covered dogs chained to trees and an understated landscaping consciousness dominated by ancient appliances and antiquated automobiles in various states of disrepair propped up on cinderblocks.

We were confronted by a toothless man whose nearly unintelligible articulation was severely compromised by his dentition situation and the disgusting reality that he was chomping on a wad of chewing tobacco big as a watermelon. Despite what I thought to be a well-rehearsed spiel—and I had the trashed eye to back it up!—we were informed that it would behoove us to vamoose at our earliest opportunity. He did not have any spare antibiotics lying around his malodorous pigsty.

Somewhere in the background, a banjo played.

(I have no doubt that the neighborhood has gentrified in the interim. The shacks have likely been replaced by high-end second homes and the tick-covered mutts replaced by well-groomed -doodle variants.)

We hiked back up to the trail with the full understanding that I would likely be going through the rest of my life sporting the descriptive sobriquet, "Ol' Mono-Peeper." Or maybe "Cyclops." I began thinking whether a pirate-looking eye patch would be more likely to attract or repel women. I'd need to get a parrot and a peg leg to complete the effect.

A few days later, I was able to hitchhike to a backwater town that sported a medical clinic that would have looked at home in rural El Salvador. The doctor removed the improvised butterfly bandages that had pretty much been absorbed into skin that had achieved a color somewhere between bruised apple pulp and dog vomit. An unappealing odor filled the room. The doctor pulled my detached lid down far enough that he could see the top of my eye. This he did several times while giggling. He even invited several staff members and a couple patients who were sitting in the lobby into the examination room to observe this once-in-a-lifetime spectacle. The doctor took some Polaroids and I'm certain every conversation in that town for weeks to come centered upon the hippie hiker whose eyelid could, with minimal manipulation, be worked both ways.

The wound was sanitized and properly patched, and I was loaded up with enough amoxicillin to see me through whatever other mishaps might befall me on what remained of that 2,100-mile trek from Maine to Georgia.

Ordinarily, you would think, after almost losing an eyeball, I would have heaved GrATash off the nearest cliff, or incinerated it in a campfire, and never again even considered carrying so much as a twig while on the trail. But the incident was not GrATash's fault; it was nothing more than one of those unpredictable, vexatious occurrences that occasionally drop into your lap without warning that you either survive or you don't, that you either learn from or you don't.

At the next opportunity, I used my pocketknife to round off GrATash's top. Then we continued hiking toward the end of that particular journey. It was three months before my eye started looking right.

GrATash stayed with me for several more years. It eventually got sucked into the black hole of my in-law's storage shed while Gay and I took an extended trip to Central America. It has yet to resurface. To this day, I half expect the hiking stick that nearly de-eyeballed me to eventually turn up when some random member of my wife's clan is rooting around in that storage shed looking for a pair of old ice skates or some such. "Hey, what's this stick doing in here?" that person will ask, right before tossing it into a dumpster. I would love to hold GrATash one more time, to revisit our time together along the Appalachian Trail, which was so long ago that I can scarcely recollect the names of the geographic features I passed or the names of the people I met along the way.

In the early 1990s, I found another hiking stick—which had been left leaning against a fence post at a trailhead in Colorado—but it and I never truly bonded. It was a tool, not a companion. It was clearly someone else's stick that mistakenly came to be mine. That stick died when I broke it over the head of a pit bull that was viciously attacking my last dog, Cali, while we were hiking on the fringe of the Eagles Nest Wilderness. I left its splintered, blood-soaked parts lying on the ground.

By that time, trekking poles had become all the rage. I was gifted a pair, which I used only for a few months. While understanding the supposed benefits—aiding in propulsion, relieving pressure on the lower back, and padding the bottom line of gear companies—I never felt comfortable with them. I often paid more attention to the placement of the pole tips than I did the placement of my feet. Plus, whenever I needed to blow my nose, get a drink, take a photo, or smoke a joint, I had to uncouple my hands from the pole's straps. It was not a match made in hiking heaven, which was a bit strange because I have long used poles while snowshoeing. I re-gifted the trekking poles the following Christmas.

Shortly after moving back to the Gila, Gay and I (read: Gay) were perusing the offerings in a dusty antique emporium downtown. Not exactly my favorite activity. To kill time while the love of my life examined overpriced rickety end tables and chipped china, I started exploring the cobweb-covered back corners, hoping to find a dusty cask of brandy or a bottle of laudanum. Instead, I found a hiking stick, the dimensions of which almost perfectly matched those of GrATash. I asked the proprietor how much. He shrugged his shoulders and said, "Uh, how about five bucks?" He was obviously expecting an incredulous counteroffer. He did not get one. As I paid up, the proprietor smirked like, "Damn, they grow 'em stupider every year."

That is the stick that elicited the compliment from the Sprinter driver. It is a plain stick that was obviously once varnished. No ornamentation. It has a crook about two-thirds of the way down. It has now been with me longer than I had GrATash. Longer than I have had Casey. I'm not certain how many more miles it has left. It used to be fifty-nine inches high. It is now fifty-five inches, worn down by time and distance. (I know the feeling.) Its body is scuffed, dinged and sports a crack running almost its full length. Breakage assuredly looms. I need to retire my stick, which I never named, before that happens. That will be a sad day. It would be impossible to calculate the distance we have covered together.

So, why carry a hiking stick?

They have practical value that, in my mind, exceeds that of trekking poles. The fact that my hand can easily slide up and down its shaft depending on circumstances makes it very versatile while traversing sketchy terrain and crossing creeks. I use it to steady myself on dicey descents. It serves as a deterrent when aggressive dogs approach. And it provides something of a psychological salve when traversing snake country. On some primal level, I believe my reflexes could out fast-twitch a striking rattler, which is pure fantasy, but who knows? Maybe adrenaline would win the day.

Plus, hiking sticks have distinct personalities, flat-out look cool, and serve as a direct connection to a bygone era when hikers wore flannel, wool, leather, and felt. I no longer wear flannel, wool, leather, or felt. So, there's only this one physical thing left that connects me to my personal days of yore.* This stick in my hand.

The difference between a hiking stick and trekking poles is similar to the difference between a wooden canoe and a plastic canoe. No one would argue that the former is more practical than the latter, but plenty of people still cast their lot with the undeniable beauty of natural materials.

There is a fairly regular crowd of hikers that congregates, then dissipates, heading off in their own various directions, every summer morning at the TS-X trailhead. To a one, they carry with them hiking sticks. In that regard, we are trail kin, a slow-dying breed that is being replaced by folks whose ensembles include trekking poles and the latest brand-name, moisture-wicking outdoor clothing made from materials with names straight out of a chemistry book.

When those of us who stick with sticks pass each other on the trail, we often compare them and relate their histories. That, of course, is silly. Most of this is silly. I'm sure in the eyes of an ever-increasing number of trail runners and mountain bikers zooming by, we must look like anachronism incarnate. A breed that will soon become extinct.

Not sure what I'm going to do when I finally retire my current stick, which needs to be done before it snaps in the middle of some activity I ought not be doing at my age anyhow.

Possibly, GrATash will serendipitously emerge from the depths of my in-law's storage shed.** Failing that, perhaps I'll order one of those fancy "staffs" available online. One containing semiprecious stones, with an owl's head carved into its peak.

* Actually, it's not "only this one physical thing." I also wear heavy leather hiking boots when conditions merit rigid footwear, and I continue to carry a tattered paper map and a compass so old its numbers are worn off. It may well be argued that these things also have less practical value than their more modern counterparts. I feel comfortable being something of a hiking museum piece. Soon, I shall be stored in the corner of a dusty antique emporium. Hopefully, next to a long-lost bottle of laudanum.

** After both of my wife's parents passed away, the family home was cleaned out and sold. There was no sign of GrATash.

DAY 153

We rounded a bend while hiking beside a paradisiacal waterway so wonderfully wild and scenic that it was once featured on the cover of *National Geographic* magazine—and there it was: My personal vision of hell, colored so attractively bright green. Pretty even, against a tall cliff backdrop with the water babbling nearby. But it could have been a wall of fire or an entire understory seething with venomous snakes, and I would have recoiled less. Instead, it was a thick carpet of knee-high foliage: *Toxicodendron rydbergii*. Poison ivy. The worst plant in the world.

It would be impossible to overstate the negative effect that one species has had on my life. For not only am I as allergic to poison ivy as a person can be, but I spent my teenage years where poison ivy goes to vacation. In Toxicodendron cosmology, the poison ivy deity says to its venomous flock, "If you are really good poison ivy and make life miserable for as

many people as possible, then you will be reincarnated in eastern Virginia."
(Here I should point out that, in the East, the poison ivy is *Toxicodendron radicans*; the Western variant is *Toxicodendron rydbergii*.)

We moved south from the northern Adirondacks when I was twelve. There were eye-openers aplenty. Atop a list that also included hurricanes, corporal punishment in school, ticks, chiggers, and stifling humidity was poison ivy, which occupied every possible biological niche. It was *everywhere*, and it took myriad forms, from little tri-leaf clusters that didn't reach above your socks to six-inch-thick vines that grew to the top of giant trees. And everything in between. Its nasty little tendrils were often intertwined with other more innocuous plants, like honeysuckle vines and blackberry bushes. You could scarcely pull off the side of the road to take a piss without standing pecker-deep in poison ivy. It was ubiquitous, insidious, and virulent.

Over the course of the seven summers I dwelled in that tick-thick part of the country, I was felled—and I mean totally incapacitated, on my back in abject misery—by cases of poison ivy dozens and dozens of times. I was taken to the hospital for steroid injections twice. Few were the body parts that were not frequently afflicted with seeping purple blisters big as silver dollars, which did nothing to help me make romantic headway with members of the opposite sex. Quite the contrary.

Poison ivy was even directly responsible for me getting knees-wobbling wasted for the very first time. Toward the end of the eighth grade—my inaugural school year in eastern Virginia—I contracted my first body-wide case, probably from doing nothing more than walking through the lush woods that surrounded our farm. Sadly, the full brunt of the allergic reaction erupted two days before our annual class trip, which was to Buckroe Beach, located near where Hampton Roads empties into the Chesapeake Bay.

Because of the severity of my condition, I had been prescribed Benadryl. Dosage was probably one pill every six or eight hours. I decided to save time by eating a big handful before we ever arrived at Buckroe Beach, which was home to a small amusement park that sported a creaky merry-go-round, a wood-framed rollercoaster that likely had not been properly inspected by the appropriate authorities for many years, and the most forlorn Ferris wheel I had ever seen.

It was at the very top of this wheezing contraption that I started feeling "a bit funny." It did not help matters any that, for inexplicable reasons, the Ferris wheel stopped dead in its tracks for probably a quarter hour while a classmate and I were at its pinnacle, which, though modest, was still high enough that, when combined with a blooming Benadryl buzz, resulted in a severe case of the spins. It also did not help matters that my classmate, who remained a close friend until his untimely and unexpected passing a couple years back, decided it would be funny to start rocking the seat back and forth.

"You're looking mighty green," he said with a wide grin, shortly before I puked off the side, which, judging from the curses emanating from down below, landed right in the middle of someone's cotton candy.

When I first arrived in New Mexico, there was zero in the way of poison ivy. All the time I lived in the Colorado High Country, I never observed so much as a single leaflet of that foul plant.

Until ...

... I went on a ten-day rafting trip down the Dolores River, which is red rock desert country. I spent most of that time assuming I would meet a bad end in some swirling Class Five rapid. (I am an admitted whitewater wuss.) The thought of catching a terrible case of poison ivy never entered my head. Best I could tell in retrospect, there was a cluster hidden in a bush onto which I was tying a bowline. I did not even consider eyeballing the verge for evidence of my old nemesis. We were hell and gone when the densest rash I had ever sported—which is saying a mouthful—appeared on my right forearm. It was like I had a third-degree burn from my wrist to my elbow. At one road crossing, I walked two miles to a country store that purveyed Calamine lotion, which I applied liberally, to no effect. I spent the next week in agony. Within seconds of getting off the river, I was at the doctor's office getting a prescription for industrial-strength prednisone. It took a month for the rash to fully dissipate.

Upon relocating back to New Mexico, I was stunned to see that poison ivy had made inroads into the darkest riparian areas of the Gila. It now carpets entire hillsides and drainages and spreads farther each year.

Further proof that we can never fully outrun our past.

My disposition inclines me toward leaving Mother Nature to evolve unfettered. New species move in, old species move out. With poison ivy, though, I have fantasy visions of aggressive ecological manipulation. I dream about buying a flamethrower—innocuously listed on eBay as a "tactical torch"—and obliterating every patch of poison ivy I can find, potential collateral damage—wildfires, getting arrested by the ATF—be damned. Gay thinks I am overreacting. She has never had her skin appear as though it is suffering from radiation exposure.

Even though I have yet to catch a case of poison ivy in New Mexico, I know my time is coming.

DAY 154

I was joined on the trail today by an acquaintance half my age, a newcomer to the Gila from the Midwest. After the usual conversational topics played out—football, outdoor gear, local women we mutually admire— he out of the blue asked what my "operational philosophy" was. I replied, without hesitation, "Don't be stupid." He remained silent. I assumed he was chewing his mental cud over the profundity of my answer. It did not dawn on me for some weeks that he might have been of the opinion I thought he was being stupid for posing the question. I hunted him down to clarify matters, since he is a likeable young man who is a lot brighter than I am.

My response was true. If I could sluice down my personal modus operandi into one succinct sentence, that would be it: Don't be stupid. This covers a lot of ground and offers up much in the way of lifestyle wiggle room. The problem is that, quite often, you don't realize you are being stupid until it's too late. This can take the form of: "It was stupid to have attempted to shimmy my way up this cliff face at my age." Or it can be of longer duration, like: "I realize these many years later it was stupid to cash out my entire retirement account so I could take that trip to Africa."

Fortunately, "Don't be stupid" is ambiguous enough that its potential fluidity factor is limitless. If, on the off chance you find yourself being stupid, you can simply adjust the stupidity bar downward a notch or two and cover your ass, which might then be hanging by its fingernails from the aforementioned cliff face, and contend that your actions were not stupid, but rather, "bold." Or, in the case of the retirement account depleted by the impetuous trip to the Dark Continent, "enlightened defiance of conventional lifestyle dictums."

The beauty of this is that you can still do occasional stupid stuff, without being *overall* stupid. As long as your actions *average out* in such a way as to not be stupid in the aggregate, you are pretty much covered. Micro-stupidity can be OK; macro-stupidity means you need to subscribe to a different operational philosophy. It also means you might be shunned, fired, divorced, incarcerated, or dead.

That philosophy also relieves an adherent of any obligation he or she might have to be smart, or to try to be smart, without actually prohibiting or demonizing any effort to rise above your not-stupid state. It's a very liberating way to journey through life. It also might be stupid.

DAY 156

Dog. Trees. Beer.
Or is it: Trees. Dog. Beer?
Or: Beer. Dog. Trees?

DAY 160

For the first time since ninth-grade geometry class, in which I earned a solid C minus (my best-ever grade in a class that included numbers), I used the word "hypotenuse" in a sentence. This long-repressed word inexplicably sprang forth from a rarely visited substratum of my subconscious while giving directions to an elderly couple vacationing in New Mexico from British Columbia.

In hiking circles, there are three types of trails: out-and-back, shuttle, and loop. Sure, there are some minor variations, such as when an out-and-back connects to a loop, but, by and large, that triad of trail food groups pretty much covers it. Thing is, when a hiker describes a loop, he or she is not exactly dragging a protractor into the discourse. Loop hikes, of course, never ever form exact circles. They meander, squiggle, and snake their way hither and yon. Still, any route that leaves a trailhead and returns to that same trailhead via different means is a loop, no matter how circuitous it might be.

Now, why, after all this time, I chose to overlay a more accurate geometric representation onto the conversational map when that couple asked me for directions, I cannot say. But I did. I told them that the first two legs of the loop upon which they were tromping were adjacent and opposite legs of a right triangle and the last section, the longest, was in fact the route's hypotenuse. That I even knew these terms and concepts will surprise those who sat next to me during any of the many math classes that confounded me throughout my formative years, classes where the words "Isaac Newton" were rarely, if ever, uttered in the same sentence as my name, if you catch my drift.

I had a spring to my step as I parted ways with them, thinking as I walked how impressed they surely were that an uneducated American could be so learned and precise. Then, about thirty minutes later, I stopped dead in my tracks when a sobering realization entered my ankle-deep stream of consciousness. "Hmmm, I'm not sure I really know what a hypotenuse is." I had sudden visions of an elderly couple busting through thick brush twelve miles off in the wilderness as darkness fell, packs of ravenous coyotes nipping at their lily-white buttocks. I could almost hear the husband saying to the wife, shortly before they both perished, "The hypotenuse HAS to be just a little farther! Surely there'll be a sign! Faster, Edna, faster!"

Later at the bar, I related this tale to my drinking buddies. There was much rambling contention regarding what a hypotenuse might or might not actually be. One person was adamant that hypotenuses were not limited to right triangles but could also be applied to obtuse triangles.

Another amigo inexplicably brought trapezoids into the discourse, which, true to inebriated form, resulted in a tangent wherein, apropos of nothing germane, words like "isosceles" and "scalene" entered the exchange.

Someone even referred to "sines" and "cosines," both of which were beyond the intellectual pay grade of most of those there gathered.

I expected at any moment that news of a missing Canadian couple would start circulating its way through our town's well-honed gossip mill. If that happened, I would volunteer to help look for them. As we did so, I would ask my fellow searchers how anyone could possibly screw up a straightforward hike around such a well-defined loop.

DAY 166

We were day hiking in the Pack Mule Mountains when a distant roar moved closer and eventually engulfed us. Casey cowered and shook. She scanned our surroundings, wondering what manner of beast could produce such a fearsome noise. If Casey was cringing, then every other critter was likewise soiling its fur. Casey did not think to look skyward, where two F-16 fighter jets were passing lower than the nearby 8,000-foot peaks. They flew back and forth for fifteen or twenty minutes, banking, zigzagging, climbing, and descending.

I assumed the pilots were mimicking planned air-combat conditions. They probably have a script. Or maybe they were simply amusing themselves in the wild blue yonder at the expense of all that lay beneath their wings.

It was November 11: Veterans Day. Compelling coincidence.

This marked the second instance in as many weeks that we got to experience the thunderous might of the U.S. Air Force. The previous time, we were hell and gone down in New Mexico's remote Bootheel when a trio of C-17 Globemasters—among the largest transport aircraft in the world—were performing maneuvers above a legally designated wilderness study area. For close to an hour, they flew in large circles in what looked like slow motion.

The Air Force has long been attempting to institutionalize the flying of fighter planes over the Gila Wilderness. I wrote a story about this for the *El Paso Times* clear back in 1980. The latest proposal is for jets from bases in Albuquerque and Alamogordo to fly as many as 30,000 sorties a year, many of which would be supersonic, with ceilings as low as 500 feet above the sacred ground of the world's first legally designated wilderness area.

As well, part of the proposal includes the discharge of 15,000 flares and 15,000 bundles of chaff annually, which, in these days of climate change, stand a good chance of igniting our tinder-dry forests, though, not surprisingly, the Air Force contends that the chances of resultant conflagrations are next to nil.

It is an understatement to say that this latest proposal is controversial.

Opponents have some practical arguments, saying that these flights will negatively impact our ever-growing outdoor recreation-based tourism industry and that the roar of all those jet engines will stress the herds of ungulates and bovines that tromp through our public lands.

Then there are the more aesthetic arguments, which are centered around the supposed sanctity of legally designated wilderness areas.

Proponents counter that more air space is needed for training purposes so that we might maintain our status as the world's mightiest military power.

When the latest updates regarding this proposal were posted on local social media sites, serious flag-waving commenced. Those who support having F-16s flying low over the Gila on a regular basis wrote things like, "That's the price of freedom!"

One man wrote, of those opposing these overflights, "You'll be sorry when North Korea invades us, and we're not prepared!"

Another man wrote, "I'd rather hear F-16s than a bunch of Subarus driving around with bad mufflers." (I had to remind him that almost all of the Subies in Silver City these days are late model and far less noisy by a factor of a hundred than the diesel-spewing bubba pickup trucks that line our highways. He responded by calling me a commie snowflake and offering to kick my ass all the way to Russia.)

I knew when I moved back to the Gila that the threat of having our local calm compromised by fighter jets was a real possibility, but given that previous proposals had fizzled, I figured—hoped—this one would follow suit. It still might.

Please understand, I am hardly unsympathetic to our armed forces. I grew up in a military family and spent most of my first twelve years living on an Air Force base.

Nor do I have anything save respect for active and retired members of the military, the overwhelming majority of whom are the kind of people you'd like to have living next door. But you can appreciate the value of our men and women in uniform and still be of the steadfast opinion that we retain some substantial corners of our country that remain relatively free of salutes, pageantry, medals, insignias, marching, bombs, blasts, recoils, explosions, sonic booms, and oh-rahs. Demilitarized zones, as it were. Sadly, in some quarters, to even entertain such a thought, much less express it, is to invite accusations of being a pussy or maybe even a traitor, someone who needs to pack up and move elsewhere. Like maybe Denmark, to dwell among the repressed socialists.

Denmark doesn't have the Gila, or anything like it.

I don't know if, this time, the Air Force will prevail in its attempts to defile the Gila with its overflights. The drumbeat feels like it's getting closer and louder than ever before.

When the fighter jets at long last disappeared over the horizon, it took five minutes for the resonating echo of their engines to completely dissipate.

I then saluted the quiet sky.

Hidden in a nearby juniper, a raven squawked.

Postscript: To the surprise of most everyone, the Air Force backed away from its proposal to fly F-16s directly over the Gila. So, we won. Right up until the next time when the roar of the American war machine once again reverberates through our canyons and across our mesas. It will never end.

Post-Postscript: Not long thereafter, a new proposal for Air Force flights over the Gila began to circulate. Those flights would come from bases in Arizona instead of New Mexico. Like that makes the slightest difference. A sonic boom is a sonic boom, no matter its origin. All part of the same empire.

DAY 171

A series of "lost dog" fliers started appearing on local trail-head bulletin boards, including the one located next to the main parking area of TS-X.

Nothing new. Canines running astray are shockingly common in these untethered parts. Local social media pages are thick with notices—some desperate, some shockingly matter-of-fact, like, "Schnerpels has run off yet again!"—for missing pets.

I consider it my karmic duty to scrutinize such fliers and, while doing so, to, at minimum, feel earnest sympathy for the person who tacked them up. In the unlikely event that the dog thereupon portrayed crosses my path, I would do my best to nab it or, failing that, to commit to memory exactly where I laid eyes upon the pooch. Either way, I would then call the number appearing on the flyer and wait for the owner to arrive, so that I might assist in the search. I have yet to be in that position. I have never, ever come across a lost dog whose picture—always taken during a happy time, like the dog standing in a creek with a stick in its mouth—appears on such fliers.

Usually, after a week or two, the fliers begin to disintegrate, and eventually they decompose entirely, leaving only tattered remnants of faded tape behind. The dog was either found, and the owner was not courteous enough to pull the fliers down, or the dog was not found and hope for a reunion eventually got blown away with the wind.

These fliers were different. They were not only replaced but updated on a regular basis. They contained status reports. Additionally, they were spread over a wide area. Generally, lost dog fliers will be found only in the immediate vicinity of where the animal was last seen. Not these. They were tacked up on telephone poles, at parks, and inside laundromats and convenience stores throughout the entire region. Either the owner was not certain where she misplaced her dog, or the dog was known to have the potential for ranging far and wide.

This particular search was dogged and ongoing. Week after week. Month after month. A woman I'll call Kay was looking for a scruffy dog named Charley—a thirty-pound border collie/terrier mix—who, via his disappearance, became something of a local celebrity in absentia. His plight was well followed on social media, where Kay was praised for her dedication while simultaneously being castigated for losing Charley and for not accepting the fact that, in an area inhabited by coyotes, wolves, mountain lions, bears, bobcats, and rattlesnakes —as well as lethal predator-control devices—the chances that Charley was still alive were next to nil. Kay was admonished to face the sad truth: Charley was gone. Get a grip. Move on.

Still, the posters remained up, regularly refreshed.

Four months after Charley went missing, I decided on a whim to contact Kay. I wanted to fathom the depths of her ongoing commitment, which, from a cynical perspective might, after 120 days, be more accurately construed as false hope bordering on delusion bordering on craziness.

217

I called the number on the Charley posters.

Couple weeks later, Kay hiked with Casey and me for two hours on a trail she often traversed with Charley—the very same trail Casey and I followed during our very first on-foot foray together, back when my newly procured canine companion was still connected to me via a sixteen-foot retractable leash.

I learned that Kay, a native of Philadelphia, who had for the previous several years been living a semi-nomadic existence in a motor home, now anchored in a local RV park, had distributed almost 600 flyers, and spent her entire inheritance and savings looking for Charley. Thousands and thousands of dollars. It had become her life's mission to find her dog or, failing that, to learn his fate.

While it may be tempting for some people—most of whom are likely not dog owners—to wonder how a person could lose track of a beloved pet, I speak from experience when I say it can happen in the blink of an eye.

The year before my quest to hike every day for a year, I bought a small camper trailer and Casey and I spent two months traveling back East to reconnect with the settings of my youth. One of those was the Appalachian Trail outside the village of Salisbury, Connecticut. The plan was to take a ten-mile stroll up Bear Mountain.

Shortly after leaving the trailhead parking lot, which was filled to the brim with vehicles, we were passed by a runner who stopped only long enough to give me shit about hiking with my dog off leash.

"You could lose your dog!" he growled.

I reflexively adopted the pose of the hard-assed Westerner who considered this particular section of trail to be barely worth my time. I mean—Connecticut! Are you kidding me? I responded, "Look, dude, my dog and I have been hiking together for many years and many miles in New Mexico and Colorado. She is well trained. There is absolutely no chance she will run off!"

He dashed ahead, leaving me to stew in my own arrogant juices.

A few minutes later, I looked for Casey. She was nowhere to be seen. I called her. No response. I hiked a bit farther, expecting her to be waiting for me sporting an impish grin, like, "What took you so long?" Such was not the case. I stopped and bellowed, her name echoing through the shadowy forest. I backtracked half a mile, calling her name repeatedly. Then I back-backtracked. Increasingly desperate. On the fifth or sixth backtrack, the trail runner came down. He grinned widely when I sheepishly asked if he had seen my dog. To his eternal credit, he was polite. He said he would keep an eye out and wished me good luck.

I absolutely could not *believe* this was happening.

After spending more than an hour searching for Casey, I resolved to do one more sweep. If unsuccessful, I knew I had to embark upon a process that would have been unthinkable when I arose that morning in my camper at a nearby state park. I would need to drive to Salisbury, look for a business where I could compose and print a series of lost dog fliers, drive back to the trailhead, and every other trailhead nearby, and start tacking them up. I would need to call the local animal shelter and radio station. I would then need to start knocking on nearby doors. Then I would start hiking until my legs wore down and my voice gave out. Somewhere along the line, I would have to call Gay, who, doubtless, would have been on the first plane to Connecticut.

This was not how I had hoped the day would evolve.

Shortly before I arrived back at the trailhead—exhausted, exasperated, freaked out—there was Casey, sitting contritely in the trail, tail between her legs. I hugged her tightly and tamped down my inclination to shout at her for wandering off. I, of course, should have been yelling at myself for not paying attention to a dog happily exploring an unfamiliar area. Almost lost in the adrenaline shuffle was the fact that, no matter where or how far she had wandered, Casey had managed to find her way back to the trail.

Good girl.

To underscore that all was forgiven, we completed the ten-mile loop we had originally planned. We arrived back at the trailhead well after dark. Casey stuck close to me the entire time. We both slept fitfully that night.

She has never again wandered off.

So, yes, I get where Kay was coming from. Mostly. Sorta. Well, not quite. Because, after all, Casey and I were reunited on the Appalachian Trail in Connecticut. Kay and Charley, as of this writing, were not.

I felt terrible for her.

Kay, who worked most of her life as a waitperson, hiked extensively—sans leash—with Charley through wildland parks that surround Philadelphia, where she had adopted Charley from an SPCA facility when he was about eleven months old. When she decided—inspired in part by the death of her human partner—to sell her house and take up a nomadic lifestyle that eventually led her to southwest New Mexico, she and Charley continued to hike at every opportunity. Though I never ran into them on the trail, their preferred routes often overlapped with those Casey and I hike upon. It seemed like an idyllic life.

Right up until July 23.

Kay and Charley were hiking with a friend and his dog in the Gila. Kay was, she says, "flirting." Her attention wandered. After a few minutes, she looked around for Charley, who was nowhere to be seen. Her friend's dog, however, was within eyesight, so Kay did not immediately worry. Shortly thereafter, she called for Charley. No response. She ventured off trail a bit and yelled his name for a few minutes. It did not take long for panic to ensue.

She spent two nights at the trailhead, calling for Charley every fifteen minutes. No luck.

Kay then began her onslaught of flier distribution. She joined numerous local social media groups and began making frequent posts. She also spent day after day searching trails she walked with Charley. She was despondent, grief-stricken, and overwhelmed with guilt. She vowed to dedicate her life and her fiscal resources to hunting for Charley.

And this is where, in her words, "things started getting a bit woo-woo."

Even as she continued to physically search for Charley and respond to the countless messages she received from people who were convinced they had seen him, she embarked upon the process of single-handedly supporting Silver City's substantial psychic/shamanic/supernatural industry. She did not exactly have to beat the bushes to locate practitioners.

All told, Kay hired twelve psychics, two shamans, and something called a map dowser, the latter vocation being one I had never heard of prior to my hike with Kay.

This aspect of Kay's search for Charley was not totally out of character. She had long been interested in alternative perspectives. After Charley walked off, she was motivated to jump into that world with both feet.

"The map dowser said Charley was down at [Trout Lake], and he gave me incredible directions for where to look for Charley," Kay said. "It's a weird thing what they do. We have all heard of water dowsers, people who use sticks or a rod to locate underground water. A map dowser is kind of the same thing, except they have a map in front of them. The idea behind dowsing altogether is that you are tapping into universal knowledge. We all have access to universal knowledge in our bodies and you can tap into that universal knowledge by following very slight electromagnetic impulses in your arms, which will tell you where the water is. Or where on the map somebody is.

"The map dowser I hired does something a little different. He apparently has the ability to see through Charley's eyes in some way. Don't know if he goes into trances or anything about how he actually operates."

(The map dowser Kay hired lives in Georgia. They communicated virtually or on the phone. Long-distance dowsing.)

"He would send me an email report saying that he saw a water-retention basin, and he saw a really rickety fence and a gray barn. As I was driving along the road, I could actually see these things, and I'd say OK, Charley came this way and then he saw this and then he saw this. When I got to the motel at [Trout Lake], the dowser sent me to an area and I would pepper that area with signs, knock on doors, and ask people. A young girl said, 'I just saw the most interesting thing. It looked like a baby bear just ambling across the street and into the woods.'

"And I said, 'Did he have any white on him?'

"And she said, 'Oh yeah, his feet were white.' And, of course, in my hopeful state, I was sure it was Charley.

"I spent four days in the area spending oodles of money with the map dowser, finding places where Charley's energy signature was very strong and trying to track him down. Of course, I never saw my dog and never connected with him."

(According to his website, the map dowser charges $175 for an initial consultation and $135 for follow-up consultations.)

Five of the twelve psychics Kay hired walked her through Charley's death. Wait! What?

Yes. Those psychics provided details of Charley's expiration, many of which were gruesome.

Seven other psychics told Kay that Charley was still alive.

"After the first psychic told me about Charley's death, I walked around [Trout Lake] saying goodbye to my beautiful dog and got a text as I was three-quarters of the way around the lake from somebody who said they had seen the signs at the laundromat and were sure they saw my dog in Silver City."

Kay dashed back to town to follow that lead down. To no avail. Always to no avail.

Kay was understandably frustrated. She stopped and asked me point-blank, her face halfway between laughing and crying: "How come these psychics and the dowser can't agree on where Charley is? Why can't they find my dog?"

"Well, there is the possibility that it's all bullshit and they are ripping you off," I replied.

"Yeah, that's a possibility," Kay said with an expression that bespoke deep pain.

Possibility is all Kay yet retains in her search for Charley.

Despite setback after setback, she steadfastly refuses to give up.

"It's defined my life, losing a partner through disappearance, and I'm still unprepared to handle it."

Kay told me that she plans to stay in Silver City until she finds Charley or is convinced he is dead.

"By now, he is completely feral," she said. "I'm not going anywhere until I have some kind of clarity. We were soul mates, this guy and me. I don't know how long it will take my crazy dog to return."

I bit my lip. The chances of a thirty-pound domesticated border collie/terrier mix surviving month after month in the wilds of southwest New Mexico—like some desert version of Buck from *The Call of the Wild*—seemed beyond remote. But stranger things have happened. We have all heard stories about pets being reunited with their people years after being lost. And maybe Charley hooked up with another person and is living happily somewhere else, maybe very far away.

In the meantime, the flier bearing Charley's likeness at the TS-X trailhead has disintegrated. It its stead was a flier for yet another lost dog, this one named Sam.

Casey and I hike quite a bit in the areas where Kay most often searched for Charley. When we do, I keep my eyes peeled, hoping to catch a glimpse of his shadow moving furtively through the trees, searching for his person.

Postscript: Almost two years after I hiked with Kay, I got a message from her saying she was moving to California. "You have to know that it was really difficult to leave the area without ever having had closure with Charley," she wrote. "So if you ever see him or hear of him, please let me know." I responded that she could count on it.

223

DAY 174

This morning, for the first time in my life, I called the forest cops.

A couple raggedy-looking twenty-somethings had been camping for three or four months alongside a fairly popular trail that follows a creek, which is one of the few places near town guaranteed to have at least a scum-covered pool or two in which dogs can cool off on hot summer days before the monsoon rains arrive.

It pained me to pick up the phone with the intent of filing a complaint against two people who at least superficially were clones of me when I was that age.

Among the many traits that differentiate the vast swaths of public land found in the Mountain Time Zone from the grimness of civilization is that they are relatively gendarme-free. That's one of the main advantages of living near a national forest that is severely underfunded. We have three law enforcement officers patrolling millions of acres of public land. It's therefore pretty damned easy to distance yourself from the increasingly long and repressive arm of the law.

That said, there are public lands management regulations with which I wholeheartedly agree.

These young people had pitched their tent right next to the trail and creek—both of which are justifiably illegal. (You need to camp at least one hundred feet from trails and watercourses.) In addition, it is against Gila National Forest regulations to remain more than two weeks in one spot. This latter rule came about because, in times past, clans of Rainbow Family types would lay sometimes aggressive claim to entire swaths of the Gila for entire seasons. Their encampments looked like Third World refugee camps, only with more toddlers running around with visible cases of ringworm.

The couple I reported had started acting territorial toward passersby, who often include young families and senior citizen bird watchers and photographers. Several people I talked with felt intimidated and had stopped going to the area.

The final straw occurred when I saw that they had been washing clothes in the creek with a bar of soap and leaving food scraps lying about. I can overlook a lot of bad behavior, but, when it comes to negatively impacting the land, that's where I draw the line.

The cop I talked with said I was not the first person to complain about the couple, which made me feel better, but not much. I felt like a nark, like I had jumped into bed with The Man. I almost cut my hair.

I wondered in retrospect if I ought not have made more effort to talk with that couple, to articulate my concerns about their conduct. I could have hiked in with a six-pack, a few joints, and a bag of burritos and played the role of mentor. I didn't. Not long before this occurred, a machete attack on the Appalachian Trail left one man dead and a woman severely sliced and diced. You never know these days. In the U.S. in the early part of the 21st century, even raggedy-looking twenty-somethings might be packing. They could have been running from the law. They might have had nothing to lose, except their little campsite in the wilds of New Mexico.

The next time I hiked on that trail, they were gone. Where to, I did not know. Perhaps deeper into the Gila. Maybe back to the grimness of civilization.

They left behind some trash, which I picked up and carried out, and a fire ring, which I destroyed and rehabilitated. I wanted to obliterate all memory of the circumstance that had me for the first time in my life calling the forest cops. When I was done, their campsite looked borderline pristine, like no one had ever been there.

But something had clearly changed.

DAY 180

Nearing the halfway point of my quest to hike every day for a solid year, I decided it was high time I got a physical—something, according to the fine print affixed to TV commercials and print advertisements relating to every activity more physically taxing than eating a candy bar, I ought to have done at the outset of this particular endeavor.

While filling out one of those *War and Peace*-length front-office medical history forms, in which I swore via my eventual signature that I did not suffer from any of the forty-three listed maladies, most of which I had never heard of ("Have you ever had a case of Amazonian Crotch Rot?"), I got to a question asking if I was currently suffering from any "aches or pains." There was only enough room between that question and the next to list one ache and one pain. So, while trying to decide which of the many options to go with—back? knee? shoulder? elbow? other knee?—I threw in the towel and wrote, "I am almost sixty." The receptionist said that would suffice.

DAY 181

It was a facial expression I will never forget. I was in the midst of a two-month backpacking trip in the late 1990s and Gay had picked me up at a point where the trail crossed a state highway. She drove me to the closest small town—some fifty miles away—where I restocked my food bag, took a shower, ate a restaurant meal, drank a few beers and, most importantly for our purposes here, went to a laundromat. I pulled my soiled hiking ensemble from a repurposed tent bag that served as a repository for both dirty (those items worn while hiking) and less dirty (those worn solely in camp) pieces of clothing. Out came T-shirts, skivvies, shorts, long pants, bandannas, then finally, as something of a crescendo of funkiness, my socks.

Gay has had the misfortune of being around befouled hiking attire ever since we first came together. She has also come off the trail with her various pieces of clothing not exactly up to haute couture snuff. (Though, no matter how grubby my wife's garments might be after a week or two in the woods, they are a veritable bouquet of roses compared to mine.) She understands full well that aromatic unsavoriness is about to come her way when her husband is unloading his clothes bag after a seventy-five-mile stint on the trail.

She should have known better than to stand so close as I was placing my clothing into the unfortunate washer. It is generally considered some manner of euphemism when you say that "someone's face turned green." This was not a situation that inspired such an innocent figure of speech. When my socks came out, my wife's face literally turned somewhere between olive and jade. I thought she might retch right there in the laundromat. She ran outside gagging. She was soon joined by several other patrons, all of whom must have assumed that I was gainfully employed as a septic tank cleaner.

I ended up washing those socks twice, and even then, they reminded no one of a French perfumery.

I have long wondered why hiking socks smell so horrible. I do not expect that they would, after X-number of hot, sweaty miles, be free of repulsive odor. But, at the same time, T-shirts and underwear thus worn, while certainly pungent in their own unique right, come nowhere near the mephitic factor of socks. I once held a crusty pair of hiking socks at arm's length and they did not sag one iota; rather, they retained their rigid shape. I could have used them to split firewood.

On Day 181—Thanksgiving Day—of my year-long quest, I laid a pair of socks I had worn for two or three straight wet, muddy days in front of the fireplace in hopes that the heat would somehow magically eliminate or at least reduce the smell. Casey, who is generally inclined to lie close to the fire when it's chilly, left the room wincing. She might have even been growling a bit. And this from a creature that has zero in the way of compunction about burying her nose in horse shit. When Gay returned home a few days later from a holiday trip to Colorado, the entire house still reeked. She asked if something had died in our den. I blamed it on Casey's notorious flatulence.

DAY 182

PART I

Alongside a trail Casey and I often traverse is found a cheap plastic chair, the back of which is adorned with the words, penned in black Magic Marker, "Please leave here. It matters to this old man." Not a million miles from the trailhead, but far enough that it definitely sticks out.

I have long wondered if the instructions carry double meaning. Does the "old man" want people who pass to "leave here"—as in "away with you"—or does he merely want the chair to be left where it is?

And who exactly is "this old man?"

PART II

One otherwise ordinary late-autumn afternoon, Casey and I approached the chair. We did not notice until we were almost upon it that an old woman was parked on its plastic slats. Her presence startled me, and I jumped a bit. Casey's hackles rose.

The woman barely registered our presence, even after I said, "As many times as I have passed this chair, I have never seen anyone sitting in it."

She said nothing as she stared at the dirt. She clearly wanted me to please leave here.

After a short distance, I turned around. The old lady was gone. The immediate area was dotted with foliage sparse enough that there was nowhere she could have hidden. She had disappeared. Vanished into thin air.

I wondered what the relationship between the old man and the old lady might be. Or might have been.

PART III

On a subsequent, otherwise ordinary late-autumn afternoon, I finally decided to sit in the chair, which by that point I had passed dozens of times. No particular reason. I wasn't tired. I wondered, given the experience with the disappearing woman, and given the wording on the chair, if it was not some manner of interdimensional teleportation device.

Where would it take me?

Shortly after my posterior landed, a wiry young trail runner trotted up. He stopped and stared.

"All these years, I have wondered who the old man was," he said, matter-of-factly. Before I could object or even clarify, he ran off.

I looked down upon my wrinkled hands before lifting up bones that felt wearier than they had scant minutes prior. I have not sat in that chair since, and now I pay it no heed whenever I pass by. I have even considered carrying it out.

How long does it take for a plastic chair to decompose?

DAY 183

I have reached the halfway point of my quest. Six months behind me, six months yet ahead.

This is already a month longer than I was on the Appalachian Trail. Four months longer than I was on the Colorado and Arizona trails.

I can scarcely at this juncture remember when I was not orienting every aspect of my life around hiking every day.

This has turned out to be one of my better ideas.

All downhill from here! (Except, of course, for the uphill parts.)

DAY 185

Wonder how many "extra" miles we have hiked because we (meaning: I) said, "Just a little farther; let's see what's around the next bend!" (Then the next bend after that.)

Answer: Not nearly enough.

So many bends; so little time.

DAY 195

Three days before my sixtieth birthday, a cloudy, chilly, mois-
ture-laden weather front moved in. It had been predicted for
more than a week and, given that not so much as a molecule of
precipitation had landed upon the Gila in two months, it was welcomed with
open arms. The rain came at 1 a.m. and people were going outside dressed
however they sleep to smell the wet and catch upon their outstretched tongues
the large drops cascading from a night sky that had not been starless since
a freak snowstorm blew through in October. In desert country, that is the
scent and taste of promise: We will not wither away. Not this time, at least.

It rained most of the morning and early afternoon. When Casey and I
left the trailhead, it was forty-three degrees and blustery. During the course
of ninety minutes that bled nearly into full darkness, it intermittently rained,
hailed, and sleeted.

It was, in my opinion, the worst kind of weather in the world.

It was great.

We only get a handful of such days every year, and rarely do they follow one another. Dreary days are oddities in the Gila. When they arrive, they feel good. Not solely for the always badly needed moisture, but for mixing things up enough to require digging around in the back of the closet for clothing rarely worn. Today, it was a midweight fleece vest. How I came to own this vest, I do not remember, but it has numerous holes of varying sizes burned clean through. So, it has a history that includes proximity to fire. That's usually good history.

There are countries where such weather is the norm. My native England, which I left when I was six months old, has a justified reputation for climatic gloominess. I have long wanted to go to Scotland, Ireland, and the Netherlands. However, I have considerable concern that the weather during my entire trip would be defined by frigid drizzle and, upon my return home to New Mexico, my skin would be the color of new-fallen snow. I cannot abide the notion of dermatological pastiness, even in the short term.

I envision the freckly residents of Scotland considering this type of day to be high summer. Like, "Gather up the kids, Fiona! The temperature has risen to forty-three, and it's merely blustery! Let's drive down to the beach for a picnic! I'll pack the haggis!" I once watched a video about intrepid Scottish backpackers camping in foul weather and going about their business—setting up the tent, cooking and eating dinner, sitting on sodden boulders, and shooting the breeze over a smoke—as though they were on a beach in Baja. It's possible they were acting tough because a video was being shot. But they appeared comfortable to me, like it was perfectly normal to relax out in a dingy drizzle. I would have been curled up in the tent.

I could never live where such conditions are the norm. I could handle maybe a week straight before I listed my house with a real estate professional and beelined to Alice Springs or the Atacama.

Gay and I once traveled to Alaska on what for her was a vacation but for me was a potential relocation scouting expedition. The idea of spending a couple years in the Last Frontier had long appealed to me—from a distance.

Gay eventually agreed to move to Alaska, so long as it was a relatively civilized city (for me that was Homer, for her it was Anchorage, for neither of us was it Fairbanks). This is a paraphrase of what she said to me on the flight home: "Husband, you are the most sun-dependent person I have ever known. If we have three days without sun, you turn as gray as the weather. Alaska has, like, six months a year during which the sun inches above the horizon twelve minutes a day and another six months of the year during which the sun breaks through the thick cloud cover for twelve minutes a day." We did not move to Alaska. We instead moved to southwest New Mexico. Fewer orcas. Better green chile.

I am a heliophile.

Gay, on the other hand, is not a sun worshipper. Quite the contrary. She has no desire to dwell in a perpetually gloomy place, but she could dwell in a gloomier place. She would like more cloud cover. I have heard her say numerous times words to the effect of (with nary an iota of sarcasm), "Another perfect New Mexico day. Damn."

Gay opted to stay at home instead of going out with Casey—who, despite her desert lineage, loves the misty coolness—and I. "Too yucky," she said of the forty-three-degree weather. She took a nap instead.

Next day, the sun was shining. All was right with the world.

DAY 196

We were halfway down the hill when Casey froze in her tracks, instantly achieving doggie DEFCON 1 alert status. Fur from nape to tail shot straight up. She began to woof nervously, as is her way when spam is about to hit the fan. I too stopped and peered ahead, wondering what sort of danger my astute canine had perceived lurking in the shadows. Javelina? Possibly. We saw a gaggle several days prior. Mountain lion? Bear? Coyotes? Wolves? Crazed redneck? All distinct possibilities.

After a minute or two, during which time Casey did not chill out even slightly, I tentatively recommenced walking—slowly. Casey followed in my footsteps, hackles still raised. Some dogs look upon it as their prime responsibility to run ahead and face down whatever danger might be lurking up ahead in defense of their human companion. Not Casey. Her default position when she's tense is to hide behind me. It's my job to protect her.

Finally, I came to understand that what had agitated my noble descendent of *Canis lupus* was none of the creatures listed above. It was, rather, a highly venomous, neurotoxic, carnivorous, hyper-aggressive, well, tree stump. Worse, it was a stump we have walked by hundreds of times. Why this particular stump, which had never harmed us before, suddenly became a cause for concern in Casey's mind, I cannot say. I made Casey pose for a photograph next to the existential threat. She somehow survived. Barely.

Several friends, upon hearing this embarrassing tale, suggested to me that it was entirely possible that Casey was wired into something beyond human perception. A recent criminal event that occurred near the stump, perhaps. Maybe a squirrel was sitting there nibbling on a nut and got taken by a hawk. Or, as one decidedly New Age lady suggested, Casey was attuned to the trauma the tree experienced when it was hacked down to stump level.

My money was on some manner of spontaneous doggie hallucination.

DAY 198

A young writer once asked me what my favorite thing to do was.

"Go someplace I have never been before," was my honest answer. He followed up with: "What if you don't like it?"

"Then I won't go back," I responded.

Today is my sixtieth birthday, the event that, six months prior, served as a springboard to my inebriated barroom decision to embark upon this year-long quest.

It has long been my habit to celebrate the anniversary of my feet-first entrance into this world by doing exactly what I told that young writer: going someplace new. I did not do that today. Quite the contrary. Scheduling conflicts did not allow us to hit the road. Gay, Casey, and I hiked upon a trail I know by heart.

Nonetheless, the loud ticking of the mortality clock did, in fact, bring me to someplace new, if not physically, then temporally.

It marked the first time I had dipped a toe into the decade that touches the decade where can be found my average life expectancy. My expiration date, as it were.

Gay, as is her annual habit, put together a nice birthday card for me. A photograph of Casey and I hiking together along a snow-covered trail.

As I hiked creaky-kneed along, I kept repeating, "Sixty is the new forty … sixty is the new forty."

By the time we got back to the trailhead, I almost believed it.

I wished I could go back.

DAY 200

Driving home from a late-afternoon hike, I noticed a small SUV parked on the other side of the road. Rain had moved in. Nearing dusk. Wind and moisture commingling and swirling. Directly in front of the vehicle, a young man was holding a foot-long wooden, Christian-looking cross, jumping up and down, waving his arms, yelling words I could not hear. There was a lone woman sitting rigidly in the driver's seat, her hands firmly attached to the steering wheel.

The young man looked to be performing an exorcism on the vehicle. Or he could have been laying one seriously animated curse on it. Or perhaps he was trying to admonish a higher power to get the SUV back on the road. Maybe he was crazy. Maybe all of the above.

Perhaps I should have stopped to ask if everything was OK, if there was anything I could do to help, like maybe rescuing the woman in the driver's seat. But my considerable experience with craziness has taught me there are times when it's best to simply drive on. My luck, I would be on the receiving end of a curse, or worse, have my demons exorcized. I like my demons right where they are. They have helped me get this far—200 days into my quest to hike every day for a solid year. Further than I had any reasonable right to ever expect while sitting on that barstool all those miles ago. Don't want to risk getting sidetracked.

Besides, where would my demons go without me? And I without them?

DAY 203

The setting for this particularly amusing form of dog abuse was purely accidental. In an area I had long wanted to check out, the number of dispersed campsites was limited, so I pretty much jumped on the first available patch of open ground I saw. It did not hurt that it turned out to be a spectacular place to pitch a tent, pop a beer and reflect upon a world clearly gone mad.

It wasn't until after Casey and I returned from a hike up a sandy-bottomed side canyon that I became aware of our campsite's acoustic opportunities. An unseen bird—I have no idea what type—sang and its lovely melody half-circled around us. I then realized we were camped in an echo chamber—which should not have been much of a surprise, as the rock wall behind us was high and horseshoe-shaped.

I began to hoot and holler Casey's name in various tones, frequencies, and volumes. She would look at me, then swivel her head and follow the reverberation as it made its way around the concave geology. Her brow furrowed in a descending combination of amusement, confusion, and frustration. The possibilities for benign canine torment were limitless!

It had been many years since I last experienced similar sound-based circumstances.

While living in the Windy City many years prior, I had the opportunity to interact with what is considered one of the most acoustically perfect settings in the world: the Whispering Gallery at the Chicago Museum of Science and Industry. The way it worked was you and a companion stood with your backs turned to each other at either end of a tunnel-like room maybe fifty feet long. When you whispered into the curved wall in front of you, your friend clearly heard what you said as though you were mere inches apart.

I went there with a woman I was dating. It will come as a shock to no one that the words I whispered were entirely inappropriate for such a highbrow setting. How was I to know that, in the short time I had turned my back, a family—dad, wife, two small children—that looked straight out of a 1950s *Good Housekeeping* magazine ad for Crest toothpaste had walked up and were now parked right next to my lady friend?

Finally, as my bad taste bombardment continued unabated, the woman, who unceremoniously dumped me soon thereafter, stated loudly enough that no auditory enhancement was necessary, "SHUT UP!!!"

I then turned and noticed a very red-faced couple who had their hands placed firmly over the ears of their offspring. My bad.

I have matured in the interim. Marginally.

After fifteen minutes of uninterrupted echoes, during which time I repeatedly mimicked coyote howls and uttered things like, "Casey, this is your conscience speaking" (in baritone) and "Where's Casey?" (in falsetto), she finally laid her head upon the ground and sighed, resigned to having to endure even more of my babbling than usual. She wondered if there were somehow now two or more of me. And she wondered if I would ever shut up. Not likely.

Casey paid me back by fidgeting nervously in the tent all night, making sleep impossible.

DAY 216

It was the kind of day every reasonably responsible American is forced by external circumstances to occasionally endure. Even those of us who only have one tentative foot dipped in the roiling waters of the mainstream. Unavoidable Walmart run. Issues with the Internet, health insurance provider, the mortgage company and, worst, the New Mexico Taxation and Revenue Department, a truly evil entity manned by people who clearly loathe semi-employed writers.

OK, First World problems, I understand, but problems that cause enough in the way of heartburn that I needed, rather than just wanted, to take a long, hard hike to decompress.

The list of reasons why outdoor enthusiasts venture into the boondocks is long, multifaceted, layered, overlapping, nuanced and often hard to define, even by the most avid devotees of realms where the human-built environment and its concomitant headaches fizzle into a glorious thin air.

We hike to listen to quiet, to get in shape, to watch birds, to access mountaintops, to meditate. And to de-stress. This is a big one for me. I am an easily agitatable person who regularly begins his hikes in a frame of mind best defined as "miffed," usually about stupid stuff. But, after a certain number of miles, whatever agitation I bring with me dissipates. Sometimes instantly, sometimes slowly, and sometimes not totally but mostly. Or at least partially. Probably, it's as much a matter of exercise-induced release of endorphins and serotonin as it is the fact that I am walking vigorously through wild country. I could likely de-stress on a cardio machine at the local gym. But that is not my way.

Which is all cool. When I return to the trailhead after an invigorating hike, I generally feel a lot better.

What I wonder, though, is: What happened to all that negative energy? Where does it go? Does it dematerialize, its constituent components becoming inert as they float toward the treetops?

Unlikely, I fear.

We've all seen diesel trucks spewing black smoke that soon seemingly becomes invisible, even though we all know its nasty molecules are still out there swirling around in the atmosphere.

And we've all seen black light science-experiment video footage where they show how far snot and spit travel when people sneeze. It sprays like twelve feet away and hovers for several minutes, potentially contaminating everything in its path of grotesqueness.

I fear that's what it's like when I use intense, frequent interactions with wild country as a scenic substitute for Haldol, Xanax, or even more beer. I worry that the dissipation of my frequent agitation and frustration actually pollutes the land through which I hike. Like I'm walking along spraying a heavy dose of psychic Roundup. Though, as I mentioned earlier, this is not an everyday situation, it occurs often enough that I am concerned that whatever level of irritation I might bring into the woods follows me like a wake. In order to feel better, do I inadvertently make the woods feel worse?

Do the trees wince at my approach the same way people do when a toxic coworker shows up at an after-hours employee get-together?

Perhaps, after a day during which I have had to go to Walmart and deal with New Mexico's Byzantine bureaucracy, I should, before embarking upon my daily hike, spend some time on a cardio machine at the local gym. Kind of like taking a shower before entering a public swimming pool.

DAY 217

Dead-smack in the middle of one of the many blank spots that define the cartography of southern New Mexico lies an otherwise unremarkable geologic feature that, solely because of topographic relativity, bears appellation that includes the word "peak."

Viewed from a distance, one would be tempted to call this feature a hill. Or a rise. Maybe a bump. That is, were one to even notice it enough to ponder a proper description. For, in addition to its lack of stature, it boasts little in the way of obvious features. It's not as though this shrimpy mountain is adorned with a magnificent arch or a series of hoodoos or a rock that resembles a human face. It is smooth, rounded, and void of foliage any more notable than prickly pear and greasewood. Were this feature found in the middle of an Illinois cornfield, then yes, it would likely be worthy of attention. But here, deep in the grandeur that defines the American Southwest, it is the very definition of "unexceptional."

Yet, what this peak lacks in altitude and apparent natural adornment it more than makes up for in setting. Its very existence causes the region's main watercourse to bend and bend again. It rises from the relatively flat plain that once was the bed of an ancient sea. Thus, it affords unimpeded views of the river that wraps around its base.

Upriver lies country as rugged and unpeopled as any in the Land of Enchantment, a paradise of jagged canyons, sinewy arroyos, hidden springs, and bones bleached white.

Downriver lies a broad, verdant valley, the bottom of which bears thick, rich, alluvial soil that has since time immemorial served as a productive agricultural area, a rarity in these parched parts.

The view from this otherwise unexceptional peak offers the best of both worlds. One direction: raw wild. The other direction: bountiful fecundity.

Given the peak's stellar location and resultant views, the Native Americans who dwelled here centuries ago—I assume they were members of the long-gone-who-knows-where Mogollon culture—obviously considered this protuberance to be extraordinarily special. There remains jaw-dropping physical evidence backing up this admittedly unacademic observation. On the backside of this peak, which lacks signage or trails, lies a cliff face that is not apparent from any of the cross-country approach angles. It is not until one reaches the summit that one realizes this otherwise humble peak is home to an amazing trove of petroglyphs. The gallery consists primarily of individual works that obviously took years to complete, works that cover entire boulders the size and scale of which compares to the giant canvasses on display at the Louvre. One after another after another. You move along the base of the cliff face thinking, "There can't *possibly* be any more!"—only to find yet another massive display of astounding creativity.

En plein air to the extreme.

It was January first. Gay, Casey, and I welcomed the New Year agog. Once daylight started fading, we hiked down and, within seconds, the rock gallery disappeared from view. What was left was nothing more than an unexceptional peak that seemed to bid us adieu with a wink and a smile.

New Mexico is like a Russian nesting doll. On acid. You never know till you start peeling away the layers what lies at the core. It could be a nugget of turquoise. Or it could be a scorpion. Or a magic spell. Or rebirth.

DAY 221

I opened Pronto's back hatch and immediately noticed something sorely amiss. Where normally there would be my faded green day pack, there was nothing save an exposed area of interior carpet, which, now that I scrutinized it more closely than usual, could use a thorough cleaning. I was momentarily at a loss. How could it be possible for my pack, which is always right there, to not be right there? Could it have been stolen? If so, it was the only item taken, as everything else—my pile of auxiliary clothing, water bottles, camp chairs, toolbox, iPod—were all left untouched.

I finally recollected that, the day before, I had taken a different vehicle to the trail—something that only happens about twice a year—and, therefore, I had moved my pack from Pronto's interior. I had (obviously) neglected to return it to its rightful place. Forgetfulness is a rather bothersome symptom of the aging process. I growled and cursed and wondered if, with no pack, life was even worth living. But, there at my feet stood a dog, her tail wagging expectantly, awaiting our imminent departure. And there was this year-long quest that needed my attention, with or without a pack. Returning home to retrieve it was out of the logistics question.

So, we left, packless. I had to stash my wallet, phone, and sunglass case—all of which are usually placed in the topmost compartment of my pack—in various random pants pockets. I had with me no water. If any manner of emergency would have occurred, then we were surely doomed. Death was likely.

I felt naked.

It was a chilly day. Since few people hereabouts are willing to venture out if the temperature dips below fifty, there were no witnesses to my abject packless ignominy.

This hike would be for an hour, and not one minute more!

It did not take long for me to realize how light I felt. How unencumbered.

I say that I prefer minimalism, no matter the venue, no matter the circumstance, no matter the mode of travel. Yet, I rarely so much as step into the bushes to piss without having on my back the means to bivouac comfortably for a week. I understand there are many people who would, under no conceivable circumstances, step into the bushes to relieve themselves. So, at least I've got that going for me. All things are relative.

We ended up exploring numerous side canyons I've been meaning to check out for years. Got back to the trailhead two and a half hours later. Bit thirsty. No emergencies. Getting dark fast. Snow forecast for the next three days. Will carry pack tomorrow. Because you never know.

You never know.

DAY 223

I have these (obviously) one-sided trail conversations with Casey in which I take on both my voice and hers. The only role Casey actually plays in these exchanges is to either ignore me or stare at me perplexedly, with an expression indicating she is of the opinion her daddy is yet again displaying symptoms of multiple personality disorder and she's wondering which suppressed character is now being manifest—not realizing it is her.

Like, if we're hiking along on a muddy trail—a surprisingly common state of affairs in otherwise arid southwest New Mexico, especially in winter—I will say something like, "Damn, it sure is muddy this afternoon."

Casey will respond, in a tone of voice pitched high enough that it's borderline falsetto with a hint of helium inhalation, "I kinda like mud. It feels good squishing between my toes."

I'll respond, "Yeah, but it gunks up the soles of my boots and makes it hard to hike without slipping and sliding. Then there's the filthiness factor inside the vehicle and in the living room when we get home because neither of us ever remembers to wipe our feet."

And Casey will say, "I don't know what your issue is, you wuss. I love mud! The more, the better! Matter of fact, I think I'm going to walk over to that sludge-filled bog and wallow around for a few minutes. With any luck, there'll be a dead animal carcass in there!"

It would be impossible to recount how many of these types of "conversations"—none of which would be described by any creature more cognitively developed than, say, a garden slug, as deeply intellectual—Casey and I have had over the years.

Those of us who are partnered up with dogs have this image of eventually meeting our pets on the other side of the theologically vague "rainbow bridge." I would not be the least bit surprised if Casey runs up to me in whatever form creatures take in that nebulous domain and, after obligatory hugs, head scratches, and face-lickings are complete, lets me know how wrong I got her voice during those uncountable one-sided trail conversations. For all I know, she, instead of a borderline falsetto voice with a hint of helium inhalation, will address me in a gravelly baritone, like she had spent the previous years (or however time is measured in that mythical post-mortal realm) chain-smoking Camel 99s.

Either way, it will be good to sit on the side of whatever kinds of trails exist on the other side and catch up, to scour the vicinity for heavenly mud. Together. Again.

DAY 228

During my end-to-end hike of the then-not-yet-completed Arizona Trail in 1997, I met only one other thru-hiker. We had camped within a mile of each other near Roosevelt Lake, but neither of us had any idea there was a kindred spirit close by. He was going north, and I was going south. We passed each other early the next morning. Talked for maybe half an hour, which is damned near a filibuster-length trailside chitchat for long-distance hikers who generally have many miles to knock off before sunset.

I remember only two snippets from that conversation. The first was that the man was a relative neophyte long-distance backpacker. A mere two years prior, he had, on a whim, with no previous experience, thru-hiked the Appalachian Trail in one hundred days, which is an impressive pace for all but the most extreme and motivated outdoor athletes. The second was that he had since become addicted to carrying a pack up and down mountains. Thought of nothing else. Had plans to complete the Triple Crown before heading to Europe. It's all he wanted to do for the rest of his life. His wife of many years had put her foot down. He promptly divorced his wife of many years.

This dude was maybe a bit over the top.

Since then, I have met many similar hiking addicts. People who legally change their given name to their "trail handle" (which I will talk more about later on). Their numbers seem to increase exponentially every year.

I am by anyone's definition a dedicated hiker, but I don't think I have a hiking problem. I swear. I can quit any time I want to. But I don't want to. I mean, what's the harm? It's not like I spend an inordinate amount of time and money maintaining my habit. It's not like I have punted a good job and moved to a remote location to feed an addiction I don't think I have. Well, OK, I have done all those things, but it's not as though I have ever contemplated leaving my wife to pursue a life of solitary hiking. (Though it is entirely possible she has had such considerations. You'd have to ask her.)

When giving thought to the subject of hiking addiction, I feel compelled to point out that, unlike other forms of compulsive behavior, the end result is a low BMI and well-developed calves. Maybe some tendonitis, sure. But, compared to, say, losing your teeth, having track scars lining your appendages, having a nonfunctioning liver, and getting arrested twenty-five times for breaking and entering, that's small taters compared to other forms of addiction. Well, OK, there's the perpetual poverty, the oft-compromised personal hygiene, and a social circle that would look perfectly at home dwelling in encampments located adjacent to railroad tracks.

Anyhow, given that, as I mentioned, this affliction seems to be growing. I think it would be of benefit to provide a checklist for those who fear that they or someone they know might be in need of an intervention.

If you answer yes to more than a handful of these questions, you may have a problem. Seek professional help immediately. There are surely support groups out there somewhere. Begin your search at an all-you-can-eat pizzeria located near a trailhead.

- Does your attraction to hiking cause you to forgo activities in which you once regularly partook, like, for instance, mowing your yard, washing dishes, and doing laundry?

- When you are not hiking, do you spend an inordinate amount of time looking at maps and thinking about hiking?

- Is your coffee table buried under a mountain of gear catalogs?

- Do you consider a trip to a gear shop to be akin to a religious pilgrimage?

- Do you consider your hiking boots to be formal footwear?

- Do you almost crave the pain and discomfort of trail life?

- When not on the trail, are you uncomfortably clean?

- Do you keep a trowel and a wag bag in your bathroom?

- Have you seriously considered legally changing the name bestowed upon you at birth by your loving parents to a trail handle bestowed upon you one rainy night by a drunk guy you met two hours prior at a rodent-infested trail shelter?

- Have you seriously considered modifying your relationship status— upward, downward, or sideways—based upon hiking?

- Does your health care plan consist of a small first-aid kit containing little more than ibuprofen, Band-Aids, and moleskin?

- Do you eat energy bars, instant oatmeal, and freeze-dried food when you're not on the trail? And actually like it?

- Are you inclined to order lukewarm Tang and Everclear when at a bar?

- Do you start pacing back and forth if you have not hiked in the past twelve hours?

- Do you use trekking poles when walking around Walmart?

- When interviewing for a new job, do you ask how many "zero days" are included in the compensation package?

- Are your dreams dominated by hiking?

Well, at least I can honestly say that I did not answer *all* of these questions in the affirmative. But only because I don't use trekking poles. And it has been many years since I actually applied for a job.

So, I'm good. No need for concern.

DAY 230

I have no idea how long I had been following the tracks in the snow. Casey and I were hiking upon one of the closest trails to town, located in what is called by land-use planners the "wildland/urban interface zone." As if such nomenclature was not demeaning enough, it is a management classification that has an official acronym: WUI, pronounced "woo-ee." A WUI can informally be defined as one part mostly fucked up and one part very likely to soon be fucked up even more.

As usual, I was about 90 percent oblivious to my surroundings. Buzzing along, happy as a pig in slop. At some point, though, the remaining ten percent reluctantly emerged when I noticed beneath my feet a set of paw prints that appeared at first blush to be canine in origin. "My, my," said I to Casey, "that was one sizeable dog." Casey, with her nose ever to the ground, appeared somewhat agitated. I kneeled and put my hand over one of the tracks. My extended digits barely covered it. Casey's prints were, by comparison, miniscule.

Then, almost immediately, I started hiking again, and my thoughts wandered toward Neverland. But something felt a bit amiss on the fight-or-flight front. Reality once more beckoned. I looked down at those tracks again and realized there was no evidence that the pooch had been accompanied by a human. Most times, where there are dog tracks on a trail, there are accompanying people tracks. This struck me as marginally weird enough that I snapped completely out of my on-trail bliss and studied the situation lying at my feet. Could it have been a coyote? A wolf? A bear? Uh … a mountain lion? Thoughts about food-chain dynamics began to percolate. This is what's known as a moderate buzzkill.

Though I am hardly an expert in the field, I do know that tracks left by a mountain lion closely resemble those of a large dog—except with the claws retracted. I once more leaned over and, sure enough, no matter how many of them I scrutinized, no matter the angle of observation, nary a claw mark was visible in the snow.

So, OK, likely those tracks were left by *Puma concolor*—the second-largest feline species in the Western Hemisphere, after the jaguar.

Given the newness of the snow cover, it was a recent passing.

My heart rate began to tick upwards. I put Casey on a leash—a rarity—and pulled her closer to me. She considered that a sure sign of imminent doom.

A bit farther along the trail, the tracks suddenly ended. I peered in every direction and, nope, nary another track was visible. No additional snow had fallen, so it wasn't like they were recently covered. They seemingly disappeared into thin air. It was then that I noticed the thick trunk of an old juniper arm's length to my left. It was also then that I wondered if I really truly wanted to look up into the branches of that tree, afraid of what I might observe observing me.

There has long been much in the way of press in the West regarding encounters between "wild" (read: living where they've always lived) animals and humans who have elbowed their way into erstwhile undisturbed ecosystems. Many have been the reports of pets becoming tasty menu items for coyotes, mountain lions, bobcats, et al. Critters with a taste for blood, bone, and sinew. A full-grown man was killed and eaten by a mountain lion outside Silver City a few years back. That caused quite the local stir.

People react differently to that kind of news. Many folks rationally argue, usually from the comfort of their den, that it's man who has moved into habitat that was forever occupied by wildlife. Therefore, such people maintain, it is incumbent upon humans to make appropriate adjustments, one of which is to clearly understand that, when you step foot into the wild, you might end up getting killed.

Others argue that the Powers That Be ought to be protecting populated areas from animal invasion, using lethal means if necessary.

Many times, though not nearly enough times, I have come in contact with wildlife. I have come face-to-face with numerous bears, I've seen a mountain lion as big as a U-Haul van, and I once had a full-grown cow moose whack me with her snout. I've seen bobcats, coyotes, wolves, bison, and a whole host of other examples of potentially dangerous fauna. And, yes, there has been some pants-wetting on my part. But never once has the thought entered my head that the authorities ought to come in and "do something about" all these pesky animals "intruding" on our well-marked trails and well-maintained suburban lawns. I can't even imagine anyone thinking such an inane thing. "Well, you obviously haven't lost a cat to a fox," one indignant lady sniffed in my direction when I uttered that sentiment, probably a bit too loudly, in a mountain-town bar.

"No, that's because I'm a responsible pet owner," I, pretty much a lifelong cat daddy, retorted.

My eyes slowly began moving their way up the trunk of that juniper. Mountain lions are "ambush predators" and, as such, they are masters of camouflage. And they have supercharged reflexes. I squinted and combed the branches, half expecting to soon be wearing a cougar chapeau. The branches above me were feline free. I was disappointed—though, of course, that's easy to say now, since there was no lion preparing to pounce upon my cranium.

I simply could not suss out how those tracks came to disappear midstride. Mountain lions are able to jump something like twenty feet. So, maybe it leaped off the trail into the thick surrounding brush. Either way, time to move along, with frequent backward glances.

When I related the story of the tracks in the snow to my chums at happy hour that evening, they all huddled closer together. Many of the people I drink with are disinclined to venture any farther into the Gila than developed picnic grounds or scenic overlooks. They are primarily urban-raised artist types, who view the wildness lapping upon the shores of our town as something frightening, something best avoided. They live here *despite* that wild country, not because of it. Yet, not one of them even hinted that the animal cops ought to go in and remove—much less dispatch—the wildlife that dwells out where the concrete ends, out where reality begins.

"Weren't you scared?" one ceramicist asked, her eyes wide.

"Yeah, but only a bit," I responded, with perhaps a bit too much alcohol-infused bravado. "But that's why I live here."

At that point, the mountain lion whose tracks Casey and I followed in the snow reverted to the realm of abstraction. Another goddamned abstraction.

DAY 232

Having spent my earliest years in the northernmost part of the Adirondack Mountains, my relationship with ice began not long after my memory began to crystallize.

When I was four, my mom—then between husbands—decided it was high time that her eldest child learned to skate, lest I lose some manner of standing in that ice-dominated part of the world before I was old enough to lament the thought of being a social pariah.

I was not so sure.

She planned no formal lessons. That was not the way for a woman who, the previous summer, had "taught" me to swim by tossing my very surprised self off a dock into the frigid waters of Lake Champlain, then jumping in to save me when I started to sink.

Once she laced me up with a pair of borrowed skates that were about twelve sizes too big, my mom flagged down a passing skater, a man she did not know. She asked him to take me around the massive municipal rink. He towered over me. He bent down and asked if I was ready. I knew it really did not matter how I answered. The next instant, I was in the middle of the biggest cheek-rippling, g-force vortex any four-year-old could possibly imagine. My body, parallel to the rink, flopped like a windsock in the man's wake. Only occasionally did my skates even touch the ice.

That is how phobias are sometimes born. Also: passion.

My mom told me I pretty much took to skating right away. Though I was never very good at it, especially when compared to the hockey players, figure skaters, and speed skaters that populated the 'Dacks, I found pleasure in sliding across ice. It was a cold-season substitute for walking through the woods.

Then my mom's next husband uprooted us to eastern Virginia, where what little ice there was generally took the form of those dreaded winter storms, during which roads glaze over and frozen tree branches snap under the extra weight, taking out power lines for days on end. Every few years, it would get cold enough for long enough that the area's many swamps would freeze to the point that local kids could frolic on this foreign substance. Those occasions were short-lived and generally concluded when youngsters started breaking through the melting ice and sinking waist-deep in stinky muck.

I outgrew my last pair of skates before high school, and they eventually got tossed.

When I ascended to the Colorado High Country many years later, I became reacquainted with ice. For better and for worse. I bought a pair of hockey skates and most every winter night before bed I would, with my last dog, Cali, drive to a rustic rink behind our local Walmart, where I would smoke a bowl and glide through the darkness. It was a meditative reconnection to a time so far past that it seemed more historical fiction than memory.

Then, one otherwise ordinary night, I fell. Though, as noted, I have never been anything more than a basically competent skater, I rarely in my entire life have taken a spill. I learned as a child that, with ice, a derring-do attitude was often followed by painful consequences.

There was a half inch of new powder covering the rink, making it impossible to see a crack in the ice. I caught the toe of my skate and went down hard, reflexively putting my right arm out to break the fall. I could almost hear the soft tissue in my shoulder tearing.

Not long thereafter, while walking down a street to my office, I stepped on a patch of ice and my foot came out from under me. Picture a cartoon character slipping on a banana peel. As my posterior was making its way toward pavement, again, my right arm went into instinctive protection mode. My shoulder tore even more, and in more different ways.

Even after two surgeries, that shoulder is worse than ever. When I hoist my pack, I do so gingerly. You don't realize how much you flap your arms while jumping across a creek until you do so with a lame wing. About the only good thing I can say about my right shoulder is that it is not as trashed as my lower back. Small favors.

One would think that, after dealing with the dark side of ice intensely enough that the consequences have come to define my life, I would assiduously avoid ice any more substantial than cubes found in a beverage glass. And, since I re-relocated to the Gila, I have done so pretty much by default.

But we got some rain earlier this winter, followed shortly thereafter by nighttime temperatures that plummeted into the low teens for several weeks. As a result, sections of numerous creeks located in shadowy canyons sported ribbons of ice several hundred feet long. I was unable to resist. Much to the consternation of my wife—who lived in the Colorado High Country for more years than I did and, therefore, is also familiar with the dark side of ice—my roots, combined with an apparent genetic inability to integrate past experiences into future behavior—pulled me toward those ribbons.

I convinced Gay to pull out her camera, which she did very reluctantly. Then I walked to the most upstream part of one particularly enticing strip of ice.

Even though I no longer desire to dwell permanently in wintry climes, I yet retain remnant strands of the skating gene.

It has long been one of my travel fantasies to skate on the canals in the Netherlands, though, from what I have heard, climate change has thawed that dream. I drool when I watch videos of people skating for miles on Nordic lakes frozen deep down with ice so clear it's invisible, so it's like skating on air.

This was a bit more plebeian.

I got a running start and began to slide. Well, OK, "slide" is not the right verb. The ice was uneven and blemished with sticks and leaves. Given that it was late afternoon, it was fairly warm, so the ice was sticky. I was wearing trail shoes with aggressive tread. So, "totter" might be more accurate.

The experience, captured on digital video, was far from graceful. There were lurches that could easily have gone either way. Casey seemed particularly worried as she followed along, her claws dug deep into the ice.

It was fun in a very childish way. The older I get, the less the word "fun" is integrated into my existence. There are plenty of experiences that are "pleasurable" or "satisfying." But flat-out fun? That seems to have diminished as my metabolism has slowed to a crawl and my bones have become more brittle.

I actually laughed.

Then I walked down to the next ribbon of ice and prepared to launch yet again. This time, Gay refused to photographically immortalize my reconnection with childhood. She had recently read some manner of old people's magazine article that said one of the foundational keys to longevity is to not do stupid stuff. She reminded me of my own operational philosophy as related to the acquaintance several years my junior with whom I hiked earlier in the year.

I tried to explain that I was not of the belief that tottering along on a ribbon of ice technically met my own definition of "being stupid." She, being the arbiter of my ill-advised behavior, did not agree and left the spousal unsaid hovering in the air. I, being an obedient husband and all, only glanced at those tantalizing ribbons of ice as I trudged by, my shoulders slumped.

The next day, though, it was only Casey and me. We purposely accessed a different creek, one that I suspected would be frozen solid. It was! I scarcely touched the trail as I tottered along on the ice, knowing full well that I needed to prepare a plausible lie in case things went awry, in case I returned home with bumps, bruises, contusions, and maybe even additional damage to a shoulder that oftentimes seems beyond repair. Something like, "Damn, Casey was about to plummet off a cliff, but I caught her just in time but, sadly, while rescuing our poor dog from certain death, I tumbled." Thankfully, nothing bad happened. And, while on that ribbon of ice, I thought back to when I was four, and my mom handed me off to a passing skater, and I was pulled like a windsock around a rink and, for a period of time that ended up being achingly short, my life changed for the better.

Gay asked how the hike went.

"Pretty much the same as always," I responded with a wink toward Casey, who winked back while shaking her head. One's canine companion should also be a convincing co-conspirator, a partner in crime.

DAY 239

About halfway through the return leg of yesterday's hike, I realized that the accessory pocket on the right side of my day pack's hip strap was wide open. This is where I keep my key ring. Unfortunately, where there would normally be keys, there were no keys. I did not know whether I had neglected to zip the pocket closed prior to leaving the trailhead or whether the zipper had somehow worked its way open while I was hiking. Didn't really matter. The keys were gone.

Though no one likes losing stuff, misplacing even small items unsettles me down to my corpuscles. I mean, it haunts me. While on my thru-hike of the Appalachian Trail, I mislaid a small handle that was designed to fit into the metal cup that covered the top of my Svea 123 cookstove. I was so agitated that I considered turning around and retracing my steps—hundreds of miles back to Mount Katahdin if necessary—until I located that handle. My blood pressure still rises at the memory. I suspect this trait is a symptom of my OCD, which gets worse every year at the same time that my ability to live up to the foundational tenet of that bothersome psychological affliction—a need to have things orderly and symmetrical—unravels.

This, however, was not some small metal handle. My key ring held keys to my 4Runner, the Yakima roof rack atop my 4Runner (for which I did not own a spare) and my house. It also holds one of those pricy computer-chip keys to my wife's car. All told, I was looking at several hundred dollars' worth of key replacement, not to mention a noteworthy inconvenience factor.

Though I, of course, had no idea where those keys might be lying, I had no choice but to trudge all the way back to the turnaround point if necessary—about two miles in—with my eyes pointed downward in the unlikely hope that I would catch sight of my keys. This process was made more complicated by the grim, though picturesque, reality that eight inches of snow was covering the primitive trail upon which I had been hiking with Casey, who was clearly a bit confused by my decision to go back to where we had just come. Sometimes Casey clearly thinks I have lost my marbles. "No," I reassured her. "Only my keys."

Well maybe my marbles *and* my keys.

Because I had spent much of the late afternoon and early evening lying in the snow, taking photos of the craziest ice formations I had ever seen, I was already soaked down to my underwear.

Adding to the lost-and-not-found situation were a total of twenty-eight creek crossings, some of which are negotiated via means that can go either way. So, the keys could be hidden under snow, or they could be submerged in opaque, fast-flowing, freezing-cold water.

After having—to no avail—meticulously covered every inch of the trail almost on hands and knees, it was past dark when I arrived back at the trailhead, cold, wet, and pissed off. I crawled under my vehicle, flashlight in hand, and for the first time ever took advantage of the fact that I keep an emergency key concealed in a magnetized box hidden in a secret spot that took me ten minutes of wallowing around in the mud to locate.

I fidgeted in abject frustration all the way back to town. At the first stoplight, while depressing the clutch, I realized something in my right front pocket was poking my leg. I reached down and, to my shock and dismay, it was the very keys I had just spent more than an hour looking for. I had no idea why I put those keys where I had never put them before. I am getting to an age where I'm trying to ascertain what bothers me more: forgetting or not remembering.

DAY 240

If a man climbs a mountain and no selfies come back with him, did he ever really ascend?

If a woman canoes down a deep green river on a hot and humid midsummer day and it was not tweeted, bleated, shared, or blared, did she ever really birth all those mini whirlpools with her paddle blade that keep on spinning well after she has passed?

If there was no GoPro camera catching the bird's-eye view, did the snowboarder ever really hold his breath and steel his nerves and launch off the cornice and proudly stick the landing?

If the rocky trail was followed with blistered feet all the way to the distant pass, and the hike was not Vimeo'd, Snapchatted, Instagrammed, TikTok'd, Facebooked or YouTubed, was the glorious pain of the journey really worth the limp-laced winces?

If there were no sponsors' logos adorning the dirty old day pack, did it ever really get carried to the bottom of the Grand Canyon and back in one long, parched day?

If the tracks down the bright white slope were not captured and collated via the mystical rays of orbiting satellites communicating with a GPS unit in real time, did the fluffy, chest-deep powder really sparkle like a million diamonds, did the skier ever really float through the snow like she was passing through the heart of a benevolent magic spell cast by Ullr?

If a mother watches her toddler staring in gobsmacked amazement at the kaleidoscope wildflowers at 12,000 feet in the Rockies in July and the vision was not instantly stored in the cloud, did that child really come to understand for the first but hopefully not the last time that life is truly defined more than anything by beauty so profound it can chase away all the monsters in all the closets in all the world without even breaking a sweat?

If an old couple walks hand in hand slowly toward a creek-side grove of aspens they have known since the trees were mere saplings and there are no likes or comments, was their passion ever truly worthy of a thousand silly little love poems penciled on sticky notes and left on the kitchen counter?

If a once-blazing campfire burns down to embers and the mesmerizing flames didn't go viral, was there ever really the kind of heat and light that, if it is nurtured and tended properly, brings the tribe together as one and births song and dance and stories that are told over and over from one generation to the next?

What if nary a soul was properly and sufficiently influenced?

What then?

DAY 243

Took a bit of a slide today while exploring a remote side canyon. Caught myself in time. Did not launch thirty feet over the slick-as-snot spillover. Couple banged-up kneecaps was all. No harm, no foul.

Though I too often pooh-pooh the possibility of suffering some manner of medical malady while wandering by my lonesome out of cell phone range, I do give the matter occasional fleeting thought. Much of that thought centers on Casey. I wonder how she would react were I to break my leg or suffer a heart attack back in the boonies. Though our dogs often know our vulnerabilities and weaknesses better than anyone else, including our spouses (I spend much more time with Casey than I do with Gay), they still—as related in a previous chapter—on some lizard-brain level look at their human companions as borderline infallible.

So, it must stun them down to their marrow when their person comes crashing down to earth.

There was a story that made national news in 2006. A woman named Danelle Ballengee, who I knew because our time in Summit County, Colorado, overlapped, took a life-threatening fall. Danelle was one of the top ultra-endurance athletes in history, winning the Pikes Peak Marathon four times, completing the Eco-Challenge twice, and doing things like running hundred-mile races in the Himalayas.

Danelle took out on what by her lofty standards was a routine run outside Moab, where she now lives. She had told no one where she was going. Similar to what I have done a thousand times and will likely do again first thing tomorrow morning. She hit a patch of ice while scrambling up a rocky section of trail and tumbled into a ravine, shattering her pelvis, which is a life-threatening injury under any circumstances. I had a close friend die after suffering a similar injury, and he was in the middle of a town with a trauma-center hospital nearby.

She lay there in mortal agony and bleeding internally for fifty-six long, teeth-chattering hours, her dog, Taz, at her side the whole time. She had no food, no water, and no protection from the elements. Even as search and rescue personnel were finally mustering, having been alerted by one of Danelle's neighbors, she looked deep into Taz's eyes and said words to the effect of, "My life is now in your hands. You need to go for help." And, miracle of miracles, Taz did just that! He ran back to the trailhead and led a recently arrived SAR team to her exact location. Danelle was saved by her dog, who lived to the ripe old age of sixteen plus.

Dogs are undoubtedly empathic. Casey knows when I am in a down mood, and I have seen her trying to decide whether the best course of action is to come over and nuzzle or to leave me to stew in my own juices. I am sure she would comprehend that something was sorely amiss were I to end up writhing in agony at the bottom of a ravine. Casey cowers when I spout loud obscenities after, say, taking a slide while exploring a remote side canyon. She does not know whether I hold her in any way responsible for the mishap. I have to forcefully ratchet down my ire and hug Casey to try to make sure she understands she is an innocent bystander. It seems as though she never fully believes me, though she also seems to appreciate the effort.

What would it be like were I to end up in circumstances similar to that of Danelle and Taz? Would the intensity of the emergency situation overwhelm Casey, who is reflexively timid, or would she be able to rise to the occasion? If I told her after fifty-six hours of mortal agony that my life was now in her hands, would she dash off in search of help, or would she simply stare at me quizzically while wondering why we have been spending all this time in such an uncomfortable environment?

I fear she might move away and tremble, figuring that somehow, she was responsible for the situation. That breaks my heart.

Casey might well pull it off. As my skeptical wife says, let's hope it never comes to that.

I concur.

I don't want to ever put her in that position.

One day, I very well might have to.

DAY 246

It was like one of those sweat-inducing dreams that haunt me on a recurring basis: I get up that which I am climbing with relative ease, but, when I turn around, I think, "Hmmm ... how am I going to get my increasingly decrepit carcass back down again?" The topography always morphs in my dreams, from merely challenging on the way up to dangerous and convoluted, borderline impassable, on the way down.

But this was reality. I was in something of a pickle.

At least I have my cell phone if I have to embark upon the process of calling for help, I thought. But, wait! My cell phone is in my day pack, which I took off before shimmying up this notch.

Well, if push comes to shove, my partner can help extricate me from my situation. But, wait! My partner is Casey, and she has been looking at me for some minutes with an expression that clearly states she feels her daddy does not always make the best decisions. Besides, she's too busy sniffing the landscape to worry about my imminent connection with gravitational vector/impact formulas.

At least search and rescue will surely come looking for me ... sometime. Wait! I yet again did not tell anyone where I was going. New Mexico is mighty big, and they would have no idea where to begin their search, a situation exacerbated by 1) the fact that, yet again, I have bushwhacked my way far from a trail and 2) the fact that Gay would likely not report me missing for many hours, as she would assume my failure to return was the result of an extended post-hike detour to a local watering hole.

I'm getting too old for this shit. It's time I started acting my age, beginning tomorrow. Next week at the latest.

DAY 247

Casey and I arrived at "Contemplation Point," where I immediately began to contemplate whether contemplation was mandatory. If so, was it OK to contemplate base-level stuff like football and sex, or was I required to raise the bar a bit and contemplate the meaning of life or the nature of the universe? I wondered what would happen if I failed to contemplate while at Contemplation Point, like, you know, if I did nothing more profound than blow my nose, get a pebble out of my shoe and resume hiking? Or, what if I contemplated poorly? What then might the ramifications be?

And what about my dog? Was Casey also on the hook for some meaningful canine contemplation? (The nature of jerky treats, perhaps.)

I mean—the pressure!

Maybe best to follow the dog's lead, to tiptoe off in the opposite direction. Pretend we were never here.

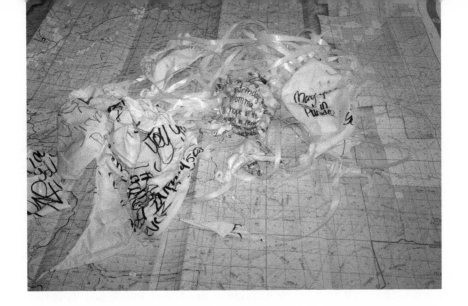

DAY 248

Gay, Casey, and I were hiking for the first time on a rough
path through the desolate heart of the Gila. There were no
discernible footprints preceding us in the dust. Though we were
on a marked and mapped Forest Service trail obviously hewn by the hands
of man, it was easy to pretend we were leaving first tracks. Until, that is, we
observed, stuck in the branches of a bush with thorns the size of daggers, a
deflated and partially decomposed party balloon that had attached to it the
kinds of ribbons one uses to wrap Christmas and birthday presents. I carefully extricated the remnants from the dagger bush and carried them home
for proper burial.

Only when the trash can lid was open did I realize the balloon had
handwritten messages etched upon its rubbery rind. "May you rest in paradise" was legible. As was: "Happy birthday, Momma. I hope all the angels
in heaven sing happy birthday to you." There were shreds of other messages,
but they were too smeared to read.

So, this balloon had likely been released by a family as part of a remembrance ceremony for a beloved relative. There was no way to tell how far it had flown before it landed way out in the beauteous middle of nowhere. How far can a lone balloon fly? Do they fly farther if they are blessed? Who knows who launched the balloon toward heaven? Whoever it was, their aim was true, for in heaven it had landed.

That balloon has now disintegrated beyond recognition, but I keep as a reminder to try really hard to live the kind of life that, when my time comes, family, friends, and hiking, drinking and poker buddies will be inclined to release a balloon with heartfelt messages penned upon its side and stand there watching till it becomes a little dot way up in the bright blue New Mexico sky.

DAY 251

One of my favorite trails was improved all to hell last summer. Yet another example of the never-ending betterment of the West. The bulk of its rocks were removed. Its grade made more benign. Erosion-control structures were installed at appropriate intervals. I was disappointed in the extreme, as I have always been attracted to trails that are rocky, rough, eroded, unkempt, poorly signed, poorly designed, and otherwise "bad."

On a purely selfish level, I know your average person, even your average hiker, is going to seek out more polished pathways—meaning there will be fewer people tromping upon these rugged trails. Those who are willing to risk fractures and sprains in the name of seeing what's around the next bend will either be fellow devotees of challenging on-foot travel, or at least those willing to negotiate difficulty if that's what it takes to access whatever lies ahead.

Of course, every once in a while, there will be an accidental traveler, one who did not know before the fact what they were getting into. Sometimes those people will be scowling and growling things like, "This trail needs to be fixed." More often than not, they will be smiling, glad for the chance to experience something at least approximating real adventure in these faux/contrived-adventure times. Or pretending to be having a good time in order to save face.

Increasingly, there are more people coming to the American West who only *think* they want to immerse themselves in true wild. They hail from places that have been improved all to hell for generations, places defined by a sea of signs, which often begin with the word "No." They want smooth grades and rock-free tread. They can have it. But not here.

Hiking by itself does not necessarily make one tough, in the sense that, say, going through Marine Corps basic training makes one tough. Under the right circumstances, though, hiking, especially on bad trails, can help make one tough-*er*. They test and enhance balance, proprioception, concentration, endurance, and desire. Of course, there's always the chance of injuring your ankle or knee. That's part of the package. Maybe even the best part. The big "maybe" that comes with each plant of your boot onto the dirt.

DAY 253

In the entire history of humankind limping its way across the landscape, how many people have hyperextended a knee ... while ... sleeping? Answer: Likely none. But one. (Guess who.) Any previous members of my specie suffering such a nocturnal malady would surely have been consumed lock, stock, and barrel by the closest saber-toothed tiger, thus removing their flawed genes from the overall pool. I am really glad we no longer have to worry about saber-toothed tigers.

Of course, while hobbling down the trail, I ran into one of my buddies, who naturally asked what had happened.

"Tweaked my leg scaling a cliff yesterday," I responded.

"Well, we're not getting any younger," he said. "Gotta be more careful."

I couldn't agree more.

DAY 255

Got to a three-way trail junction today at the exact time that two other people—one man, one woman—arrived at the same intersection from different directions. All three of us had a dog. The woman's was a purebred-looking standard poodle. The other man's was a purebred-looking golden retriever. Then there was my mixed-breed mongrel.

Almost instantly, the three dogs, who had never before met each other, proceeded to do what dogs do: They starting sniffing each other's poop chutes. In short order, they had formed what I would consider being a very undignified ass-sniffing triangle.

I said, "Man, I'm really glad humans don't greet each other like that."

The woman, who seemed mortified that her pedigreed pet right then had its nostrils up my mutt's posterior, verily growled, "Well, we'd all probably get along a lot better!"

I exchanged a furtive glance with the other man, who, like me, seemed a bit perplexed by her response.

"You first," I said to the woman. She grunted theatrically, yanked her poodle by its leash and harrumphed off.

"Guess she was right," the other man said to me while shrugging his shoulders before we parted ways.

DAY 258

There's an informal trail that follows a plus-or-minus perennial creek a thirty-minute drive outside town. Because for most of the year there is water—a relative rarity in these increasingly arid parts—it is known by local residents, but because of its unofficial status (there is no signage, it does not appear on national forest maps, and the parking area can accommodate only three cars), it is not used as much as some other nearby trails. Yet, mainly because of the inability of many social media addicts to keep lesser-known trails lesser known, that diminutive parking area is starting to see more vehicles, many of which bear out-of-state license plates.

What most trekkers along this informal trail thankfully do not realize is that, while hiking, they will pass a well-camouflaged side canyon that accesses an astounding mesa—I'll call it Arrow Mesa—several hundred vertical feet above the plus-or-minus perennial creek. To proceed, you have to first know where to go, then be willing to negotiate loose rock and thrash your way through sections of overhanging brush, much of which bears thorns. The reward takes the form of astounding rock formations, remnants of Native American habitation, a wide array of unhabituated wildlife and unimpeded views that extend for more than fifty miles.

And solitude. Only one time have I ever seen other people on Arrow Mesa, and they were as surprised to see me as I was to see them. We each pretended the other was not there.

I learned about Arrow Mesa half a lifetime ago by wondering, "What's up there?" And answering that question the hard way—by scrambling, bushwhacking, and slowly piecing the topography together over the course of many scratches and abrasions to form my own mental map. Close as most of us ever get to integrating the word "exploration" into our personal vernacular in these dark Google Earth times.

A few years ago, I was disheartened to notice some rock cairns had sprouted up. Upon further investigation, I came to understand that those cairns delineated the easiest route to Arrow Mesa. Having seen many times in my life what can happen to a little-known locale once cairns are constructed, I could not knock them down fast enough. I hoped that whoever built them, upon his or her next visit, would reflect upon their transgression and realize the error of their ways. They did not. Since those first mounds appeared, I have been engaged in an ongoing battle with the unknown cairn-builder of Arrow Mesa. The process of eradicating those cairns has become some-thing of an obsession, as I'm certain the process of building them anew has become an obsession with my nemesis.

I would love to meet the cairn-builder (who I am sure is a very nice and well-intentioned person) of Arrow Mesa to get a grip on his/her thought processes for continuing to point the increasing number of people hiking alongside the aforementioned plus-or-minus perennial creek to a place they otherwise would not know about—unless they opted to leave the informal trail and start exploring, as I did half a lifetime ago.

Because there is a distinct possibility the conversation might get tense—especially if we were to meet while he/she was building cairns and/or while I was knocking them down—I will set this imaginative chitchat on neutral ground—in a bar of the cairn-builder's choosing. Over a convivial pint of ale.

Me: OK, asshole, what's up with all the damned cairns?

(Maybe that would be a textbook example of getting off on the wrong foot. Start over.)

Me: I am very curious what compels you to continually build the cairns showing people how to get to Arrow Mesa. Why do you do it?

Cairn Builder (CB): I would ask what compels you to tear them down?

Me: Yours is the underlying action, so you first.

CB: It helps people find the best way up there.

Me: But your cairns often delineate suboptimum routes.

CB: They didn't used to. Before you started knocking them down, they without a doubt showed the best, least-impactful route. Now I have to establish lines I hope you do not find.

Me: So, if for whatever reason they don't delineate the best route, why continue?

CB: Because it's a beautiful area that I'd like people to know about. Even if the routes I mark are not the best—because of you—they are still environmentally relatively unimpactful. I'd rather people follow routes I establish than have them wandering willy-nilly up there and tromping riparian vegetation, expediting erosion, and maybe getting lost.

Me: If you didn't bring people's attention to the area by building your cairns, then they wouldn't go up there in the first place. At least most of them. That would be the least environmentally impactful option.

CB: You go up there, right?

Me: Yeah, but I don't drop a line of breadcrumbs behind me.

CB: What's wrong with showing people the way to a beautiful area? People become better people when they interact with natural beauty.

Me: Arrow Mesa is not an art museum. The more people that go up there, the more environmental degradation will occur as a result. I have seen it many times. There will be more trash. Campfire rings will ensue. Folks will start constructing rock art. The wildlife will retreat. More than that, though, you eliminate the sense of adventure that people feel when they access a place that is relatively untrammeled. It's a subtle point, I know, but an important point. Finding your own way into and out of a remote area is far more rewarding than following a line of cairns. Besides, it's borderline illegal for someone not affiliated with a land-stewardship agency to mark a route.

CB: I don't think our local Forest Service law-enforcement personnel would consider this worth their time. They would likely consider it a net-positive safety issue, that my cairns make it easier for people to stay found. Again, I line out routes that are on durable surfaces. Under any circumstance, given the relative remoteness of Arrow Mesa, I don't think we'll have many people going up there. Besides, it's not legally designated wilderness, of which, as you know, there is a million acres nearby. I think the more people we can attract into the backcountry, the more people we will have fighting for land preservation. I think it's worth whatever minimal trade-off we might experience on Arrow Mesa. Besides, they're small cairns. You have to be an experienced hiker to even notice them.

Me: I assure you that if those cairn routes are left untouched, Arrow Mesa will see increased visitation and that people—maybe you—will start building bigger cairns and brushing out a trail, which, in turn, will attract even more visitation. There was a time when hardly anyone knew about the social trail that follows the plus-or-minus perennial creek down below. Like I said, I have seen it too many times to stand by and watch it happen to yet another relatively pristine area.

CB: Well, you have your opinion and I have mine. In any case, I will continue to erect cairns on Arrow Mesa. And I assume you will continue to destroy them.

Me: I do not consider it destruction. I consider it returning the area to its natural state. The most salient point I can make, though, is that I have at least as much right—legal and philosophical—to knock those cairns down as you have to build them. Before we continue this conversation, though, I gotta take a leak. Could you point me to the men's room?

CB: Find it yourself.

DAY 260

Yesterday was wintry. Snow blew sideways the entire time Casey and I were out. Temperature did not rise above freezing. A clothing rarity in these usually balmy parts: hat, gloves, and coat while hiking. Frosty breath. Casey looking at me like maybe this was not such a good idea. Accumulation deep enough to hide the ankle-breaking rocks that define many of our trails, but not deep enough to form a solid base atop those rocks. Consequently, cautious going.

Rounding a bend, we were surprised—given that the trailhead parking lot was empty when we pulled in—to see another hiker, who, like me, was trudging along with his chin tucked in against the chill.

We both looked up at exactly the same time. His eyes went wide. My eyes went wide.

For we both realized we were facing ourselves. Me looking maybe twenty years forward; he looking maybe twenty years past. Like gazing into a temporal mirror right there on the side of the trail. Like one of those computer programs police departments use that show how people are going to age.

As I stepped off to the side and put Casey on a sit/stay, it seemed as though he was considering my appearance even as I was considering his.

His beard was scraggly like mine, and exactly the same length, but completely silver. Wild hair that had not seen shears in at least a year cascading haphazardly from beneath a wool hat that went out of style when Carter was president. Head shape the same as mine. Eyes the same color. Same height. Same build. Similar gait.

He carried with him a hiking stick almost identical to mine. He sported wire-rimmed glasses. Wore an ancient Ragg sweater. Beneath the cuffs of blue jeans, I could see worn leather boots with Norwegian welts and Vibram soles.

It was like I dressed many years ago.

An older me dressed like a younger me.

"Looks like a killer canine you've got there," he said as he warmly beheld Casey, whose face brightened at his approach, like she recognized him. It was almost verbatim the kind of statement I have often made to other hikers with dogs that obviously posed no threat more serious than a tail wag. Seemed like someone who has hiked with dogs.

"She might lick you to death," I responded. His brows raised, like he would have said something similar had our companion-animal circumstances been reversed.

At that, we parted ways. I turned to look back, and he did the same. I wondered if my expression was as puzzled as his. It was like neither of us knew who or what we had just passed on the trail. Doppelganger or long-lost relative did not come close to doing the situation justice.

I liked what I saw. He was out on the trail despite the nasty weather. More importantly, he appeared happy, not just in the moment, but with life in general.

He looked alive.

I hope he liked what he saw. That he felt I also looked alive.

He followed my downward tracks upward and I followed his upward tracks downward.

It was almost dark when we got back to the parking lot, which still contained only my vehicle, and it was snowing harder than maybe I have ever seen it do in this part of the world. The only prints in the snow were left by Casey and me. By the time we pulled out, those prints had already vanished under a blanket of white.

As I drove away, I regretted not having initiated a deeper conversation with the man we passed back on the trail. Could have kicked it off saying, "You look familiar. Would you consider submitting to a DNA test?" But the inclement weather was not conducive to trailside discussion.

All during the slippery drive home, I was thinking "that was extremely weird" and wondering if the experience was not one of those parallel universe/ interdimensional situations like the Misty Mountain tale related earlier.

Next day, at exactly the same time, I went back out to where we had passed.

There was no sign of me.

And I have not been back since, even though I go there several times a week.

DAY 264

Quite the sobering experience to walk up to an icy trailhead after a midwinter hike and notice that Pronto is nowhere to be seen. Gone.

Casey sits there with a perplexed look on her face, like, "Where's Pronto? I'm cold! How could you possibly misplace an SUV? Keys, I can understand. But a *vehicle*?" Like, not for the first time, she's wondering if there might not have been more acceptable human-companion options available back when she was on the adoption block. Like, maybe the very next day, some tightly wrapped individual might have walked in. The kind of person who does not misplace his or her vehicle.

Casey is a trusting soul. She does not grasp the concept of larceny, except as it applies to another dog trying to make off with one of her chew toys. Then, she becomes a proponent of restorative justice.

The mental gears get churning around the subject of how big a pain it will be to deal with a stolen-car situation, which would be a first for me.

Cops. Insurance companies. Rental car agencies. Stern spousal inquisition. Negotiations with salespeople who tell me they have to go talk to the manager before approving the deal on whatever replacement ride I decided to procure. Stacks of papers with really small print to sign. More stern spousal inquisition, this time accompanied by a skeptical glower. Damn!

I mean, how desperate must a person be to steal a vehicle owned and operated by me? Cigar stink imbedded in the upholstery. Inch-thick dog fur covering every surface. And not just any dog fur. Dog fur that has been seasoned over the years with a combination of muck, fish guts, slush, and mud. Mildewing PB&J sandwich fragments under the driver's seat. Unidentifiable stains. Dents. Scratches. Rust.

(Memories.)

As I pull my day pack off to retrieve my cell phone, getting ready to dial 911, I fleetingly remember how blissful life was back in college when I had no vehicle. I was in tip-top condition due to riding my bicycle everywhere. I hitchhiked long distances, meeting a wide variety of fascinating characters in the process. No vehicle-related expenses whatsoever, except occasionally chipping in for gas when I mooched a ride from one of my hiking buddies. I was free!

Casey is still sitting there staring at me like I'm retarded. As I peer into her steely eyes, a flicker appears at the midway point between my hippocampus and prefrontal cortex. It is clearly trying with all its might to fight through the cranial fog. A disassociated image begins to form. It's like something from a dream, but it has heftier substance. At last, it coalesces into retrievable form.

And then I realize that I had in fact parked at a completely different trailhead some miles distant.

Never mind.

Casey shakes her head and dutifully follows close behind—sighing and snorting the entire time—as we trudge through the snow as the light begins to fade and the temperature begins to drop.

DAY 266

Which is worse: indecision, or making a bad decision?

Tough call. I go back and forth. I can't decide.

This is more than a theoretical question for me, as I raise indecision to an art form, and I am almost preternaturally inclined toward bad decisions on those rare occasions when I actually make a decision. My decision-making process would resemble an M.C. Escher painting were it translated to pigment.

That said, here I am not talking about the decision-making process in the context of work, love, or the long-term course of one's life. I'm sticking to the subject at hand: hiking in the boonies, which—unlike work, love, and the long-term course of one's life—I know something about.

At least I think I do. Sometimes, I'm not so sure.

To help address the question that introduced this chapter, I solicited input via social media and barroom conversations from numerous of my outdoor-oriented amigos, whose oft-contradictory responses were either decisive or not.

If nothing else, I consider the following to be a form of inexpensive therapy for those of us equally inclined toward indecisiveness and adept at making bad decisions.

Here are some of those observations (names withheld). Extra credit if you can guess which is mine:

- A bad decision is a bad decision. Indecision has the potential to be a good decision once decided; potentially more so because it's more thought out. Hamlet's soliloquy, perhaps the most famous in literature, is about indecision.

- What good story was ever told in regard to indecision?

- If you choose not to decide, you still have made a choice.

- Decide and deal, that's me.

- Bad. All day! Way more fun. If anything, you come out with a good story. That is, of course, if you come out at all.

- From an old-time search and rescue perspective, indecision is far less likely to get you dragged out of the woods on a stretcher.

- Bad decision is worse. Clearly. But it's not cool to claim that in the Red Bull/X Games era.

- To this point, bad decisions have always taught me something and haven't killed me.

- No decision, no lesson.

- Making a bad decision after indecision has got to be the worst.

- It's YOUR decision to be indecisive! Don't ask me!

- Depends on the situation. In a circumstance of potentially fatal outcome, a bad decision is decisively worse. With indecision, your options remain open.

- Indecision only delays the inevitable, but a bad decision accelerates it. However, making good decisions is a function of the experience that comes from making bad ones. I say, "Go for it."

- One of my best friends taught me: When you are not sure what to do, do nothing!

- Making a bad decision, 'cause it just cascades from there.

- Indecision can result in bad decisions, but, when bad decisions mount, they can cause indecision. As well they should.

- If shit does not hit the fan as a result of your decision, then it was by default a good decision. Or at least not totally a bad decision.

- Not all bad decisions are bad. Or *totally* bad. For one thing, you don't realize you have made a bad decision until you're, say, midway through some soon-to-be-fatal fall.

See what I mean?

Tough call.

Once again, I can't decide.

DAY 269

I asked Gay how she wanted to celebrate her birthday. Her answer did not include any references to scaling a cliff. Surprise!

DAY 271

One of the best reasons for bringing a canine companion into your life is that it gives you a good excuse to throw things. Not that you need an excuse to hurl various items, but it helps if there is another creature involved in the process, especially one inclined to retrieve whatever you might toss, be it a stick or a ball, so you might more easily throw that item again and again.

My last dog, Cali, would fetch till her legs fell off.

Enough years ago that my heart aches recalling the distant memory, I was on a high mountain pass in Colorado. A newspaper reporter and a photographer were interviewing me in situ shortly after a backpacking book I wrote hit the street. Cali was, as always, with me for what turned out to be a multi-hour jaunt to a nearby peak. While we were getting our ducks in a huddle at the trailhead, I noticed a muddy tennis ball discarded in the parking lot. I absentmindedly tossed it off the side of the pass. Cali went after it. Turns out the ball had bounced its way a thousand or so vertical feet downward. As I hoisted my pack, I thought, "Hey, I haven't seen Cali in quite some time." Shortly thereafter, she crested the lip of the pass, panting hard, tennis ball secured in her mouth. Cali was very serious about fetching.

During the new-dog shopping process—which terminated when we adopted Casey—one of the items on my checklist was a breed inclined to fetch. Labradors, even Lab mixes with extremely suspect double helices, are not only on that list, but they appear near the very top. As stated, I like to throw things. I grew up skipping stones on Lake Champlain, and I was a quarterback on my high school football team. Full-contact snowball fights were especially appealing to me. During my youthful-offender phase, I often recreated by throwing rocks through windows. I once even lobbed a crudely constructed Molotov cocktail. Great fun!

Additionally, playing fetch with your dog is a bonding exercise.

It did not take long to realize that Casey was not inclined to fetch. This was disappointing. Most times, she stands there, a look of bored bafflement on her face, like she is wondering what possessed me to discard a perfectly good stick or ball. Very rarely, she will halfheartedly trot in the basic direction of my toss, like she's part of my follow-through. Once in a blue moon, she will actually pick up the ball or stick. About twice has she ever brought the item back to me, and, both times, it appeared to be more of an accident than an earnest effort at traditional retrieval, like she just happened to be passing in my general direction with a ball or stick in her mouth that I lately threw.

Yet, I persist, in hopes that one day Casey will suddenly realize that fetching is part of the human/canine contract, that it is her job. I mean, it's not as though her day-to-day responsibilities are so overwhelming that she simply cannot fit another thing into her busy schedule. She hikes with me. She sniffs. She eats, sleeps, chews on bones, goes to the bathroom, and graciously allows me to rub her tummy. Seems like we could easily squeeze fetching in there somewhere.

On day 271 of our quest to hike every day for a solid year, we drove to a snow-covered trail north of town. On a whim that pretty much covers the definition of insanity, I picked up a stick and threw it without much aim in hopes that my Lab mix would live up to her species' reputation. Casey, perhaps energized by the snow, leapt into action. She sprinted after the stick, picked it up, returned it, and dropped it at my feet, where she stood, wagging her tail expectantly. I was stunned. Finally! The dog trait I had long hoped for appeared out of nowhere! I praised Casey mightily and threw the stick again.

Nothing.

I tried to coax her. "Go get it, Casey," I effused. "Yeah, you can do it!"

Casey looked at me like, "Hey, I was happy to return the stick to you once, but after that, you're on your own. You want that damned stick back, you know where to find it."

And that was it as far as Casey's fetching career goes. She has not gone after a ball or stick since. She was willing to give it a whirl. Meh. Didn't appeal to her.

End of story.

Whenever the mood strikes, I will throw a rock or stick, solely because I enjoy the motion. I will stand and listen as it thuds somewhere off in the distance. And I will then watch my dog run off in an entirely different direction.

I can live with that. (I have no choice.)

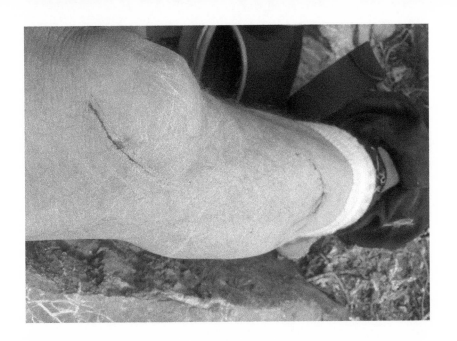

DAY 272

In retrospect, maybe I should have worn long pants while ascending one of the most remote peaks in the Lower 48. And maybe purchased some moisturizing lotion.

DAY 275

Her reputation preceded her. Out of nowhere, she had become the talk of the trail: "the Woman with the Gun," who threatened to shoot people's dogs. Gossip mill basic description: probably in her seventies. While some said she was diminutive, most said she was big and burly. The possession of firearms, it seems, makes people seem larger than they really are. Take their gun away, though, and they shrink. Sometimes entirely away, till there's nothing left save someone who is scared and defenseless.

Her pistol was supposedly housed in a holster attached to the pectoral strap of her day pack, and, when hikers accompanied by canines approached, she planted her hand on the grip and displayed a menacing expression. A young lady I do not know wrote on one of the local Facebook community group pages that the Woman with the Gun pulled her weapon and pointed it at her aged, arthritic dachshund. The young lady related how she had to get between the Woman with the Gun and her venerable, vulnerable wiener hound. She called the Forest Service cops, who tried—but probably not very hard—to hunt down the Woman with the Gun. This situation occurred at almost exactly the same time I was nearby with Casey.

For the next few weeks, I hiked in a perpetual state of red alert—not exactly the optimal mindset to bring with you into the beautiful New Mexico countryside.

I wondered what my reaction would be should I come across the Woman with the Gun. "Lady, you pull your gun, and I will stuff your head into the dirt," is about the best I could come up with. If she actually shot my dog? I mean, there's Casey lying on the trail, screaming, blood spewing forth from a gaping bullet wound? I would surely go berserk. My next mailing address would either be the hospital, the morgue, or prison. Ditto for the Woman with the Gun.

I thought that, but hell, maybe I would freeze in my tracks and beg the Woman with the Gun for mercy.

I have had guns pointed at me numerous times, mainly by ill-trained teenage soldiers in Third World war zones and, worse, by a very agitated rent-a-cop in a mall who was under the not-entirely-unreasonable impression that I was up to no good. None of those weapons were pointed at my dog.

Fortunately, I never ran into the Woman with the Gun. References to her eventually dissipated to the degree that they might very well never have existed. Could be she changed her ways. Could be she moved away. Could be she was eaten alive by a herd of unleashed dogs. Could be she was an urban legend. Or a boogeyman-type myth concocted to frighten people into using leashes or hiking elsewhere.

Then, one otherwise ordinary morning, Casey and I were on the fringes of TS-X, and, suddenly, there she was—the Woman with the Gun—coming downhill as we were going up. She was, as advertised, in her seventies. Silver hair. Short but stocky. Whatever baseline sociability she might have once possessed was long ago buried under the tectonic folds of a deep scowl that seemed chiseled into bedrock. Like the faintest grin would break her face into a million disjointed pieces.

Casey had bounded ahead—meaning she was closer to the Woman with the Gun than I was. It would have been tough for me to intercede had things gone badly awry. The woman placed her hand upon her gun, but she did not pull the weapon—a 9mm semi-automatic (we had a similar pistol on our farm when I was in high school)—from its holster. I moved toward her with a purposeful stride. She stopped dead in her tracks, grimaced, almost like she was in pain, backed up a step and asked if I would please call my dog, which was embarrassing, because that's our automatic protocol when Casey and I come across fellow hikers. It was one of only two times in an uncountable number of dog/trail miles that I have been so deeply lost in thought that I did not notice an approaching hiker quickly enough to step off the trail with Casey at my side. And, usually, Casey will do so of her own accord. Dog and dog owner suffered simultaneous brain farts.

Of all the times for us to screw that up!

The Woman with the Gun—her hand still resting atop that 9mm—said, almost apologetically, that she had recently been bitten while hiking, and as evidence displayed a hand that appeared to have numerous scabbed-over puncture wounds. Thing is, when word of the Woman with the Gun first started making the rounds some months prior, people said she always claimed to have lately had her digits gnawed upon while on the trail. So, either the Woman with the Gun had especially bad luck with dogs, or something else was going on.

Maybe the Woman with the Gun had a traumatic experience as a child. Maybe she is haunted by bad dog dreams. Maybe she really does routinely get bit on the trail. Maybe her oft-bitten hand perpetually smells like a roast beef sandwich. Maybe she has bad juju that passing dogs pick up on. Maybe she should keep her hands in her pockets while hiking.

I watched the Woman with the Gun until she was well out of sight. Can't be too careful. There's a lot of crazy blowing around these days.

The Woman with the Gun and I have crossed paths twice more. Both times, Casey and I, as is our habit, stepped off the trail as I issued the commands—loudly enough for the Woman with the Gun to hear—"sit" and "stay." The Woman with the Gun, giving us a wide berth, thanked me profusely both times, saying how much she appreciated our courtesy.

But she never took her hand off her gun.

And I never took my eye off her.

DAY 277

We have a kitchen drawer in which we store various types of energy bars. Today, running a bit late, I grabbed whichever one was on top without looking. At the trailhead, I took a bite, again, without so much as a cursory glance at the pedigree of the food product I was ingesting. Taste did not appeal to me (chocolate dipped coconut). Only then did I examine the wrapper. Turns out, it was something called a Luna Bar, "the first nutrition bar for women. And to inspire women to be bold and blaze their own trails."

Praiseworthy on all levels, of course, but still, this was cause for immediate concern. I would have spat out that first bite, but it was too late. A piece of masticated chocolate dipped coconut Luna Bar was already halfway down my alimentary canal, likely wreaking gender-specific havoc on genetic programming that has long served me well.

My ramble was suddenly defined by an irresistible desire to sniff every blossom alongside the trail.

When I passed a group of fellow hikers, I worried about my hair being overly mussed.

I looked down and was appalled both by the amount of mud on my boots and the fact that my hiking attire was crumpled and mismatched.

My rancid T-shirt made me look fat.

I noticed that the trail was badly in need of a good vacuuming.

I also noticed that a nearby boulder would have looked much better a few inches farther toward the arroyo. But not too far. Or maybe over there by the cliff face.

I decided it was high time to get Casey professionally groomed.

At my regular imbibery several hours later, I ordered chardonnay instead of my usual bottle of ale. I asked for a glass. A clean glass, at that. While lifting it toward my lips, my pinky reflexively shot out.

Fortunately, I was back to normal by morning. I decided the clothes I wore hiking yesterday (and the day before that) were still clean enough to wear today.

It is an understatement to say I am now more careful when pulling energy bars out of the kitchen drawer. That was too close for comfort. I mean, what if I had inadvertently eaten the entire Luna Bar? Likely something truly awful. Perhaps I would have developed a taste for musicals!

Whew!

DAY 283

I have no tattoos. My vehicle is adorned with nary a bumper sticker. My clothes bear no company logos. Do I even exist?

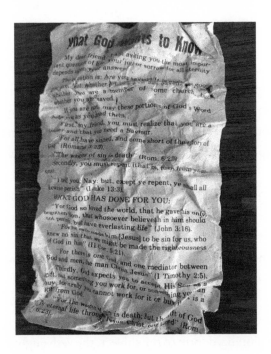

DAY 285

A few years ago, some (probably well-meaning) person or persons unknown made it an annoying habit to spread the Word via these little pieces of paper with dense, Old Testament-type, wrath-of-God-type Biblical wording on both sides printed in six-point type. (Only those with 20/20 vision are ripe for potential conversion.)

Sadly, the main venue for this anonymous means of proselytization seemed to be placing them under rocks, tacked to trees, or simply tossed on the ground. Then, quick as it started, the distribution stopped. I assumed the perpetrator must have been Rapture-ized, incarcerated, or converted to some denomination less inclined to leave pieces of paper out in the Gila. Like, maybe the Friends. I really can't picture Quakers condoning littering in the name of a supreme entity.

Lately, they have begun to appear again. I found one a couple days ago under a small makeshift wooden cross next to a trail junction I often pass. Given that I loathe all forms of trail trash, I pick these messages up and, same as I do with gum wrappers, cigarette butts, and orange peels, take them to the closest trash receptacle, all the while wondering how many people actually become born again via this particular strategy. I'm guessing: not a one.

Before disposing of the message, I read through the text, hoping that somewhere in the fine print there might be an offer for a free pizza or half-price happy hour appetizers or some such. (The only free offer was for something called "Salvation," which would be a perfect name for a cocktail or a particularly potent strain of recreational cannabis.)

One sentence caught my grammar-Nazi attention. It was from something called "Rom. 6:23." (Romanians? Romulans?) It read: "The wages of sin is death."

From a sentence-structure standpoint, I was flummoxed. It seemed to me that, given the pluralized form of the subject, the verb ought to be "are." But then it would read, "The wages of sin are death," which also seems awkward because "death" in this context is a singular direct object. Sure, "death" (the word, not the concept) carries an implied plural of incalculable proportions.

When I got home, I opened my copy of the Good Book (Strunk and White's *The Elements of Style*) in hopes of gleaning clarification. None was forthcoming.

Upon reflection, my best guess is that "[T]he wages of sin" part of the sentence is technically a noun clause, which gives it the ability to function in singular form, thus making it agree with the verb "is"—by the skin of its teeth.

Still, you would think that, with a supposedly almighty entity at the creative helm, the wording could easily have been a bit clearer.

Satisfied that this seeming grammatical sin was satisfactorily explained, I dismembered the cross and scattered its pieces and, upon returning home, dropped the note in the trash can. Then I walked down to my favorite libation emporium and ordered some Salvation. All I got was an exasperated expression from the bartender and a bottle of my usual. Purgatory, it seems, is not so bad.

Postscript: While filling up at my preferred gas station, I looked two vehicles over and noticed a Toyota pickup truck that appeared to have many dirt road miles under its chassis. The owner was out of hiker central casting—battered name-brand boots, sweat-crusty hat, T-shirt with more holes than fabric. When he noticed me noticing him, he came over, seemingly recognizing a kindred spirit. I assumed he was going to ask me about local trails or some such.

Instead, he handed me, from a hefty stack, one of the little pieces of paper with the grammatically challenged wrath-of-God wording.

I nearly tripped over my tongue.

"Are you the asshole who's been putting these all over the Gila?" I asked.

"It's an important message," he replied without flinching. He was a man obviously used to standing on solid ground.

As he returned to his pickup truck, I shouted, loudly enough that other customers turned and looked, "Quit the goddamned littering!"

I understand it's impossible to see a smirk while observing only a person's backside.

But see a smirk I surely did.

When I sat back in Pronto, Gay asked what that was all about.

I told her the full story.

She shook her head.

I'm not sure at who.

DAY 290

 With a little help from a friend, part two.

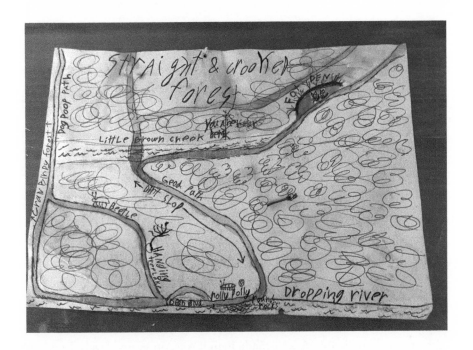

DAY 294

A few years back, Casey and I wintered in a valley far from our home. I did not want to be there, but economics called, and I dutifully answered with my head bowed low and my empty wallet held high. Directly across from the residence where I hung my hat was a saving grace: numerous hiking trails that skirted one of the best-known rivers in the Rocky Mountains. Even though I considered those trails—more urban park than wilderness—to be a downgrade from my usual haunts in New Mexico, they amounted to a much-appreciated psychic salve, given my circumstances. I traversed them so often that every undulation, tree, bog, and rock became seared in my memory.

One snowy day, I observed nailed to a trailside tree a watercolor etched upon a sheet of artists' sketch paper. It was a hand-painted map of the area. The piece was titled, "Straight & Crooked Forest." Its renderings were accurately oriented by the obligatory "You are here" mark. It included a fox den

I did not know about. An irrigation ditch was named "Little Brown Creek." It had a "Good Path," a "Dirt Slop Path" and a "Dog Poop Path." The river was named "Dropping River."

As I hiked on, I could not help but wonder about the artist, who I assumed, based upon the composition, was a child. Given that the winter weather would soon ruin it, I decided that, if the map was still there when I returned the next day, I would lay claim to it. Sadly, it was gone, likely retrieved, I thought, by its maker or another hiker who admired its composition and did not want to see it fall victim to the elements.

Three months later, when the snow melted, I walked by that same spot and—lo and behold!—the map was face up at the bottom of Little Brown Creek, which was fast filling with runoff. It remained in mint condition despite the long winter. A well-made map it was, on several levels. I rescued it. I tried in halfhearted vain to reunite the map with its creator by way of social media.

I love maps, to the degree that I have a collection of analog cartography that covers most of the planet and fills several large boxes. I spend my evenings perusing maps—of my backyard, of national parks and monuments, of Europe, of Antarctica.

Yet, the map of the Straight & Crooked Forest is the only one tacked to my office wall. I often gaze upon its simple complexity before leaving on my daily hikes. It reminds me to scrutinize, or at least attempt to scrutinize, the details of the landscape through which I pass. This is something I need to be reminded of.

It is my fervent hope that I will one day serendipitously cross paths with the artist who laid pigment to paper. She or he could tell me the story of how and why the map came to be, and why he or she opted to leave their creation in the very same area it depicted. I could then tell she or he how I came to possess their wonderful work. I would offer to return it. I wonder if she or he would accept. I would be happy to go either way.

DAY 298

I don't remember exactly when Casey pieced together the concept of taking shortcuts, mainly via cutting switchbacks, which, I have explained to her many times, is both environmentally irresponsible and, well, cheating. What would the high priests and priestesses at Leave No Trace say?

Once she progressed to the point that I let her hike off leash, Casey started looking at trails more as themes than plots. Like most young dogs, she would wander hither and yon, as far as I would allow her. The actual tread provided little more than basic orientation as she wandered in such a way that she probably traversed ten times the distance I did.

As she became increasingly familiar with the territory through which we frequently passed, Casey started blatantly cutting switchbacks wherever topography and floral composition and density would allow. She would then manifest a smug look, like, "Ain't I clever?" (She still does that.) She clearly wonders why I am so inclined to stick to the trail, no matter how indirect it might be.

I could at least understand how she figured out shortcuts on our regular trails. Then she started doing it on trails we had never before hiked upon. How she pulls this off, I cannot say. I mean, her eyeballs hover about twelve inches at most above the ground. She, therefore, cannot see far enough ahead to know where the trail goes.

She simply figures it out. Somehow. She has spent years hiking with me. She has developed directional skills based upon, I would guess, experience combined with intuition. Maybe some intertwined guesswork. A little bit of luck mixed in with the occasional screw-up. Pretty much the manner in which I have long moved through life.

Daddy's girl all the way.

Whatever the foundational methodology, Casey definitely moves in her own direction, at her own pace, and to her own distinct beat. And she definitely is clever.

It has been wonderful to watch her grow.

DAY 300

Another arbitrary numeric milestone. This one, however, a bit more potentially impactful, insofar as it marked the first time in this year-long quest that I started seriously ruminating about the existence, as well as the ramifications, of the finish line—even though the temporal terminus was still more than two months away. About the same amount of time as it took me to hike the Arizona Trail. Chronological reality aside, I felt deep down in my weary bones that, barring some unforeseen catastrophe, I would make it. A potential fizzling of motivation was no longer a potential part of the equation.

I don't know why 300 was more noteworthy than, say, 299 or 301. I did some cursory research. All I found were some mathematical properties that 1) I did not even slightly understand (I mean, what does it mean to be a triangular number that is the sum of ten consecutive primes?) and 2) did not appear to have any perceivable relation to the subject of hiking.

As stated many thousands of words ago, I commenced this venture with the understanding that I would simply Do the Thing, or try to, and see where I landed. My lifestyle modus operandi since childhood. I now found my hand moving closer to a tiller that thus far had remained largely unmanned. Quite unexpectedly, creeping up the base of my spine over the course of the previous couple months was the notion that I wouldn't mind it if I actually gained something palpable from this sweat-logged undertaking. I wanted the effort to have a modicum of lasting significance. At least relative to my inconsequential little corner of the universe. This notion was not entirely unwelcome, but it definitely upped the interior-reflection ante.

DAY 301

I have never been inclined to bring a music device with me on the trail. Though I own a fully loaded iPod, it stays in Pronto while I am hiking. I prefer the sound of silence, or of birds jabbering, or of a creek babbling. I also want to be able to audibly perceive the approach of a mountain biker or a gaggle of javelinas. I especially want to be able to hear a rattlesnake rattling.

But, in a sense, I *do* bring music with me when I hike. Whatever the last song that was playing when I turn my vehicle off at the trailhead has a way of latching on to my eardrums and staying latched till I return. That song, whatever it might be, will feedback-loop its way through my mental sound system whether I am out for an hour, a day, or a week. Ergo, I make damned certain to select my pre-hike tunes with care. Much as I am a fan, no Tom Waits or Leonard Cohen. Gregorian chants are out. Way out.

It was some years ago that I learned this irritating (understatement) affliction actually has a proper name: earworm. Like a disease from a dog's digestive tract somehow made its way into your head.

My deep-rooted understanding of this maddening malady—also known as "stuck song syndrome," "musical imagery repetition" or "involuntary musical imagery"—began during the early stages of an 850-mile, sixty-two-day hike along the Colorado section of the Continental Divide Trail from the New Mexico border to Wyoming.

Though I do not remember the genesis or gestation, I eventually realized, as I was hiking through the lovely South San Juan Mountains, that I had embedded between my ears a tune that did not seem inclined to go away, or even moderate.

It perhaps would have been one thing if the channel would have changed occasionally, like a radio station or an iPod set to shuffle. It would have been one thing if the tune in question was a Bach violin concerto, or, say, side one of *Abbey Road*. Or, hell, if it would have been "Rikki Don't Lose That Number" or even "Hey Hey We're the Monkees!" I was not so graced. Rather, the tune that dug in like a tick, as though it had been implanted by a lab technician out of *Brave New World*, was, of all hideous and torturous things, "The Hokey Pokey."

How such a thing transpired, I have no idea.

And, step after step, uphill and down, in heat and cold, in dryness and in rain, in the early morning and in the evening, as I purified water, set up camp, cooked dinner, and sat back staring up into the cruel heavens, "The Hokey Pokey" was always with me, like crab lice infestation that would not go away.

And, worse (as though there can possibly be anything worse), I was desperately ignorant when it came to the entire lyric set of "The Hokey Pokey." So, rather than being able at least to "listen" to what subsequent research showed me are a full ten verses, I was cursed with less than one. I now know that the entire first verse consists of: *You put your right foot in, / You put your right foot out; / You put your right foot in, / And you shake*

it all about. / You do the Hokey Pokey, / And you turn yourself around. /
That's what it's all about!

Additional verses make their way through much of the exterior of the human anatomy (sadly, leaving out the most captivating parts), so that, when one is happily past the right foot, one has the golden opportunity to Hokey Pokey oneself to the left foot, both hands, both sides, the nose, the backside, and the head, until, finally, one reaches the near-Nietzschean nebulousness of one's "whole self."

I was not even blessed with so much as one complete body part. I had no idea as I hiked along the CDT that the song commenced with a right foot, and, therefore, had no idea that it then traveled from the left foot, and subsequently to the hands, and so on. For 850 miles, the words that played over and over (and over and over and over, ad infinitum) in my mind's ear were limited to the last three lines that follow all ten of those verses: *You do the Hokey Pokey / And you turn yourself around. / That's what it's all about!*

I had an awful lot of time to muse on every facet, every implication, every subtle nuance of those three rousing lines of "The Hokey Pokey." And if there's one thing I wished, more than anything—more than a hot shower, more than a big bag of potato chips, more than an icy six-pack, more than sex—while hiking along the Continental Divide Trail that summer, it was even the faintest knowledge of what the goddamned Hokey Pokey, as related via that limited lyric set, actually was. Was it a meditative state? A component of the Kama Sutra? A series of martial arts katas? A chess strategy?

Without knowing a damned thing about the Hokey Pokey—aside from those lyrical snippets —how could I possibly progress to the point of learning what "it" is, and thence, to learn what "it" is "all about?" Basically, I can tell you with absolute certitude that there is no way. By the time I got to Monarch Pass—the halfway point—I was starting to feel as though the whole hike was a waste of time. Like, if I couldn't get to the bottom of the Hokey Pokey, what chance did I stand of returning home a more enlightened individual? None! I stood no chance.

Clearly, the Hokey Pokey was driving me to distraction. I was going downhill fast. Madness was nipping at my heels.

(Here I feel compelled to point out that "stuck song syndrome" can become serious enough that it requires medical and/or psychological intervention.)

Roland Lawrence LaPrise—who died in 1996 (curse his bones!)—concocted the song—properly named "Do the Hokey Pokey" (making it grammatically imperative)—in the late 1940s for the ski crowd in Sun Valley, Idaho. His group, the Ram Trio (with Charles Macak and Tafit Baker), recorded the song—the basic tune and concept of which had roots that grew all the way back to ancient times in the Scottish Highlands—in 1949 and gained a copyright for the song and the lyrics the following year. Though it never made its way onto any national music charts, it proved to be a popular post-World War II tune, getting significant radio airplay.

So, this was not some silly melody birthed by a flaccid "A Mighty Wind"-type folk ensemble in Greenwich Village. This was—given its Sun Valley heritage—serious mountain music created to deliver a serious mountain-based message, and here was I, slogging my way through the most intense mountain country in the Lower 48, and this one fragment of this one song came to me and stuck with me like a Zen koan for a *reason, goddammit!* I was obviously too dense to comprehend what that reason might be.

And, so it went, past Leadville, through Summit County (where I then dwelled) and the Eagles Nest Wilderness. (Unenlightened!) Over James Peak. (Still not understanding what "Do the Hokey Pokey" was trying to teach me.) Through the Indian Peaks. (*Still* not getting what "it's all about," and wanting more than anything to touch the hem of Hokey Pokey wisdom.) Past Grand Lake, into the Never Summers. (Nothing.)

Nothing!

Until, at last, I arrived at Rabbit Ears Pass, where my buddy, Chris Nelson, was due to meet me for the last six trail days. I shared my Hokey Pokey-based angst with Chris, who said, "I can help you with this."

324

I stopped dead in my tracks. Perhaps Chris had already ventured down the Yellow Brick Road of Hokey Pokey-ism. Chris and I had trained together for years in tae kwon do. He's a professional firefighter who has faced death in many forms many times. He's also, like me, a bowler, a sport that in my mind serves more than any other activity as a metaphor for life and all its myriad intricacies and complexities.

It would not have surprised me if Chris, wise man that he was, would be able to share some Hokey Pokey insights, therefore allowing me to learn what "it" was, and, then, maybe solder everything together and learn what "it" was "all about." Just think—I could then perhaps become a revered Hokey Pokey master!

Chris looked me square in the eye. His lips pursed, as though he was considering kissing the atmosphere, which, given the depth and gravity of the subject at hand, seemed appropriate. Instead, he started whistling the melody of the theme song to *The Andy Griffith Show*. At that instant, "Do the Hokey Pokey" dissipated from my mind, never more to return. I had learned all I needed to know about "Do the Hokey Pokey."

I had made it almost to the end of my two-month hike, and perhaps "Do the Hokey Pokey" had helped me along the way, helped me to put my right foot out, and then my left, to persevere through rain and fatigue and hunger. Maybe that was "it," and maybe that was what it was "all about!" Maybe "Do the Hokey Pokey" was analogous to backpacking and living and trying to grow as a human being!

Either way, the journey-at-hand was not yet complete. I still had a few more trail days. For every step of the remaining way, the melody from *The Andy Griffith Show* went with me. No deep lyrics to dwell on, no hidden messages to decipher. Only the tune. Which, of course, might mean some-thing profound. I wondered what *that* was all about.

DAY 303

Easter worship, pagan style. Hallelujah.

DAY 305

On the final backpacking trip I took during my quest to hike every day for a solid year, the site where I chose to camp—the only semi-level spot for miles—was thick with bear scat, like there had been a gathering of ursines addicted to Ex-Lax. I had to kick one especially prodigious load away to make room for my tent, and the pile was so steaming fresh that it stuck to my boot. I almost sprained a hip trying to kick away the caca, which, upon closer inspection, resembled some of the higher-priced organic breakfast-food products available at our local food co-op. Maybe the local bears have been dining upon our sizeable aging hippie population.

Many people would have considered the bear-dropping situation cause to immediately seek alternate accommodation. Rapidly.

Guess I am not that smart. Besides, the bear was clearly gone.

When people consider potential negative animal-human interactions in southwest New Mexico, rattlesnakes undoubtedly top the list. Not far behind come bears. We do not have grizzlies hereabouts, but they used to live here. Their ghosts still wander around the Gila, searching for a foothold I hope they one day will find. We only have their smaller cousins, black bears (which, nomenclature notwithstanding, can be black, brown, and almost blond).

Though I have never seen a grizzly in the wild, I have seen many black bears. There was a time on the Appalachian Trail through Great Smoky Mountains National Park when, in the barely past-dawn mist, I about stepped on the front paw of a medium-sized bear that was inexplicably reposing in some dense vegetation right next to one of the busiest sections of tread in the entire country. The bear was as startled as I was. We both shrieked and jumped several feet in the air. It went one way at a brisk pace; I went the other way with a degree of avidity I can't usually muster at that hour.

Many years ago, I did a two-week solo trip through the Gila. While hiking along a creek, the trail diverted to bypass a thick stand of Gambel oaks. In the middle of that copse was a bear foraging under rocks for slugs or grubs or whatever it is bears forage for under rocks. The bear, which had not yet noticed me, was heading in the direction I was coming from. So, I slinked around those oaks in an attempt to slyly outflank the bear. After having done so, I turned to make certain the coast was clear. I was startled to observe the bear charging, head down, full bore, directly at me. I dropped my pack and skedaddled. I found a tree and shimmied up like a possum on speed. Sadly, my perch did not afford a clear sight line to my discarded pack, which I assumed was right then being ransacked by a bear that fully intended, upon polishing off my stash of Snickers bars, to amble over, climb the tree in which I was precariously perched and kill me.

I must have stayed in that tree for an hour. When I finally mustered the nerve to climb down, I found my pack undisturbed and the bear nowhere to be seen. Best I could figure, the bear got to a point going up the creek where it caught my scent on the trail, so it turned and galloped in the opposite direction, not realizing that, by that time, I was standing dead smack in the middle of its revised route. An unpredictable set of compounding coincidences if ever there was one. I was, and remain forevermore, happy there were no witnesses to my frantic retreat.

In Colorado, black bears often venture into populated areas, where they ransack dumpsters, break into cars and, occasionally, trespass into abodes. These things rarely happen in New Mexico, where the bear population seems to grasp that much of the human population is well armed and generally inclined to shoot first and ask questions later.

There are occasional incidents. A few years back, a Texan camped at a popular campground got bit in the middle of the night. His glutes were right up against the wall of his tent. The bear must have wandered by and thought, "You know, I may come to regret this, but it's something I've long wanted to do." Then, it sank its considerable dentition deep in the Texan's hind end. That was it—no follow-up attack, no subsequent mauling. Just one solid chomp. The wound was severe enough that the Texan had to drive to the nearest hospital—two hours away—in the middle of the night with a badly bleeding bum. It's my guess that the drive was uncomfortable. It is further my guess that it was probably difficult for the attending medical professionals to maintain any semblance of decorum when he entered the emergency room. He became the butt of many local jokes. Fish and Game officers tried to hunt the offending bear down. They were unsuccessful. I wonder how hard they tried.

My most recent bear interaction occurred when Gay and I were backpacking to a well-known hot spring in the Gila. On the first day out, we stopped to dine upon a couple Subway roast beef sandwiches I had thoughtfully added to our otherwise Spartan backpacking larder. Halfway through our greasy repast, I looked up the arroyo next to which we were sitting and noticed an adult bear wandering in our direction. I said to Gay, who had not yet noticed our impending lunch guest and who, to the best of my knowledge, had never seen a bear in the wild, "Well, that's interesting." She turned and proceeded to slowly hand me her sandwich. At first, I thought it was pretty tacky that the woman with whom I share a bed would reflexively sacrifice the supposed love of her life by transferring what amounted to a large lump of fragrant bear bait to my possession. With scarcely an iota of hesitation, I might add. I soon reconsidered, understanding that, were it not for me, she would certainly not be in such a situation. Basically, better for one of us to have to run while being chased by a hungry bear while holding two roast beef sandwiches than both of us running holding one sandwich each.

For what seemed like a lot longer period of time that it probably was, I weighed the value of those sandwiches, wondering how much resistance I might be able to muster in defense of our lunch. Short answer: not much. So I, holding two Subway roast beef sandwiches, each the size of a canoe, counted under my breath, "One, two, three," and jumped up, ran down the trail ten or twenty yards and heaved those sandwiches as far as I could. When I did so, the bear, until that point being totally unaware of our presence, bolted back up the arroyo, tail between its legs. Gone, just like that.

There is a certain look that a wife can bestow upon a husband that 1) needs no explanation but 2) covers much in the way of conceptual territory. Sluiced down, it basically translates to: How did I come to be married to such an imbecile? And here I thought I would receive hugs of gratitude for my prompt and decisive action.

Sadly, Gay chose to augment that look with some actual verbiage. The woman who so lately was perfectly willing to contribute to my imminent demise by handing me—a man, I should add, who was more than willing to endure being torn to shreds by a wild animal twice, maybe three times his weight, to protect his wife—her roast beef sandwich with a bear coming toward us, growled, "What are you doing?"

I meekly, and somewhat indignantly, responded that I was preparing to sacrifice my life for the greater marital good.

Turns out, she had handed me her sandwich not because she was so blithely willing to see me rather than her torn to shreds but because she had hoped to be able to surreptitiously retrieve her camera without scaring the bear and without having a fast-food product dripping with salad dressing, mayonnaise, and mustard hampering her manual dexterity and soiling her pricy photographic equipage.

Oops.

So, not only did Gay miss the opportunity to take an award-winning photo of a bear, but we no longer had any roast beef sandwiches, which were surely by then covered in ants and flies that were rejoicing in their good fortune, which had inexplicably fallen out of the sky right into their laps.

I suggested to Gay that a PowerBar would be better for us anyhow. She grunted.

I do not give bears as much thought as maybe I should. Of course, when camping, I do not tempt fate. I do all the right things. I cook well away from my tent. I hang my food bag in a tree on the far distant horizon. As for lying awake at night wondering if I'm going to get my glutes bit, no. Whatever insomnia I might suffer while camping has roots back in civilization.

But here is the thing: The law of aural amplification applies, especially when you are lying alone. A mouse sounds big as a coatimundi when it's scurrying through the bushes at night. A coatimundi sounds big as a bobcat. Clear up till you're lying there, thinking it surely must be a Bengal tiger rooting around right outside the flimsy nylon walls that separate you from the food chain. Have I cautiously unzipped the front of my tent to scan the area with a flashlight? Many times. But the scariest thing I ever caught in that thin beam of photons was a porcupine that immediately sprinted—all things being relative in the porcupine world—up a nearby tree. Gay named him Ernie. Or maybe it was Elroy. Either way, he was still in that tree the next morning when we awoke and was still there when we packed up and hiked away. He might be there still. Reminded me of me when I was up in that tree hiding from the bear.

Here's the thing: Knowing there are creatures out there, some of which are capable, and maybe even inclined, to fuck you up, is one of the attractions of hiking. I *want* to see bears, mountain lions, javelinas, wolves, and even rattlesnakes. Such sightings make my day. They form the backbone of subsequent bar stories. I understand full well that, one day, I may change my tune if something bad ever happens, if I—or my wife or my dog—get attacked or bit while sleeping. I doubt it though. That "tune"—sometimes melodious, sometimes cacophonous, sometimes with lyrics I cannot fully comprehend— is the soundtrack of my life and has been since I was a wild child roaming the boreal forests of the northern Adirondacks. May it continue to be so, clear up to the point where I am no longer able to shimmy up a tree at all, much less like a possum on speed.

DAY 306

Seemed like my toothbrush tasted a bit gamey. Perhaps, thought I, it had contracted a bit of rot from my most recent backpacking trip. But, in addition to its earthy flavor, the bristles seemed to be, well, moving independently of the usual small-circles teeth-brushing motion.

I pulled the toothbrush from my mouth and, much to my groggy, early-morning consternation, observed a now barely alive moth entombed by a thick layer of Aquafresh. I mean, what are the chances of a winged insect lighting upon the bristles of my toothbrush during the night? And, further, of me not noticing it before applying toothpaste and placing it in my mouth? For the record, I can say confidently that Lepidoptera-flavored oral-care products stand little chance of ever taking commercial wing.

DAY 308

When I pulled over and offered a ride to the young man—obviously a long-distance backpacker (a breed of hiker I can recognize from miles away, partially by bearing, partially by filth factor)—he rested his pack, which looked to weigh about eleven ounces total (ultralight, minimalist gear being de rigueur these days) in his lap as he buckled into Pronto's passenger seat, Casey lying on the floor behind him. He extended a suitably grimy hand and introduced himself as Wildman. Actually, I do not recall how he introduced himself. Could have been Treebeard, Aspenfoot, or Windwalker. There have been so many over the years, I can't keep them straight.

Though the Continental Divide Trail wraps around Silver City, its route is broken. There is an eleven-mile gap west of town that, despite the best efforts of many people and many entities over many years, has never been fully connected. The CDT abruptly dead-ends on both sides of the gap—located pretty much in the middle of nowhere—which causes thru-hikers to splice together a makeshift route that invariably leads to much road walking, the bane of everyone who has ever hoisted a pack. One of those roads passes near my house. When driving down that road, I almost always pull over and ask hikers if they want a lift to the CDT trailhead. About half say thanks, but no thanks, citing the ethical need to hike every step of the way from the Mexican border to the Canadian border. About half say hell yes.

Not one of the uncountable number of CDT hikers I have chauffeured has given a name like Bill or Susan. Every single person has presented a "trail handle." Names like Mud Dog and Bearclaw. It amounts to people adopting a new identity when they shoulder their pack and head out on a properly named long-distance trail for months on end. You can become whoever you want for 3,000 miles because almost nobody else you meet on your trek will know that Windwalker is actually Stanley Schmuckluck who lives in his parents' basement in Ashtabula.

On my southbound thru-hike of the Appalachian Trail many moons ago, I was Jumpin' Jack, the Hallucinogenic Hiker. The first part of this lengthy sobriquet came my way via a fellow backpacker who at first dubbed me Jackrabbit John because of my habit—which is still part of my trail MO—of hiking at a rapid pace, then stopping to catch my breath, then hiking rapidly once more. Somehow, somewhere, that morphed into Jumpin' Jack. Maybe I was humming the Rolling Stones' "Jumpin' Jack Flash" within earshot.

The last part of my trail handle was likely self-administered. (Yes, we were dropping a fair amount of acid.)

Jumpin' Jack, the Hallucinogenic Hiker was given semiformal status in a book called *Chained Dogs and Songbirds: The World's Slowest Traverse of the Appalachian Trail*, penned by a man whose *nom de sentier* was once one of the most recognizable in the world of long-distance backpacking: O.d. Coyote. (For reasons I am not privy to, the second initial of O.d. Coyote's trail name is intentionally lowercased.)

In his book, he wrote of our chance encounter (penned exactly this way, almost as if, given a bit more time and effort, our interaction could have evolved into a proper Shakespearean sonnet):

Out of all this appeared Jumping Jack, the Hallucinogenic Hiker.
He climbed out of the brush and floated up to me
with this big goofy grin on his face.
We talked business for a short while.
These weird little bees kept stinging my legs, so I didn't stay long.
He looked into my eyes real funny, and we went our ways.

In those days, less than half the hikers (rough guess) on the AT had trail handles. The person who came up with "Jumpin' Jack," for instance, did not. Neither did his two companions, who I have remained close with. I hiked for several weeks in close proximity with at least ten other southbound hikers, most of whom proceeded bearing the name given them at birth without noticeable nomenclatural encumbrance. One guy I met in New Hampshire was called "the Philosopher." (He acted as though he was the second coming of Camus). In Pennsylvania, I hiked with two women who were known as "Pooh" and "Boots." In North Carolina, I met up with another thru-hiker known as "Slowpoke."

And that was about it. Everyone else was Bill, Steve, or Amy.

It had been quite some time since I reread O.d. Coyote's recounting of our trailside encounter —which occurred in the Blue Ridge Mountains of Virginia—in *Chained Dogs and Songbirds*. While so doing, I tried to mentally reconnect with Jumpin' Jack, the Hallucinogenic Hiker, to remember who he was and what made him move the way he did.

Unwise undertaking, because Jumpin' Jack was pretty much an inconsiderate jerk. Incessant blabber, especially when stoned. Perpetually stoned. Knew everything even though he knew next to nothing. Capable of treating people badly. The only direction he had in life was defined by the trail upon which he was walking at any given time. Was quick to share his drugs, especially with women, but usually with ulterior motives. Prone to mooching and wearing out his welcome. Unreliable in the extreme. Full of piss and vinegar. Would argue with a fence post. Scarred by his violent upbringing in ways he did not yet perceive.

But he was not without a few redeeming qualities. Laughed easily. Was a good hiker. Was able to glide through life with little more than what he could carry in his pack. Could survive for months on Rice-A-Roni and instant Cream of Wheat. Young.

Above all else, young.

Jumpin' Jack stayed with me for a while after I completed the AT, but he did not fit well into the real world. I never made a specific decision to part ways with him. Jumpin' Jack just faded to black. There was one time when an ex-girlfriend I ran into years later asked whatever happened to Jumpin' Jack, whose untethered ways she had once found appealing. I responded that he had hiked away, to points unknown. I still tried to hit on her, to no avail. She had been attracted to Jumpin' Jack, not me.

My subsequent long-distance hikes—all of which I completed more than a decade after Jumpin' Jack and I separated—did not lend themselves to trail names. There were too few fellow hikers to establish any sort of coherent and ongoing sociability.

So, the opportunity to resurrect Jumpin' Jack, or to adopt a different trail name, never presented itself.

Shortly after I moved from my longtime home in Colorado back to Silver City, I ran into an old college buddy at a bar. We had both aged enough in the interim that recognition was not instantaneous. "Is that Jumpin' Jack?" he asked. It wasn't. I kind of wished it was.

When Treebeard, Aspenfoot, or Windwalker—or whatever his name was—got settled in Pronto's front seat, I extended a hand. It was tempting beyond belief to say, "Name's Jumpin' Jack." He would have then known we were kindred spirits, brothers of the boot.

As we approached the CDT trailhead, I started to wonder how my life may have turned out had I never let Jumpin' Jack wither away, or even if, at some point, I would have resurrected him or chased him down to some nasty trailside watering hole. There is a distinct possibility I would have spent my life traveling from trail to trail, from the Ouachita, to the Pacific Northwest, to GR20, to the Trans-Caucasus, down to the Route of the Parks in Chile. And a hundred others. It could have happened.

It didn't happen. Fuck … it didn't happen.

"Name's John," I said at last.

When I dropped Treebeard, Aspenfoot, or Windwalker off, I sat in Pronto, watched him putter with a few last-minute details, hoist his pack, and walk northward toward Canada.

My heart sank at the same time that I grinned and wished him Godspeed. Then Casey and I hiked off in the other direction.

DAY 312

While sitting barefoot in shorts next to a creek on a warm spring day, a lone ant ascended my left thigh.

From a basic design perspective, this ant—reddish brown in color—was nothing special. But, by ant standards, it was large—maybe a half-inch long. It had protruding mandibles that looked like they could lay some serious hurt on insects of similar or lesser stature.

When I got home, I measured the height of my left thigh while sitting on the ground. About seven inches. In terms of relative proportionality, the climb that ant made basically without breaking stride would be the equivalent of me scaling a vertical wall 966 feet high with no handholds save human hair follicles and no protective gear.

The ant proceeded to walk down my leg, as though it was not searching for anything in particular, but keeping its eyes peeled in case it came across something of note. Exploring. Reconnoitering.

Some people instinctively smoosh insects, even harmless ones, if they light upon them. I did not smoosh that ant, mainly because I am inclined to live and let live. The other reason being that, if you smoosh an ant on your bare leg, then you have ant smoosh on your bare leg. I allowed it to continue on its journey. If it bit me, though, I was going to smoosh that ant, ant smoosh notwithstanding.

I could have preemptively avoided the potential smooshing scenario by flicking that ant away. I'm not sure how far you can flick a half-inch-long ant. If you're truly motivated, your ant-flicking technique well-honed, and your concentration intent, I'm thinking a half-inch-long ant could be flicked a solid five feet. Far enough away that it would likely not return. Once again, thinking in terms of proportionality, that would be the same as my five-foot-nine body getting flicked a mile and a half. Whereas my battered body would lie in an unidentifiable heap of goo were I to be flicked that distance, all the ant, with its Ironman-like exoskeleton, would do is dust off and stand there wondering what in the world just happened. "There I was, walking along on a fairly featureless landscape one second, and the next instant I was launched by a giant finger that came out of nowhere all the way to the next time zone." Not sure how reflective ants are. Maybe at that moment it would commence entertaining the possibility of a higher power. Maybe that one flick would spearhead the eventual development and institutionalization of an ant cosmology. Probably, if it gave the matter any thought whatsoever, it would simply count the experience as yet another vagary that likely defines ant existence from egg, to larval and pupal stages, into adulthood, to the end of a life expectancy of only ninety days.

I did not flick that ant. I decided to let it continue walking down my leg. It crossed the knob of my knee and slalomed its way through the sparse hair growing on the side of my shin. It eventually reached my foot, from where it descended headfirst back to earth. I pretty much thought that would be the end of what was otherwise a mildly amusing interspecies interaction.

But, no. The ant turned around and gazed upon the tantalizing fullness of my reclining body. Then it latched its relatively substantial jaws onto my left ring toe! It didn't hurt because I have callouses covering both feet. It then commenced yanking with all its might. This half-inch-long ant that, out of the goodness of my heart, I had neither flicked nor smooshed, was trying to pull me I assume back to its nest! Ungrateful little shit!

Big cojones on that ant, though, according to my research, almost all the ants one sees anting about are female. Still.

Back to proportionality. A medium-sized ant weighs about ten milligrams. I weigh eighty-six million milligrams. So, I'm like eight million times the weight of this ant. By comparison, a blue whale—the largest creature known to ever have inhabited the Earth—weighs about 330,000 pounds, which is "only" about 1,700 times more than I weigh. Relatively speaking, I am twenty-four times more massive to the ant than a blue whale is to me. Yet, there it stood, tugging with all its might on my left ring toe.

By extension, I could not then avoid wondering what it would be like were that ant the size of a human, which is physically impossible on several levels. Like all insects, its legs would not be able to support its body weight and its respiratory system would not be able to supply enough oxygen to keep it alive. Were it able to somehow overcome those not-inconsequential challenges, since ants can lift as much as ten times their body weight and pull as much as fifty times their body weight, a human-sized ant would be able to wrangle a grown elephant back to the condo complex, or wherever a human-sized ant might reside. They would be able to reach speeds of more than fifty miles per hour—so only a couple of terrestrial animals would be able to outrun them. Scary thought.

I tried to ascertain what personality trait I should ascribe to a half-inch-long ant trying to pull a full-grown human to its nest. Maybe it was really community oriented, like, "This load will be well worth the effort, as it will feed us all for an entire year!"

Maybe it was into bravado, like, "Everyone's going to cheer me when I bring home this big chunk of meat! There will be a parade in my honor! Songs will be sung!"

Or maybe it was thinking in terms of trying to score points with the queen, which would be a waste of time, because, in the ant world, there is no upward mobility. You are what you are, and will remain what you are, clear up till you die, and no one in your nest will remember you. Reminds me of some economic systems invented and promulgated by my fellow humans.

Good possibility this ant was simply a little slow on the uptake.

At that point, I moved my foot. The ant lost its grip, shrugged its shoulders, and scurried away. I hope it spent the evening regaling its fellow ants with a story about the one that got away.

DAY 319

Yesterday, while stopping to moisten the trailside foliage, out of the blue, a tarantula decided to crawl up my hiking stick. Every once in a while, those of us who call the Land of Enchantment home have the good fortune to experience what we call "only in New Mexico" moments. Consider this one of those. I mean, tarantulas are hardly rare in these parts, but having one ascend your hiking stick, well, that's something new.

I carefully transplanted the spider well off the trail in deep grass and wished it luck.

DAY 320

Last night, a well-coiffed, young, hipster bartender eyeballed me shortly after I had finished a dusty half-day hike and said, "Dude, you look like you just spent seven years in the Sahara Desert."

Though I do not believe he meant it as such, I took the observation as a compliment.

DAY 325

The lady, a fellow senior citizen I did not recognize, was clearly flustered. She held a map in front of my face when we met on a TS-X trail. "Do you know where we are?" she growled, as though I were somehow personally responsible for her directional discombobulation.

After pointing her toward a trailhead that was far more distant that she had hoped, I asked about the map, which I had not seen before.

Given my familiarity with TS-X, I certainly did not need a map to find my way around, but, since I am a serious cartography junkie, I wanted a copy for my extensive collection. Couple days later, the local Forest Service office obliged by digging through a stack of musty files that had seemingly not been touched since the days of Geronimo.

The map was nothing special. A photocopy blowup of a standard 7.5-minute quad with the individual TS-X trails overlaid in colored ink. A short section marked as a "non-system trail"—which is a weird thing for an official Forest Service map—caught my eye. I had never noticed that particular trail, though I had walked by its two end points uncountable times.

In my trail-centric world, this was akin to stumbling upon a gold mine. I could not beat feet to the site fast enough. If I could locate this trail, my storytelling one-upmanship at the local watering hole would receive an uncontested shot in the arm. My compadres would be green with envy—even though I would withhold all details regarding where the trail was actually located. Proprietary information, as it were.

According to the map, the trail bisects a well-worn, properly named loop that sees much use. When I arrived where its eastern terminus was supposed to be, I faced a nearly impenetrable line of thorny foliage. So I wandered around to where the map indicated its western terminus was supposed to be and, again, found nothing resembling a map-worthy footpath. Could there be a mapmaker with a wicked sense of humor working for the Forest Service? "Let's see if there's anyone stupid enough to search for this trail," the sadistic bureaucrat might have said while downing shots of mescal and drawing a random line upon the undulating contours.

I was not going to be easily dissuaded. After a bit of strategic bush-whacking, I located evidence that there was indeed the remnants of a barely discernible trail right where the map indicated. It had not been recently traversed, but there was ample physical attestation that, once upon a time, people passed this way on a regular basis. There were trees shorn of branches, lines of trailside rocks hidden by deep grass and the slightest hints of tread. There was even a long-abandoned fire ring.

It took several hours to link both ends of this lost trail, which is no more than a mile long.

Though pretty enough, there were no earth-shattering discoveries along the way. No hidden canyons, expansive vistas, or breeding grounds for an unknown subspecies of badger, or alien crash sites. Only nice clusters of blooming wildflowers, prodigious piles of caca—bear, elk, javelina, coyote—and a bit of a mystery that likely will never be addressed, much less answered: Who built this trail, and why was it not, like many of the other proximate trails, absorbed into the extensive, official TS-X system through which it passes?

It became a habit to detour every week or two from the properly named loop onto the abandoned trail I had located. I did so furtively, lest other hikers see me slink into the brush. Were that to ever happen, I already had an explanation at the ready: need to take a leak. I would glance in both directions. I would jump from rock to grass patch to make certain there was no evidence of my passing.

The trail became my little secret.

One day, I saw another set of boot prints following the route. Though the outline was distinct, the details were eroded.

My disappointment was profound.

I hoped those boot prints would soon end, like the person took a few steps and said something along the lines of, "There doesn't appear to be anything of note hereabouts," shortly before turning around. That, sadly, did not happen. I further hoped the prints would diverge from the route I had painstakingly located, that they would head off in the wrong direction, never to be seen again. That did not happen either. The person knew exactly where to go. The cat was out of the bag. My little secret was mine no longer.

My disappointment morphed into overt irritation.

What was I irritated about? That someone else had come across the same map that initially piqued my interest? That he or she, like me, had decided to see what lay up this way? That someone else was inclined toward wandering? Rather than being miffed, I should have rejoiced in the existence of a kindred spirit.

With each succeeding step, however, my teeth gnashed more. I muttered expletives and lamented how there is no longer any virgin ground upon which a person (read: me) can tromp!

Damn the human race!

Then I came upon one boot print that remained somewhat pristine. I leaned over and squinted. I stepped right next to the print and realized that the tracks were in fact my own. I was the person I had been following. I had been pissed off at myself, which opens up a big can of psychiatric worms.

Heraclitus of Ephesus (whose nickname, appropriately enough, was "the Obscure") is supposed to have said the much-appropriated and misquoted words: "You could not step twice into the same rivers, for other waters are ever flowing on to you." I guess the same can be said of trails. Am I the same person I was when I left the tracks I came to follow? Am I the sum of my own footsteps?

I sure hope so, for that implies wisdom gained from age and experience.

I sure hope not, for that implies I have become little more than a creature of habit.

Next time, I hiked that lost trail from the opposite direction.

Next time, I will come at it sideways.

Maybe one day I will forget it even exists.

Maybe one day those boot prints will vanish entirely.

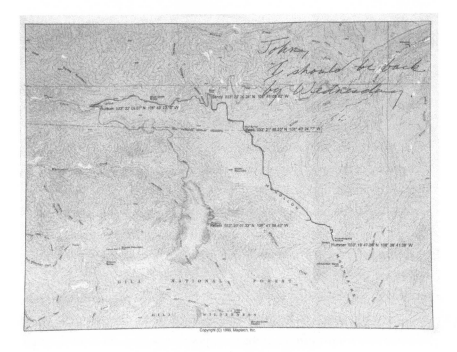

DAY 332

Having been on the road for more than a week, my mail was stacked up high when I got home. Usual heap of past-due bills, unsolicited pleadings for money I did not have and advertisements for things I would not own even if they were free. At the very bottom of the pile was a folded-up piece of printer paper that was not in an envelope. That portended at least something entertaining. Maybe a ransom note. Or some manner of summons.

Turns out, it was a color printout of a topographic map covering part of the Gila Wilderness. Outlined was what appeared to be a backpacking route.

In the upper-right corner was a hand-scrawled message from a drinking buddy I will herein call Solomon, who happened to live a couple doors down. The note read: "John: I should be back by Wednesday."

Apparently, I had—for the first time in my long and winding trail life—been designated as what is known in outdoor circles as a "responsible party"—the person who jumps into action if, in this case, my drinking buddy, Solomon, did not return on schedule. This is a duty I take seriously. The problem was, my drinking buddy, Solomon, had not informed me before the fact that he was bestowing upon me such an honor.

It was Friday and, since I had been gone, I had no idea whether the Wednesday in question was the previous Wednesday, the Wednesday before that, or the upcoming Wednesday.

Adding to the ambiguity was the fact that Solomon appeared to have spilled a beverage on part of the route, which was badly smudged.

I walked over to Solomon's house to see if there were any signs of life. There were none.

So, I thought the most responsible strategy—me being an official responsible party and all—would be to saunter down to the watering hole where Solomon and I most often imbibe in hopes that perhaps some of the regulars had a bit more skinny regarding his itinerary.

The question was received with stares even blanker than usual.

"Solomon's gone?" someone asked.

"When's he supposed to get back?" another person asked, despite the fact that the conversation commenced with me querying all there gathered in straightforward fashion related in universally accepted barroom vernacular—liberal use of foul language combined with slurred articulation—if anyone knew when Solomon was due back.

Sigh.

There was little recourse except to sip a pint and wonder whether Solomon was at that exact moment lying broken and bruised in the Gila Wilderness, his waning life being sustained by nothing more than a faint flicker of hope based upon the fact that he had left a map with a party he deemed to be responsible. "I will be rescued any minute now," he might well be thinking as the vultures start landing close.

"I'm wondering if I ought to call the Forest Service," I tentatively ventured.

"Why?" was the general response.

Somewhat frustratingly, I growled, "Because Solomon's very life is in my hands!"—which were right then cradling yet another pint.

"When did you say he's supposed to get back?" I was asked by the same person who had already asked when he was supposed to get back.

"Wednesday!" I growled even louder.

"That's today!" someone else chimed in, not realizing it was Friday.

When I corrected him, he sat silent for a minute. "Well, sounds to me, like, if he's not back by now, he's probably dead," he said. "I vote we go break into his house and steal all his stuff. He won't need it if he's dead."

"Yeah, I really like that oak desk he inherited from his dad," another person said.

"And his map collection is impressive," added a guy down at the end of the bar.

It wasn't long before a scheme was being hatched to burglarize the residence of the man who had entrusted me with his well-being.

As the sun started to set, the guy at the end of the bar lifted his head and asked, "Hey, anyone seen Solomon lately?"

I gave up.

"Sorry, Solomon," I thought, "you messed up big-time choosing me to be your responsible party. You're toast."

Postscript: Solomon returned safely the following Wednesday. He thanked me for being his designated responsible party. He said his mind was at ease knowing that, if anything bad happened, rescue would have been rapidly forthcoming.

"Anytime," I responded. "You can always count on your friends."

Post-Postscript: Midway through the process of penning this book, Solomon passed away unexpectedly. On his deathbed, he verbally bequeathed to me all his camping gear. A reward for me being so responsible.

DAY 334

There is a trail that commences close to our most popular tourist destination. It follows one of the few waterways hereabouts that can rightfully claim the name "river." A short distance from the trailhead, hikers are faced with a crossing that, though easy enough, requires either the removal of footwear or a willingness to get that footwear wet.

Most people familiar with the trail choose the latter, because, shortly thereafter, are two additional crossings. De-booting and re-booting three times would be a very time-consuming way to begin a trek—but an efficacious way to get your mind dialed into the fact that you are about to enter the world's first legally designated wilderness area, a tract both holy and rough.

My perspective has long been that whatever inconvenience they might present is more than offset by the fact that those crossings have long weeded out a certain percentage of casual hikers looking to stretch their legs a bit.

Early this afternoon, Gay, Casey, and I paid a long-overdue call to that trail. We were shocked to observe that the federal land-stewardship agency charged with managing the area had erected a series of double-strand bridges, thus eliminating the wet-feet/de-booting conundrum associated with those three river crossings.

I was incensed. I raged about the ever-increasing gentrification of the outdoor experience. I harbored the fleeting thought of coming back under cover of darkness to remove those abominations, but thought better of it when, upon closer scrutiny, I realized how much effort it would take. I would likely throw my back out badly enough that I wouldn't be able to hike for a month.

Out of sheer, senseless spite—which would only be witnessed by my wife and dog—both of whom have observed enough of my stupidity over the years that they each could write a book titled something along the lines of *My Imbecile Husband* and *My Moronic Human Companion*— and both of whom would scarcely take notice of my flaccid protest—I seriously considered ignoring the newly constructed bridges and walking straight through that river, as I had done many times before, head held higher than usual.

I, however, did not. My wife strode across those double strands without compunction, nary an iota of moral conflict affecting her gait.

"Hey, this is nice," she said from the other side. I wondered if there wasn't some manner of ancient divorce ceremony that I could unilaterally conduct right there on the bank of that little river. One that would hold up in court. Like shouting three times, "I revoke thee, corrupted wife," while shaking a pine bough in her general direction.

I thought better of that as well. My luck, she would sing the "Hallelujah Chorus" and, during communal-property dispersal proceedings, be awarded custody of Casey and Pronto.

Casey then mocked me by leaping into the water and frolicking.

"Oh, OK," I growled as I reluctantly followed in my wife's footsteps. As I did on the second and third bridges. As I did on all three of those same bridges when we returned some hours later.

Even Casey utilized the bridges on the way out. My water-addicted dog had, sadly, been taken over by aliens during this half-day hike.

This was depressing.

Another challenge removed. Another outdoor experience softened. More people accessing the wilderness.

Of course, many of the hikers taking advantage of those three bridges will be children perhaps witnessing the wild for the very first time, and perhaps those children will grow to be the next generation of wilderness warriors. And, even if they do not, they will spend a day marveling at the beauty of the Gila with friends and family. Splashing in the river, getting some exercise, and maybe seeing eagles or foxes. And, in so doing, perhaps mitigating the nature deficit disorder that is plaguing our country.

Those people have as much claim to this land as I do.

The whole hour-long drive home, I felt like a traitor to all those semi-pure, or at least not-too-impure, ecological/land management/environmental beliefs I have for so long held near and dear. At least my feet were dry. That was something.

Every few years, a massive flood roars down from the Gila's highest mountains and takes with it whatever infrastructure might be in the way. I'm talking about paved highway bridges, parked cars, power poles, camper trailers and structures.

Those three little bridges will be no match for the latent ferocity of the wild. Their time surely will come.

As I have written before, there is always hope.

Postscript: On a recent trip to that part of the Gila, I was gladdened to observe that those bridges are now gone. Washed completely away. Guess the next generation of wilderness warriors will have to get their feet wet after all.

DAY 345

It is Mother's Day, and while fiddling around with my poorly organized files, I came across a snippet I did not remember writing titled "A Dog Blog," which was ostensibly penned by Casey.

The actual memories of my earliest days are so hazy I can scarcely remember my own mother's face, though when my tail is wagging while I dream, I like to think it's because my subconscious recollects her loving licks. I don't know where she is now. I hope she is OK, but I fear she is not. If she is gone, maybe a little bit of her is looking after me from the place where dreams are made.

After I was rescued while running loose with no collar and no microchip on the streets of a dusty little desert town, I was taken to a foster home. I liked it there. I was able to play with three other dogs, including a big black Lab named Dalton that had also been rescued. But my foster mother had already adopted Dalton, and she could not keep me permanently. Though I was treated very well and had a nice yard to play in, I knew I was there only temporarily. That knowledge hurt, of course, because I would have loved to play with Dalton forever.

Several strangers came to my foster home and looked at me and went with me out to the backyard. I saw them talking to my foster mother. They never came back.

Then, a few days before Christmas, a man with wild hair and a bushy beard and a woman with a gentle spirit arrived. The man took me out back and spent more time with me than the other strangers. He knew how to play the way a dog likes. He knew all the best spots to scratch. Like those before them, they left me at the home that was not my home. I played some more with Dalton, who I was starting to think of as my big brother, and I forgot about the strangers that had come to look at me.

Then, three days after Christmas—when I got my very first gift—a big chewy stick!—the man with the bushy beard and the woman with the gentle spirit came back. They talked with my foster mother for a few minutes, and then they took me out to their car. They picked me up, because I was too small to jump into the back and because I was too scared to even try. I didn't know where they were taking me. I cried when I saw Dalton standing in the yard watching me leave. He was crying too.

We stayed in the car for a very long time. I crawled into the lap of the woman with the gentle spirit, and she let me stay there. She spoke kindly to me and petted me and laughed at every move I made. Then I went to sleep on the floor behind the passenger seat.

After what seemed like forever, we pulled off a very curvy road and we all got out. The man with the wild hair put me on a leash. We walked down to the banks of a small creek, which was surrounded by trees. There were many birds and squirrels, and the smells were overwhelming. The man with the wild hair let me eat snow and let me walk in the little stream. I had never even imagined such a glorious setting!

Then we got back into the car and drove some more. We finally arrived at a little brick house in the middle of a town, and I was led to the front door, where the man with the wild hair knelt down next to me and patted me on the head and said, "Welcome to your new home."

Home. *My* home.

Like my foster mother, the man with the wild hair called me Casey.

I was still frightened, and I still didn't trust the man with the wild hair, or even the woman with the gentle spirit, but I soon learned that I would spend many days hiking with my new people, the ones who came back for me, the ones who grew to love me and who I grew to love.

I still wonder about my mother. I wish she could see me now; see all the fun things I have done and the cool places I have visited. And I will always miss Dalton. I wish he could have come with us. I hope he remembers me the way I remember him and that he has had a good life. Like mine.

DAY 346

I'd like to think I am not the only one who jabbers disjointed grammar-challenged baby talk to his/her dog. Stuff like: "Oh, what a goody-doody yumble-scrunchious baby girl I got! How'd I get the bestest little doggie-woggie in the entire history of the universe!"— usually uttered with over-the-top enthusiasm after a long hike, head weaving back and forth, arms flailing. The way I look at it, it's a good method for bonding, positive reinforcement, and entertainment. Besides, Casey does not exactly hold an advanced degree in linguistic analysis. I could very well be reciting lines from *Macbeth*, so long as I did doing so while jumping up and down, acting like a clown and using her name every fifth word or so:

> *That but this blow **CASEY***
> *Might be the be-all **CASEY** and the end-all here,*
> *But here **CASEY** upon this bank **CASEY** and shoal of time **CASEY**,*
> *We'd **CASEY** jump the life **CASEY** to come **CASEY**.*

Of course, before doing this, I make absolutely certain there is not another sentient being within twenty kilometers.

If there is indeed another human being close by, I will throttle my doggie-blather drastically back and, with a pat or two, utter something in a clinical monotone like: "Casey, you exhibited excellent on-trail comportment during today's hike. I appreciate your continued exemplary behavior. Here's a jerky treat."

Yesterday, though there were a half dozen or so vehicles parked at the trailhead, nary a two-legged soul was to be seen. So, I went full bore and, rubbing Casey briskly with both hands from stem to stern, effusing something along the lines of: "Out of all the yummy-lummy-wummy good girly-wirlies in the worldy lurdly, I got the very wery derry top-shelf best one. Oh yes, I did, yes I did!"

You get the picture.

Suddenly, I heard an understated chuckle. I turned and sitting in the driver's seat of the vehicle closest to mine was an elderly gent reading a book with his window rolled all the way down. I mean, I would have been mortified had the man been parked on the other side of the lot, on the far outer reaches of earshot. But—no!—he was sitting not four feet away. How could I have possibly missed him?

I was suddenly speechless—a rarity for me.

"Uh, hey, how you doin'?" I eventually limp-lipped to the man, while attempting, and failing, to achieve a dignified pose, like I had not been recently released from the nuthouse. I briefly considered quoting *Macbeth* to let it be known that I was more or less of sound mind, though, I suspected, that would only complicate matters.

"Don't worry," he responded. "I had a dog for a very long time, and she was a yummy-lummy-wummy good girly wirly too," he said, his use of the past tense telling.

"Well, OK then. You have a good day," I responded, smiling, knowing I had just met a kindred spirit.

"You as well," he said while looking wistfully at Casey.

I then drove off with the bestest little doggie-woggie in the universe cutting gruesome farts in the back seat all the way home, both of us happy in the knowledge that communication takes so many wonderful forms.

DAY 349

 Sometimes, the wrong direction is the right direction.

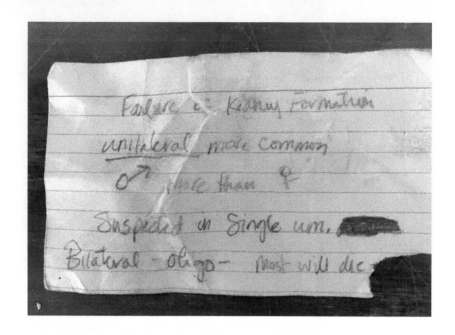

DAY 356

It was a standard 3x5 lined index card with penciled handwriting lying upon the very trail where, earlier this year, I interacted with the Colorado man and his -doodle dog. On the unlined backside was written: "Renal agenesis is—"

It was probably a flashcard-type study note, perhaps from a nursing student attending the local university who decided that a walk in the late-spring sunshine was the perfect antidote to the rigors of academia. It likely had slipped from a larger stack of similar cards bearing the names of horrible maladies that needed to be memorized.

The words on the front of the card were sobering: "Failure of kidney formation. Unilateral. More common in men than women. Suspected in single woman [name herein withheld]. Bilateral oligo. Most will die."

Those last three words definitely reoriented what had been to that point a fairly typical mindless on-foot foray in the Gila. I opted to quicken my pace, with the intention of outdistancing whatever it was that suddenly seemed to be nipping at my heels.

DAY 358

I recently decided to aggregate all of my usernames, passwords, PINS, and IDs so I could transfer them to one of those online services that manages such things in such a way that all you have to do is memorize a single user name, password, PIN, and ID. I was dismayed to learn that my list was more than fifty items long, and included a wide array of perplexing concoctions that included at least eight characters and at least one capital letter, one number, one form of punctuation, and one bloody thumbprint to access bank accounts, insurance companies, Internet providers, social media accounts and a plethora of businesses that require a shocking amount of private information so that I might be able to give them my money. Petco, REI, Amazon, Samsung, et al.

How drunk must I have been to come up with some of the more convoluted mnemonic passwords, none of which I would ever stand a chance of remembering were they not scribbled down on a sticky note that was subsequently stashed in a secret place I also stood no chance of remembering? Far as I can tell, one of those mnemonics, for instance, must have been something like: The 7 diabetic turnip $$$ greens bounded merrily ^^^ down the drainpipe while chugging tequila that was on sale for only a DOLLAR!!!

How did it come to this?

I mean, I used to live happily with all my possessions fitting into a trunk and a backpack!

Somewhere out there past the horizon, there *has* to be a password for enlightenment.

Or a user ID for wisdom.

Or a PIN for passion.

A security question for truth.

A hard drive backup for beauty.

A subject line for awe.

A login for love.

I tried the "Help" function. It was not helpful.

I've spent this past year looking hard.

Might need to log out, shut down, and restart.

DAY 359

As my quest to hike every day for a solid year gained modest traction on social media and in the watering holes I frequent, people would invariably ask how many miles I had hiked. More than anything, they wanted measurable data, to be able to translate my experience to a mental grid they could more easily comprehend. Why distance seemed to trump time, duration, and glee, I could not guess.

I usually responded that I did not know, and I did not care.

For one thing, many of the places through which I trekked were not blemished by trail signs containing distance-related information.

(I have long wished that trail signs contained snippets from poems rather than objective information.)

For yet another, on some days, I was able to keep a steady pace on well-groomed paths, while other routes were thick with brush or included many challenging stream crossings or traversed steep ground covered with loose rock. Things that thankfully slow you down.

And I carry no electronic distance-measurement devices.

For those who need actual data, I will try, but not too hard.

If I spent a minimum of sixty minutes a day on the trail—which I exceeded to a degree that the following calculations are all grossly understated—that came to a total of 367 hours. If I averaged two miles per hour, which is, likewise, undoubtedly on the low end, I covered 734 miles, or one-and-a-half times the length of the Colorado Trail and about a third the length of the Appalachian Trail.

In all likelihood (Gay and Casey agree with me on this), I averaged more like ninety minutes a day on the trail, over the course of 367 days, that comes to a total of 550.5 hours. At two miles per hour, that comes to 1,101 miles, or more than twice the length of the Colorado Trail and almost half the length of the Appalachian Trail.

In even more likelihood, I averaged ninety minutes a day and two and a half miles per hour. That would amount to 1,376.25 miles. That's 1.7 Arizona Trails.

No matter the exact stats, all this amounts to a lot of boot prints left in the dirt.

This makes my effort seem more grandiose than it really was. Unlike my thru-hiking brethren attempting to complete long trails, I did not have to carry food, fuel, stove, cook kit, spare clothes, tent, sleeping bag, sleeping pad, and vodka. With the exception of those few times when I embarked upon multiday forays, I could return home from the trail, take a shower, eat a big plate of burritos, and sip adult beverages while sitting barefoot on my front porch listening to music.

Still, not bad for an old man and his young dog. Not bad at all.

A week away from completing my quest, I was beginning to feel a sense of pride.

DAY 364

A friend, after several pints, looked me directly in the eye and asked if I ever once cheated during my quest to hike every day for a solid year. Once word started to spread about my year-long quest, I began to suspect that question would perhaps one day arise.

I mean, how could it not?

A group of hard-asses I know once took it upon themselves to descend, on foot, over the course of multiple weeks, a series of river corridors in an area of Mexico where I have spent a lot of time. Their goal was to do so *puro en el rio*—that is to say, not ascending to higher ground under any circumstances, even when those rivers boxed up and/or were defined by the kinds of rapids one would normally navigate in a kayak or raft. They swam, ambled over house-sized boulders and squeezed their way through tight cracks. They knew there would be skepticism, given the rugged nature of the terrain through which they passed, and since there was another team—well funded, with a large media following—attempting to pull off the same feat, and given the fact that they were a bunch of cigarette-smoking New Mexico dirtbags rather than heavily sponsored, professional endurance athletes dressed in the height of outdoor-recreation fashion. So, in that pre-GPS era, they documented almost every step of the way via still photography and videography, much the way mountaineers did in the old days to prove they had successfully ascended some lofty peak.*

The thought of doing something similar during my solid-year endeavor never entered my head, though Gay and I did take a lot of photos. Maybe I should have somehow engaged the magic of satellite technology. That thought did not enter my head either. Ergo, my ability to "prove" that I did not cheat does not exist.

There was one close call.

We were in Colorado visiting Gay's family for the Christmas holidays. Despite the density of the unavoidable holiday festivities, I managed to find time to drive out with Casey to a trailhead I had heard about. Much to my chagrin, there was a large sign declaring that the trail I intended to hike upon was no longer open for public use. Some property-rights issue had caused a closure that might be permanent. With daylight waning, and with unavoidable family obligations looming, I was worried that my solid year quest might end prematurely.

Then I noticed off to the side a small sign advertising something called the Bluff Trail, which, the sign declared in a terse tone, was "rugged, steep, and unimproved," which sounded like an enticing invitation rather than a warning. I prepared for adventure unseen and unknowable, which is pretty much the definition of a word that is now irreparably corrupted by things like ziplines and guided "forest bathing" tours through well-groomed state parks. I soon learned that the trail, which actually consisted of two small loops, and which was, by my unimproved standards, neither rugged nor steep, totaled only an eighth of a mile in length.

I hiked those two loops individually one way, then the other way. Then I connected them, hiking one way, then the other. I hiked them both ways in figure eight fashion. After an hour, we returned to the gluttonous holiday festivities taking place at my wife's family's home.

That hike marked the closest I came to cheating on my sixty-minute requirement. Like, who would have known, or cared, if, under such circumstances, I only hiked for forty-seven minutes around the Bluff Trail? Me. *I* would have known. I would have winced a bit every time someone asked how my quest was going.

The next day was December 25.

Ten miles outside my wife's hometown is a lovely tract of public land called Red Canyon Park, which holds special meaning to Gay and me. It is where we first realized we were in love. (I guess I should be more specific: in love with each other.) Every Christmas that I had spent in Gay's home range, I had gone out to Red Canyon Park for a hike. Which I did on this particular day. I followed the park's namesake geological feature till it petered out. I went up every side canyon I could find. It was a perfect counterbalance to the previous day hiking laps on the Bluff Trail. I totally lost track of time. When I returned to the house in which my wife grew up, with her large family assembled, Christmas dinner was in full swing. Seconds of turkey, dressing, and green bean casserole were already being ladled onto plates lately emptied of victuals stacked far higher than the top of the Bluff Trail. I could tell Gay was a bit miffed at my tardiness. Though I was late, my frail mother-in-law, the matriarch of the gathering, beamed when I walked in. She asked how my hike went. She was enthusiastic about my endeavor and asked often after my progress.

The day after Christmas, we left early to begin the long journey home to New Mexico, which had to be scheduled in such a way that I could stop near an extensive trail system located right next to the highway. As usual, Gay's family members lined up on the front porch to wish us safe travels, with expressions that indicated—not exactly for the first time—that they could not comprehend what manner of madness had possessed her to move down to rural New Mexico with a man who always seemed to be attired in tattered rags. There were hugs and kisses galore, as my impatient foot tapped, and I not-so-subtly glanced at my watch. "What more could there be to say after being in each other's company for the past four days?" I asked under my breath as my teeth ground. Turns out, there was much more that could have and should have been said.

The La Tierra Trails system lies adjacent to the Santa Fe Relief Route. It was blizzarding when we pulled in and Gay wisely opted to nap in the car while Casey and I slipped and slid our way along icy/slushy/muddy trails through snowfall that showed little sign of abating. I mistimed my hike and arrived back at the trailhead after having been out for only fifty minutes, so I turned around and slipped and slid five minutes back in and five minutes back out.

We had to pull off for the night in Socorro as New Mexico was being hit by a vicious winter storm. Most of the state was shut down for almost a week.

Normally, when we travel between Colorado and home, we follow a highway that intersects with a plethora of trails. Unfortunately, the road, which crosses a sinewy, undulating mountain pass, was closed because of the weather, so we had to detour via an alternative route that runs due south of any public land. It was slow going on blacktop being traversed by drivers very unaccustomed to winter conditions. We made it back to Silver City in the nick of time for me to continue my quest, sprinting to TS-X, which was lined by yuccas and agaves peeking their heads above a rare blanket of white, looking very disoriented. The world was muffled.

Overall, the previous four days highlighted the logistical difficulties associated with trying to hike every day for a year while still keeping one foot in the door of real life. This was one of the few ways in which my quest was more challenging than embarking upon a multi-month backpacking trip on the Appalachian, Arizona, or Colorado trails. I was not taking a break from my regular existence; I was trying to integrate hiking day after day into a world of domestic chores, work, and spending time with faraway family members for the Christmas holidays.

It took a degree of resoluteness that was perhaps not fully evident, given the often-lighthearted tone with which I have opted to relate this tale.

A month later, my mother-in-law, one of the sweetest people I have ever known, passed away. She had been a part of my life longer than my own mother. Her death was not a surprise, as she had been in and out of hospitals—cheating death, as it were—for more than a year. She was surrounded by her family when her next journey began.

The memory of her enthusiastically asking how my hike went during Christmas dinner will remain with me till my days are done.

The list of things I am not is long.

Among them (maybe atop them): I am not a good family member. As a result of my own personal history, family in all its countless forms causes me stress. I can handle family, even functional family, only in small doses and at arm's length. My mother-in-law instinctively accepted this without ever giving me grief or asking about the root causes. She countenanced me standing on the sidelines of her clan without judging the distance I maintained. She accepted that, on Christmas Day, I would head out by my lonesome to where Gay and I first knew that we would be together forevermore.

Had I known that would be the last time I would see my mother-in-law, I would have happily ended my year-long quest on the spot so I could spend a couple more hours in her presence. She would not have wanted me to. She always loved my various adventures.

When my drinking buddy asked whether I ever cheated, I was able to return his gaze and say, "No. Never once."

I'll save any inclination I might have to cheat for more important undertakings.

* Those journeys are recounted in the book, *Canyons of the Mind*, by Russell James Ray, the expedition's organizer.

DAY 365

Casey and I hiked to the far edge of Arrow Mesa. My long-time nemesis, the Cairn Maker, had been busy, so I had the opportunity to restore a slew of his/her stacks of rocks to a more natural condition. Provided me with the opportunity to focus on something other than the fact the end of the line—or at least the end of this particular line—was staring me right in the face.

We walked to a rock spire that is a bit dangerous to access. Casey always whimpers nervously when we approach this point. I issued a stern "stay" command and launched from one precarious nub to the next. This I have done enough times that I have the moves down pat. Yet, each one carries with it the risk of significant orthopedic consequences should my aim or my increasingly suspect proprioception let me down. The last leap was the most concerning, as it required enough thrust to reach the top of the spire, but not too much, as an overshoot would terminate in a multi-hundred-foot vertical drop. It is a kinesthetic test I will continue to attempt until my confidence wavers. Or I go over the edge.

I sat on the lip of the spire, my feet dangling above the void.

And here, now, after 365 days, my psychic chickens have at last come home to roost.

I stared off into a distance that spreads clear to Arizona.

I was unable to stay long, because Casey, who could not then see me, would start to fidget. I did not want her panicking and deciding to try to follow me. She would not make it.

For the past several months, I have been intently thinking about what, if anything, this year-long quest means. I could be flippant, as is my nature, by saying that it means nothing more than time to drink some celebratory cervezas while planning whatever harebrained scheme next pops into my inebriated noggin. There are plenty of cocktail napkins upon which to jot disjointed thoughts. I guess that would be OK. There are far worse fates.

Here's the thing: I'm not feeling flippant at this moment. Something has been not quite right in my little world for a very long time. Not necessarily wrong and not necessarily bad. Just not quite right. And I have arrived at a conclusion after all these days and miles: My life has become too heavy. I have too many possessions. I have too many grown-up responsibilities. Too many passwords and user IDs. I spend too many weekends working on my house and in my yard. I hate that shit. It is wearing on me. I am neither genetically nor socially disposed to be an adult—which is a tough realization when you are sixty years old.

I determined that it was high time I started searching in earnest for Jumpin' Jack, the Hallucinogenic Hiker. He's out there somewhere, moving lightly through the expanse of untamed land that defines this glorious part of the world. He might be hard to find. But I'm going to give it a whirl, to play the role of private investigator searching for a past version of M. John. My back and knees and shoulder might not hold up. But I *need* to at least try. Don't know what'll happen if I find him out there among the tarantulas and cacti. He might be older than I am now. He might be stooped and slow. He might not recognize me. He might be dead.

Not sure Gay would like Jumpin' Jack, but she might. At least some parts of him.

I stood, turned, and began in reverse order the precarious series of leaps back to the edge of Arrow Mesa, where sat Casey, still adhering to her "stay" command. When I told her she was free, she jumped up and down and wagged her tail, relieved that, once again, her human companion did not meet a bad end on her watch.

On the way out, I removed my trail shoes—the second pair I had worn out over the course of the past year—and took a picture of their eroded soles. A photographic memento, as it were. Circumstantial evidence. Likely not admissible in court.

I gave Casey a good long hug and said to her, "We did it."

Then we began the hour-long return trip to Pronto, where Casey got a few extra jerky treats.

I stopped at one of my favorite watering holes and borrowed a pen from a bartender I know well, who, while handing me a fine-tipped tool that carries through its dark circulatory system the potential for both liberation and destruction, shook her head and smiled.

I spent the rest of the evening in the company of the usual cadre of ne'er-do-wells, one of whom asked, "So, what have you been up to lately?"

"Nothing much," I answered. "You?"

I stuffed the crumpled-up cocktail napkin in my shirt pocket, where it remained forgotten until I did laundry several weeks later. I pulled it out and read the words I had penned: "Every so often, we need to do something that reminds us who we are." I couldn't agree more.

THE END

Casey and I hiked for two more days, but, given that we had already reached our one-year goal, they felt more like a cool down or a decompression than a continuation.

Then we left town.

Pronto's primary-care physician had moved to a city a long drive away. Pronto was in need of medical attention and, since Gay had family in that area, we used my vehicle's condition as an excuse for a road trip neither one of us really wanted to take because the entire Southwest was experiencing a record-setting hot spell.

We left Silver City in late afternoon, pulling into a motel halfway to our destination well after dark. By the time we arrived the next morning at a shade-free trailhead that accesses one of the most spectacular wilderness study areas in the country, it was already more than a hundred degrees. We ambled through the convection oven for maybe fifteen minutes—long enough for Casey to empty her pipes—before retreating at a brisk and sweat-soaked pace to Pronto's marginally air-conditioned interior.

We entertained the notion of waiting for the relative coolness of evening, while Pronto was having surgery, and searching for an appropriate trail close to town upon which I could keep my quest alive. That notion was half-hearted at best.

We ended up lollygagging for an hour on a paved urban trail located between a river and a busy highway. It in no way met the criteria I had established a full year prior.

Gay asked if that walk "counted."

I told her, "No."

"So, this is it, then?" she asked, pride and relief intertwined into her intonation.

"Yes."

When we returned to Gila Country later that week, I was once more beckoned to consciousness at 5:30 a.m. by the stoned elves who dwell within the hidden confines of my iPhone and, with Casey at my side, we ventured out to hike through the Gila.

Because, as the lyrics of "Do the Hokey Pokey" clearly state, that's what it's all about.

Postscript

Two years after my quest ended, with no predetermined time commitment, I decided to see how many consecutive days I could hike. This was not an attempt to recreate or expand my previous experience, but rather to establish some palpable context as my effort to pen this book started gaining traction at the same time that my memory of the year-long experience began to simultaneously diminish and expand into other realms, some of which were related, some of which were not.

I made it forty-eight straight days—which still stands as my second-longest streak—and was inclined to continue. Sadly, during a trip to Aspen, I contracted a case of the flu, which put me down for three weeks.

That made me realize in retrospect both how fortunate and how resolute I had been during my 367-day quest. I had dealt with an injured ankle, several near misses with rattlesnakes, a blind dog, logistical challenges galore, a slew of hangovers, intercourse with ghosts from my deep dark past, an expired lunch cook, and who knows how many near misses I was too oblivious to even notice.

Context, in my humble opinion, was indeed firmly established.

Post-Postscript

On a hot Sunday morning, two days before the summer solstice, when she was twelve years old, Casey passed away in our arms in the back seat of her beloved Pronto after a long battle with cancer and diabetes. As she took her last breath, she looked up at me and smiled. I spread her ashes in several of her favorite spots in the Gila. When I pass by, I always tell her what a goody-doody yumble-scrunchious baby girl she was.

ACKNOWLEDGEMENTS

I would like to extend my heartfelt thanks to:

Craig Childs for taking the time from his shockingly busy schedule to pen the preamble for this tome.

Marvel Harrison and Jared Kuritz of Mimbres Press for their belief in this project and their patience in dealing with a hardheaded writer who is too often set in his ways.

Shelley Chung for her invaluable editorial insights and her expertise in subject/verb agreement and proper comma placement.

Alan Stark, Tara Flanagan, and T. Alex Miller for reading through this manuscript and providing a slew of helpful observations, none of which included the words "burn this shit immediately!"

David Cremean, retired professor of English and Humanities at Black Hills State University in Spearfish, South Dakota, for his metaphoric assistance.

My longtime amigo, William E. Paxson, for his incalculable perspective.

For their decisiveness: Andrea Stein, Mike Medberry, Ed Lynch, Charlie Campbell, Sam Yarbs, Lauri Beckwith Pohlman, Katie Roberts, Albert Halverstadt, Kenneth Hulick, George Crusher Gipson, Hamish Tear, Sam Camp, Malcolm McMichael, Bob Ward, Pete Kolbenschlag, Jack Taylor, Tricia Cook, Frederick Rivera, Robin Waters, Andy Stonehouse, Steve Howe, Davis Hoza, Tom Nichols, Jonathan Lee Wright, Cal Vin Gogh, Kathryn Davis Grohusky, Craig Erlandsen, Andrea Stein and Leon Joseph Littlebird.

Karin Teague, for speaking to me.

Mark Fox, for everything.

My wife, Gay Gangel-Fayhee, for putting her life on hold, yet again, while I walked off with a pack on my back.

And, most of all, to Casey, for being herself. Good girl. Very good girl.

ABOUT THE AUTHOR

For twelve years, M. John Fayhee was the editor of the *Mountain Gazette*. He was a longtime contributing editor at *Backpacker* magazine. A two-time Colorado Book Awards finalist, his work has appeared in *Canoe & Kayak*, the *High Country News*, *REI Co-Op Journal*, *Overland Journal*, *Islands*, *Adventure Travel*, *Men's Fitness*, *New Mexico Magazine* and many others.

Fayhee has hiked on five continents and has completed the Appalachian, Colorado, Arizona, and Inca trails, as well as the Colorado section of the Continental Divide Trail.

Fayhee is, improbably enough, a New Mexico Humanities Council Scholar.

He lives in Gila Country with his wife, Gay Gangel-Fayhee.

Milton Keynes UK
Ingram Content Group UK Ltd.
UKHW010655101123
432322UK00007B/432